THE LIFE OF

RICHARD CARDINAL CUSHING

THE

WORLD'S
CARDINAL

by
M.C. DEVINE

Second Printing

UT COGNOSCANT TE

ST. PAUL EDITIONS

Library of Congress Catalog Card Number: **64-24360**

Copyright, 1964, by the DAUGHTERS OF ST. PAUL
Printed in the U.S.A. by the DAUGHTERS OF ST. PAUL
50 St. Paul's Ave., *Jamaica Plain, Boston, Mass.* 02130

Acknowledgments

Grateful acknowledgment is made to Leonard Casper, Ph.D., author, and Professor of English, Boston College, for his reading of the manuscript and helpful suggestions; also to all who have kindly supplied information and urged publication of this book.

CONTENTS

11

TO OUR BELOVED SON
RICHARD, CARDINAL OF THE
HOLY ROMAN CHURCH, CUSHING
Archbishop of Boston

PAUL P.P. VI

BELOVED SON:

Health and Apostolic Benediction.

A day which you have long awaited will dawn for you, Our Beloved Son, in the passage of the year, and will bring to your soul a great outpouring of religious joy. There will then be completed 25 years since the reception of your episcopal orders.

By reason of the benevolence and singular esteem in which we hold you, we offer our congratulations, we extend our best wishes and we offer our encouragement.

We could not let pass without our merited eulogy that which you have accomplished with the help of divine grace for the greater glory of God, for the growth and beauty of the Archdiocese of Boston, and for the strength of the Catholic cause.

As a good and watchful sacred shepherd, for whom to rule is to serve, and for whom to lead is to help by love and to love by helping, you have so expressed your concern and care for the flock entrusted to you in Christ, that as far as possible there is nothing lacking to them of those helps which could lead to the furtherance of divine worship and the nurture of Christian life in its growth and flowering. The Archdiocese is so directed, indeed, with prudent care that it flourishes with special vigor in the number of its priests, religious communities, Catholic schools and colleges, social action, the teaching of Christian doctrine and in new projects of beneficence. In carrying out your pastoral charge, as a good father to a family, you give from your treasure things both new and old (Cf. Matt. 13:52), knowing that new ways are proper for the new needs of men, but not neglectful of those methods which usage and experience have proved to be the most solid. Generous in spirit and in deed, special merited praise is due your manner of life and that of the faithful of Christ to whom your counsel gives leadership and direction.

How much has already been brought to pass and is still being accomplished, especially in the foundation of missions in the various regions of Latin America: There the generous outpouring of your help for the many needs of the churches has not been without its visible fruit and happy increase, in particular with the help of the most providential work founded by you, which takes its name from St. James the Apostle.

Wishing for you now all happiness and health, we pray Christ Jesus, the eternal High Priest, the crown of those who rule, the Author and the end of our faith, that He may adorn and enrich you with even further gifts of His loving care. Of these gifts, the most desired and the greatest would be that you follow more and more in His holy way, both by good works without interruption or end, and in the growth and intensity of His love.

We wish that in your journeys and in your thoughts there shine forth the moving and sweet phrases by which Saint Gregory Nazianzen commended himself to the service of Christ: "I live for you, I speak for you, I sit for you. O Christ the King—toward you I trace my footsteps, because you have taken me by the hand —Guide me even now to a good journey." Carm. I. 1, 36 vv. 31-33: Migne P. 6. 37.

Accept freely for yourself these words of good wishes and of encouragement with which we greet you on the day of your anniversary, as you would rightly wish us to share the joy which is yours from the fulfillment of so many worthy hopes.

To make your anniversary day more fruitful, we freely give to you the privilege, after your solemn Mass, of blessing the faithful there present in our name and by our authority, granting a plenary indulgence to be gained according to the law of the Church.

Finally, to you, Our Beloved Brother and to your devoted Auxiliary Bishops, as well as to the entire flock which you guide as their sacred shepherd, we lovingly impart, as a pledge of our special affection, the Apostolic Benediction.

Given at Rome, at Saint Peter's, the twenty-second of May, in the year 1964 the first year of Our Pontificate.

PAUL P.P. VI.

1

SOUTH BOSTON BOY

It was a brisk winter day in 1907. A tall lad of about twelve emerged from 44 O Street in South Boston's City Point district and hurried through the snowy streets, with a frightened eight-year-old sister in tow. They were on their way to Carney Hospital.

His mother had said he would have to take her. They had gone sliding together, she had gotten hurt when hit by a sled, and now he would have to take her to Carney. It was not at all to his liking,

15

this business of taking a quaking little girl to the high, forbidding building that was the old Carney Hospital. With every step, he was tempted to turn back, but he trudged ahead through the snow. The idea of facing the worried look in his mother's eyes with an admission of failure was, after all, completely inconceivable.

At last the Carney came into view, and the boy heaved a sigh of relief. The nuns would take care of his sister.

On the porch he came to a determined standstill and to the bewildered little girl announced firmly, "You go in by yourself, Anna. I'm waiting for you right here!"

He had been faithful to duty, he had obeyed, but there was no need for overdoing it, was there? He was a typical boy, one of a multitude in a crowded area. Perhaps his sister, young as she was, knew instinctively that argument would be futile. At all events, in she went, alone, while Richard James Cushing took up his resolute stand—outside.

Such was the third child of Patrick and Mary Cushing, at the age of twelve. He was his mother's pride and joy, as a member of the family put it, but he was in every way a real boy.

Anna survived the ordeal, and life in the homey apartment at 44 "O" Street flowed smoothly on once more. It was a good life and a full one, for both the parents and their five children. Looking back over the years to that day in 1890 when at

Gate of Heaven Church, South Boston, Mary Dahill of County Waterford, Ireland, became the bride of Patrick Cushing, himself an "Old Country" man from Glanworth, County Cork, the devoted couple could find many causes for rejoicing. True, they both had to work hard from the day they landed in America, yet work was an element in which they thrived.

Mary Dahill, the oldest of six children, had left her home town of Tournegehee in the late eighties to board the Cunard liner, *Pavonia,* as a steerage passenger. Once arrived in the States, she found work as a cook in the Boston home of a judge, and was soon sending money back to Ireland to bring the rest of the family "out." The whole family settled in a tenement near the South Boston waterfront. Mary's two sisters were employed in domestic service or in local factories. Her brothers, James, Thomas and John, became day laborers.

Mary met her future husband, an Irish immigrant like herself, when she took a job as cook in Mrs. Ness's Boarding House, on the corner of K Street and Broadway in South Boston. He was employed as a blacksmith's helper at the time and made it a practice to go to Mrs. Ness's establishment for his meals. If Mary prayed for a husband who would be her loving companion and unfailing support for the rest of her life, her prayers were certainly answered the day Patrick Cushing made her his wife. She had sacrificed herself generously on behalf of her family, and in reward, God was to give her a family of her own. She and Patrick could not know on that happy day in 1890 that a son of theirs would some-day become a Prince of the Church; they simply began their married life with that deep faith in God and trust in one another which is the foundation of every good Christian marriage.

Their first home, an apartment in a three-story house at 806 East Third Street, saw the birth of their three elder children: Elizabeth (August 7, 1892), Mary Jane (December 19, 1893), promptly nick-named Dolly because of her diminutiveness, and Richard James (August 24, 1895), who was probably named for Patrick's brother Dick, at that time re-siding with the couple. The day after his birth, Richard was baptized by Rev. Thomas Brannan in Gate of Heaven Church. In their second home, at 44 "O" Street, to which Patrick and Mary moved while Richard was yet a toddler, two more children were born to them: Anna (June 21, 1899) and John (May 13, 1903). The great joys Patrick and Mary experienced as their family increased were not un-mixed with sorrow, however. Their fourth child, a little daughter whom they named Rebecca, died as an infant. This loss the couple accepted with that serene resignation which was just one of the many effects produced by the firm faith they shared.

Religion for them and their children was not simply a part of their Irish heritage, something ex-pected of them by the community in which they lived, and therefore, almost obligatory. It was neither of these nor was it mere external show. It was a way of life. If you were a Catholic, you were to be a good one, and that was that.

The earliest recollections of the Cushing children include the vivid memory of the whole family saying the Rosary together in the evenings. This traditional Marian devotion was a daily practice in their home, and one which Richard was to continue all his life. If as a boy, he had any one outstanding devotion, it was to the Mother of God. He learned to have confidence in her in those moments when as part of the kneeling circle, he watched the beads slip through the powerful hands of his father and the capable, work-worn hands of his mother.

Did he not have his own home in mind when in his column in *The Pilot*, Archdiocesan newspaper of Boston, he wrote on March 1, 1958: "The family is the unity of society, the kindergarten where we learn to live as children of God. Here fathers and mothers devoted to their vocation bring up children to shoulder their own independent lives."

Indeed, it was easy to learn to live as a child of God in the Cushing home. It was not only that there were the traditional devotional objects, the holy pictures, the crucifixes on the walls, the holy water fonts, but there was the living example of a father who never sat down to a meal without saying grace, and a mother who told her children time and again that her one desire was to see them grow up good.

Was not Mary Cushing's oldest boy thinking of her when he related the following anecdote?

" 'Have you said your prayers?' a wise mother asked her ten-year-old son as he rattled down for breakfast.

" 'No, Mama, I forgot.'

" 'What are you—a heathen?' "

"With a shocked look on his face, the boy went back upstairs and said his prayers."

Patrick Cushing was a blacksmith by trade, employed in the carbarns of the Boston Elevated Street Railway Company. There he worked ten hours a day, seven days a week, at the forge, repairing wheels. He was of average height, had greyish brown hair and blue eyes. His children, to whom he was always "Pa," remember him as a quiet, humble man of great strength of character and love of hard work. He was content to stay home in the evenings with the family which was his whole life and for which he was such a good provider.

His wife, Mary, was a tall woman, with dark brown hair and eyes as blue as her husband's. She matched him in energy and devotion to her family. All the financial affairs and the management of the home were in her skillful hands, and she kept everything running smoothly. Despite the fact that the family circle was increasing, Mary never had to go to work outside her home to help support it. Her quiet, humble man never failed her. He brought the wages home; she saw to it that they met every need. In fact, from the memory her children have of the meals she served them, it would seem that there was more than enough of everything.

Mary Cushing was one of those mothers who know how to win the hearts of their children without depriving them of the opportunity of developing into strong personalities. She enjoyed the entire affection and generous love of her oldest lad's heart, and she kept his loyal devotion to the end of her days. Yet though she cooked his favorite foods and showed her love in the innumerable ways a mother can find, she never pampered him. From the time he was a child, she let him understand that love is shown by deeds, not only by words. He learned the lesson early—a lesson he was never to forget—and as one of his favorite 'deeds,' made it a practice to go to the neighboring beach to gather firewood, bring it home and chop it up for his mother to use in the kitchen stove.

This desire of Richard's to be of help to others, a desire which early became his 'predominant passion,' made him popular with his grandmother, too. The good woman was afflicted with rheumatism and had great faith in the 'salt water cure.' Consequently, little Dick, as he was called at home, made it his duty to keep her well supplied with salt water.

Such willingness to be of service to members of the family and even to relatives, which the little boy was not to lose as he grew up, led him to write as Archbishop of Boston: "Youth has its own schedule, and visiting grandparents, granduncles, grandaunts can be a bore—let us face it. Yet how often a grown man finds satisfaction in the evenings he gave to that generation, recalling how much comfort his visits afforded."

As a child, the future exemplar of charity could be quite loud in his demands for recognition and approval at times. Long before he was old enough to chop firewood, he would go up to his mother and ask, "Am I the best boy in Boston?"

"No," would come the decisive reply from this wonderful woman, who passed on to her Richard the love of playful teasing.

At that answer, the little fellow would be thoroughly dismayed and show it with a good loud wail, which lasted only until Mother stopped her work and hugged her small son to her, laughing at his tears and assuring him of his special place in her heart.

Yes, Patrick and Mary Cushing built a home in which love was indeed manifest, but not so much by a great many outward signs of affection as by an atmosphere of loyalty, relaxing good humor and readiness to be of service. Friends liked to go home with the Cushing children, even very small friends. It was fun to play cards for hours in that cheerful, happy household. Every member of the family found pleasure in just being with the others. Aunts and uncles, too, liked to pay a visit to the Cushings. At times, Patrick Cushing, "Pa" to his family, would take up the flute he had made himself and play to a delighted audience. Indeed, he spent most of his evenings right in his own kitchen, where the pot of tea was always on and where the whole family congregated, or in summertime on the doorsteps chatting with his wife and their neighbors. When he did go out, it was very often to make his children happy.

One of his favorite ways, in fact, of treating his little ones was to take them for car rides. In those days of nickel carfare, such excursions could prove quite exciting, especially when they knew that the day would not end without an ice cream treat. And on many holidays, the whole family spent a delightful afternoon at Norumbega Park, a favorite amusement spot still popular today.

Christmas was a time of special family joy. Each year the children hung up their stockings in great expectation, and were never disappointed. Of course, once in a while, they would find the traditional piece of coal, to their dismay and the amusement of their parents, but the longed-for toys and goodies were soon forthcoming. There were sure to be big, juicy oranges, and a colorful jack-in-the-box, not to mention the old favorite: crackerjacks.

On Christmas Eve, there was always a pot of Mother's homemade chicken soup, which everyone agreed was delicious. Indeed, Mary Cushing's meals were excellent every day, it seems.

Her oldest son never made it a secret that he was 'crazy about her cooking,' as one of his sisters expressed it, and would always eat whatever she cooked. Here was a mother who used her talents first where they were most appreciated, in her own home.

The South Boston in which Richard grew up was, and still is to some extent, a tightly-knit community with all the friendliness and neighborliness of the typical small town. The folks living in the tall, closely built houses lining the long, narrow streets not only knew each other, they knew about each other and felt close to one another's joys and sorrows.

In the late afternoons when the Irish immigrant fathers and their oldest sons got off the trolleys and started down those streets pulsing with life and activity, they and the women waiting for them in the warm kitchens felt in their hearts what the residents of South Boston even today call "the spirit of Old Southie." It was a spirit felt perhaps most of all by the boys who played together on the ball fields and the "L" Street beaches, mingling their shouts with the high-pitched shrieks of the sea gulls circling continually over the ocean and the land.

Years later, when one of those boys was a priest, a distinguished gentleman who was an authority on Massachusetts genealogy, said to him after hearing him deliver a speech in his inimitable style: "I was convinced, Father, as I listened to you tonight, that you must be one of the Cushings—the famous Cushings of my own town."

The priest chuckled. "No, sir," he said, "I am one of the Cushings of *South Boston.*"

This same love of his birthplace and delight in glorying in it is never lacking even now that the priest has become a Prince of the Church. Once, after introducing a visiting clergyman as a Canon of a great Roman University, the Cardinal announced with a laugh, "I'm a Canon from South Boston!"

It is not surprising that he should so love to identify himself with "Old Southie," for the Cushing family fit well into the life of that hard-working community.

From the joyous and affectionate relations of his home and neighborhood environment, it was easy for Richard Cushing to create the same friendly atmosphere around himself when he started school. He attended, in all, three South Boston public grade schools: the Pope, the Lincoln, and the Oliver Hazard Perry. Strong and healthy always, he brought to his schoolwork all the vitality and drive that were to be particularly characteristic of him all through life, and the results were good. He was considered by his teachers "a bright boy, one who would go places."

"Richard was a fine little fellow, quiet and studious," recalled one of his primary grade teachers, Miss Mary Dee, on the occasion of his elevation to the See of Boston. "When others in the room were raising high jinks—and they often did—I can remember him sitting there, reading his book and paying no attention to the noise and confusion around him. He never gave me the least bit of trouble." (Instead, he brought her deep joy when he sent her a telegram of good wishes on the day she retired from the Boston School System.)

Although Dick was quiet, serious, and given to studying hard, both at home and at school, yet he was by no means shy. When he had something on his mind, he would stand up straight and tall and 'deliver' with all the fire of a true orator.

Monsignor George Casey, columnist for the Boston *Pilot* and Perry School classmate of the Cardinal's, recalls, "He was always smart. When a question was asked, he'd be on his feet with his hand in the air while the rest of us were still thinking about it. And I remember him reciting the Gettysburg Address from memory."

Dick was a much sought-after companion in after-school hours and liked nothing better than to be doing things with the crowd of boys, to whom he was "Jimmy." Spring and Fall found them playing ball or off on a hike, while on the hot summer days they headed for the City Point beaches to swim and play in the ocean waves. Other favorite sports, as might be expected, were boating and fishing.

Popular with his classmates, Dick was equally popular at home with his own sisters and little brother. Nor had his entrance into school in any way lessened his closeness with his mother. Once when he was still in the lower grades, he went to Medford, a small city north of Boston proper, to spend a vacation with former South Boston neighbors, since the boy of the family and he had been great friends. Before the vacation was over, Mary Cushing said to one of her daughters, "Dolly, come with me to Medford. We'll bring Dick home." She could not stand to have him away from her!

At the end of his sixth grade year in the Perry School, Richard was rewarded for his excellent scholastic record with a double promotion. Consequently, September of 1908 found him an eighth grader, in the same class with his sister Dolly. Many an evening they did their homework together, and his sister later recalled that she took plenty of teasing from her brother, who found schoolwork much easier than she did. Although he would always come to her rescue, he was too much of a boy to resist calling her by the decidedly uncomplimentary nickame of "Brickhead!" Even today the recipient of this original title laughs at the memory of it.

Toward the close of his grade school days, much of Richard's free time was spent with a particular friend, Reverend Mortimer E. Twomey, first pastor of St. Eulalia's Church (now called St. Brigid's.) Opened in 1900 as a chapel and mission of Gate of Heaven Church—the Church in which Richard had been baptized, received his first Holy

Communion, and made his Confirmation—St. Eulalia's was given full standing as a separate church and parish in May of 1908. Dick was a favorite of Father Twomey's, and for his part, he was naturally drawn to this priest, who can best be described as a great individualist and a hard worker—qualities which were certain to win him the respect of his parishioners. They were indeed alike in many ways, these two. Both were not afraid to stand up and fight for what they strongly believed.

It was certainly in the interests of the boys of South Boston, like Richard and his friends, that Father Twomey led and won the battle to keep the South Boston beaches free of such commercial enterprises as amusement park merry-go-rounds and roller coasters. And perhaps it was from this priest that quiet, unassuming Richard drew the spirit that made him unafraid to "stump" for one good cause after another. For St. Eulalia's Church itself, he was always "yelling for money," as one member of his family put it. He early showed that marked ability to raise funds which made him famous as Mission "Academia" president in the seminary and much more famous as Boston's spiritual dynamo of charity.

Father Twomey had another quality which surely endeared him to Dick: a great sense of humor, not unmixed with a delight in teasing. One day, his young helper became the unsuspecting victim of a typical Father Twomey joke. He was walking down Broadway, one of South Boston's main streets, at a time when it was particularly crowded. Suddenly he heard Father Twomey's voice calling to him from the other side of the street.

"Young man, what did you do with the lead pipe in the rectory cellar?"

Snitching lead pipe in those days was an act which distinguished one as a near delinquent. Father Twomey's prank was more than successful, for poor Dick stood there, highly embarrassed, before all the passersby. Characteristically, however, he later shared the great amusement of his priest friend over this incident.

So it was that Dick Cushing divided his time between home, school, church, and fun with the boys. When he was not down at the beach "scaling stones," or home studying and working, he could be looked for at St. Eulalia's, helping Father Twomey with a lawn party or some other fund-raising affair.

As a matter of fact, Richard was practically one of the "pillars" of St. Eulalia's. Later on, he would be in charge of the bowling alley operated in the basement of the school Father Twomey had built and it would be he who hired the pin boys. His strong hands wielded a paint brush on the church and thus saved Father what it would have cost him to hire a professional painter. But one day, while fixing the church roof, Dick lost his grip, fell in an inglorious heap to the ground, and broke his arm.

Many an afternoon as she watched this tall,
lanky son of hers set out for the church, Mary
Cushing must have wondered if it would be he
who would satisfy her oft-expressed desire to see
at least one of her children in God's service. She
must have often searched that appealing boyish
face with its strong lines and square chin, and
noted the serious expression in the quick, bright
eyes so like her own. True, he was always ready for
a joke, and his good-humored disposition did much
to dispel the serious air, yet there was something
about Richard. . . .

Then, too, he had always been an exemplary
son, never answering back either her or his father,
although, of course, he was not above an occasional
quarrel with his brother or sisters. He was hard-
working and dependable, not at all given to moodi-
ness and almost never discouraged or upset. Were
not these qualities fit for the priesthood?

It would be only natural for a good Christian
mother like Mary Cushing to entertain such thoughts
as time and again she saw her son go off so willingly to help out the parish priest.

On other days, however, when Dick came
bursting in from school to eye appreciatively the
snack she always had waiting for him on the table,
she undoubtedly regarded him with a smile and
thought affectionately,

"Whatever else he is—bright and good and all
that—he is, after all, a real boy."

2

STUDENT

AT A JESUIT HIGH

"Well, now look at himself!"

The Reverend Mortimer Twomey must have muttered angrily something to that effect one day in 1911 when he came across his "junior helper of St. Eulalia's" atop a wagon, stumping for a local candidate for the Massachusetts legislature. Young Cushing, now a sixteen-year-old sophomore at B.C. High, was waxing eloquent for the benefit of the crowd around the tailboard of the horse-drawn wagon. The enthusiasm glowing in the serious eyes which dominated the thin face held attention as much as the easy geniality and command the tall, big-framed boy displayed—that is, until the Reverend Pastor of St. Eulalia's angrily dispersed both the enthusiasm and the crowd. Making his way with fierce determination through the gathering, he grabbed Dick and giving him a resounding boot in the britches, spat out grimly, "You'll be either a politician or a priest!"

A priest, indeed, he would become, but at that moment, young Cushing was just a high school sophomore.

Dick's high school career, like that of many another boy, had its moments of darkness and light, but contrary to the impression he himself retains, in keeping with his characteristic humility, the "ups" would seem to have outnumbered the "downs" by far.

Boston College High School, the school which Dick attended, was a highly respected institution with a strong tradition and a history of continued progress despite many difficulties. It had had its beginnings as a part of Boston College and the two institutions still shared the same building, on James Street in Boston's South End. Staffed by the Jesuit Fathers, whose residence faced neighboring Harrison Avenue, it numbered over three hundred pupils and boasted high scholastic standards.

The school spirit was strong, as is evident from the newsnotes devoted to the High School Department in the college's *Stylus* magazine. There is a noticeable pride in the ruggedness of the studies and the virile qualities required of those who would make the grade. Witness the obvious air of smug satisfaction in this student comment: "There are several vacant chairs in our class as a result of the weeding-out process, applied to those who did not believe in the proverb: 'In the bright lexicon of youth there is no such word as fail.' "

Young Richard Cushing was both a serious student and a natural for winning popularity. His constant good disposition, his ready grin, his openness to one and all made him well known and liked. Yet, as in his grammar school days, and indeed in after life, he never singled out any one special friend. He just liked everybody, and everybody liked him.

His first days in B.C. High were marked by an embarrassing episode. The Cardinal tells this story with gusto:

"We had to serve Mass in turn and finally it came to my turn. Well, I had never served in my life, but I took my turn, and I thought I did pretty well. At the end of the Mass, while the priest was taking off the vestments, he would tell you what mistakes you had made. By way of criticizing how I had served, he said, 'I'm not going to ask you if you ever served a Mass before—did you ever *see* one?!' "

On the high school baseball team, Dick was considered a good infielder and a batter, but though he had always liked the game, it was debating and public speaking that won his heart. B.C. shone in this field, and debating in both the high school and college was highly organized. The Bapst Debating Society was open to the high school students, the Marquette Society to college freshmen and sophomores, and the Fulton Society, to the upperclassmen. The debating prizes were hotly contested and the outcome of all the debates closely followed by the student body. The boy who thought nothing of addressing a crowd from the tailboard of a wagon certainly felt at home on the debating platform.

Richard also distinguished himself for having the biggest "jug record" in his class—or so he says. Boys were "put in the jug"—kept in school after class hours—for breaking discipline. After his time in the jug was over, a repentant Richard always muttered, "I'll never do it again, Father!"

Free after-school hours found Dick working for Father Twomey. "Work never killed anyone," was always to be one of his favorite expressions, an expression he probably picked up from his father. One summer, in fact, he worked for his father's company, the Boston Elevated, in the "Maintenance of Way Department." Doubtless because of the memories aroused of his Dad, often, even as head of the Archdiocese, he took advantage of his right to march as an alumnus with the Boston Elevated employees in their annual procession and to attend the memorial Mass.

Even in summertime, Dick was a familiar figure around St. Eulalia's. Father Twomey, his friend and confidant took a great interest in his helper—witness the stumping incident—but all was not earnest guidance and formation in their relationship. There was never a lack of bantering when they were together. Seeing the imposing figure of the priest coming into the drug store where Dick worked while in college, the boy's first act would be to duck down behind the counter and keep Father Twomey waiting as long as he dared!

Young Cushing was also a familiar figure in the South Boston Public Library, for he somehow found time in his busy days to do a great deal of reading on his own. It might well have been in high school that he began to keep a "commonplace-book"—a record of literary gems met in the course of reading. Writing of this practice years later as a Cardinal, he was to say:

"Since refinement of literary taste grows so slowly, almost imperceptibly, one stands in need of encouragement, along the way. A commonplace-book, I have found, offers that encouragement. It is a good practice to read with pen in hand, marking what is liked or doubted. It rivets attention; it enables one to see what progress he makes with his own mind. One of my professors, a commonplace-book-keeper, once confessed to me that he was amazed at the quality of what he had copied ten years previously. He said he couldn't imagine what had appealed to him in certain passages. That was proof positive of his progress in literary taste. The pages of our commonplace-book will represent so many stages in our development and should incite us to renewed effort to achieve greater sureness of literary taste."

Doubtless his commonplace-book served the ambitious young debater well, but more important, it reflected the keenly observant mind and highly selective discernment responsible for the lasting quality of the words which have always seemed to pour forth so effortlessly, yet so eloquently. His was a searching, disciplined mind penetrating the spirit of great religious and secular writings, noting beauty of style in famous authors, watching for the inevitable expression, for the perfect description of any person, place, problem, phenomenon or situation. Richard J. Cushing was willing always to pay with hours of hard work to obtain desired results.

Such single-minded dedication to the things of the intellect was bound to bring success in school. Thus it comes as no surprise to find that in the June, 1911, listing of B.C.'s prize winners, the Sophomore Section "B" boasts the name of "Richard J. Cushing —Honorable Mention." He was without question, a "bright boy," as his teachers often put it.

Yet, despite this well-established fact, the second semester of Richard's Junior year brought with it the inexplicable but equally well-established fact of near failure, of probation, of a letter sent home by the Prefect of Studies. The mid-year exams had been his undoing, it seemed. This dark moment is the only moment which the future Prince of the Church was to choose to recall of an otherwise successful high school career. He was to recall it years later and to narrate it for the encouragement of "other young lads who find the going rather difficult":

"Three words of my father's that changed my life I can never forget. On a street car he spoke them between two clangs of the motorman's bell, three words to help and hearten a teenage boy. They help and hearten him still, that boy grown old and Archbishop of Boston.

"Long ago this happened on a late winter night in 1912, when my Dad was a blacksmith in the South Boston carbarn; and myself at seventeen, a probationary junior at the Jesuit high school, whom only his parents thought capable of college, and they prayerfully and in spite of the letter I had brought home that day from the Prefect of Studies.

"Dismayed by my midyear exams, the good Jesuit Father had sent in haste for my Dad. An evening appointment it had to be, for the street lights were on when my father left for work, and were burning again before he reached home. Ten hours he worked, seven days a week; a big man and gentle; a good provider, the neighbors said, and Father Twomey, our Pastor.

"Well I remember that fateful night, with the letter waiting for Dad to read. Over forty years I can see our kitchen, and the supper waiting while he read the letter and said when he'd done, 'Never mind the stew, Mary, we'd best get started. Put your rubbers on, Richard, it's beginning to snow.'

"At eight o'clock, we were there, in the rectory of the Jesuit church, listening to the Prefect of Studies. The young Father spoke gently, explaining my status, questioning the wisdom of keeping me in high school. 'After all, Mr. Cushing,' he said, 'God calls His children to many vocations—a comparatively few to the life of the intellect, and fewer to the dignity of the priesthood.'

"Big and straight in his chair, my father listened, his good hat in his lap, firmly held with both hands. Only once and quietly he spoke in my defense: 'It could be, Father, he's been working too hard, weekends and evenings for Father Twomey.' And with modest pride added, 'Assistant Janitor, you might say; a good boy and willing.'

" 'No question of that,' said the young Priest, rising, 'nor must you feel bad about it all. Saint Joseph was a carpenter. God will find work for this Richard of yours.'

"My father thanked him. 'Good night, Father,' he said.

"As if it were yesterday, I recall the cold wet dark of the street car stop, and the rain that was snow in the oncoming lights of our southbound car.

We rode homeward not talking, each with his thoughts, and mine unhappy. At last I said, pretending indifference as boys will, 'They can have their diploma. I'll get a job and help at home.'

"Dad answered me quietly, words I missed in the crowded aisle. Then three I didn't miss, clearly heard between two clangs of the motorman's bell. 'Carry on, son,' he said.

"And when we got off at City Point, there were a few words more from my immigrant father, inarticulate often, but to me that dark night, the best of teachers. Hurrying homeward, 'Do the best you can,' he told me, ''tis all God asks. He'll do the rest.' Commonplace words, but who knows better to help and hearten child or man, teenager or bishop?

" 'Carry on,' said my father long ago. With God's help I will—we will, His children, you and I. I pass it on to other young lads who find the going rather difficult."

Ruling out the impression given that here was just an average lad with a routine problem of failure on his hands, we ask ourselves: what really did bring on this crisis?

In a rare moment of relaxed reminiscing, the Cardinal recently told this same story of near failure to a group of young friends, but on this occasion the story was complete: "I used to make speeches for various causes and was well paid for them. Naturally, because of that, I wasn't doing so well in my studies. So the Jesuit Prefect sent for my father,

God rest him, to find out why I wasn't doing better
in school. Of course, my poor father didn't know I
was making money on the side."

At all events, "carry on" Richard certainly did,
for his high school career was terminated in glory.
The Senior Year found him a leading member of the
Bapst Debating Society and also the speaker at the
graduation exercises.

If these recollections—so rare with the Cardinal
—are important for the story they tell, they also provide a real insight into the home and family Richard
loved. The supper on the kitchen table, the mother
and son anxiously watching the big blacksmith read
the letter, and then his decision: "Never mind the
stew, Mary, we'd best get started"—this is a scene
expressive of the union and love between a quiet-
spoken man, a humiliated son and a worrying mother. "Big and straight in his chair, my father listened
to the Prefect, his good hat in his lap, firmly held
with both hands"—this is understandable pride
speaking, pride forever linked to a son's memory
of his Dad, of his "Pa's" honest, powerful hands,
of his immigrant father's calm and consideration for
his boy ("He saw me through a lot, he really did").

Perhaps the poignancy of the moment was aug-
mented by the fact that, as the Jesuit Prefect pointed
out, it was not merely a matter of a high school
education; it was a question of a vocation to the
priesthood. The gloom that settled over the lad
leaving the Jesuit residence and the thinly-disguised

pain in the words, "They can have their diploma; I'll get a job and help at home," sprang from the sudden vision of a cherished dream shattered. "God will find work for your son," the priest had said to Patrick Cushing. And as things turned out, He certainly did, but contrary to the young Prefect's view, that work was in the vocation to which Richard himself, his parents, and Father Twomey believed he was called—the priesthood.

One of his sisters recalls that it was during his high school years that Richard first spoke out about his desire to be a priest. In addition, the Jesuit Prefect would seem to have been well acquainted with this desire, judging from his advice on that memorable evening. Father Twomey, too, did not hesitate to remind him of this same desire when he broke up his political speech. It was, then, an accepted fact with those who knew him best. And when asked as a Cardinal when he had first thought of the priesthood, he answered after a moment of rather surprised silence: "What do you mean? I always wanted to be a priest."

A priest he would be! And for a while it seemed quite definite that he would be a Jesuit. So it was that the young graduate delivering the stirring commencement address, entitled, "The Press as an Intellectual Force," to an audience of proud parents and B.C. High alumni on that great day in June, 1913, had more than one cause for joy. He was happy over the prize he had won in Latin and Greek and the Honorable Mention given him in Mathematics. But most of all, he was happy because he had brought joy to a proud father and mother, and because the way to a bright future lay open before him.

It was a beautiful and solemn moment, but not to hear the Cardinal tell of it now: "I was one of three graduates in short pants, the 'young' ones! All the others had on trousers! In any event, I gave the speech."

With graduation behind him, Dick made up his mind to join the Jesuits. He applied and was accepted, along with three other boys he knew. Patrick and Mary Cushing were, of course, delighted with this turn of events. Their Richard—one of the four candidates selected by the Jesuits! Seeing their pride in him, Dick must have felt anew the blessings of that love with which they had always surrounded him. As an Archbishop, he once urged a young woman to take good care of her parents with the words, "Be good to them while you have them, for when they're gone, you'll find that no one can take their place."

So everything was settled for Richard—or was it?

"I joined the Jesuits and quit the night before!" remarked the Cardinal on one occasion. This joking, enigmatic comment has a basis in reality.

The night before he was to leave to begin his studies with the Jesuits, Dick decided against it.

The other boys who boarded a pullman that next evening on their way to the Jesuit Novitiate in Poughkeepsie, New York, were very curious as to what had happened to him. One happened to see a card on the berth above his, and the card bore the name, "Richard Cushing." But when the train pulled out, no Richard Cushing had appeared.

Why? In telling the story of the empty upper berth, the Cardinal simply concluded, "But I never went. Why? I don't know, but I never went."

After enrolling at Boston College for the fall term, Richard spent the summer of 1913 as a private tutor. Two dollars an hour he earned teaching wealthy pupils Latin, Greek, and other subjects. This was certainly a good preparation—financially and intellectually—for a successful college career.

He had not yet entirely relinquished the idea of becoming a Jesuit, however. It was to stay with him during the next two years, at the end of which he would have to face a second difficult decision.

3

A COLLEGE CAREER

INTERRUPTED

The auditorium was packed, and an air of expectancy, of impatient expectancy, prevailed throughout the B.C. Glee Club's rendition, two orations by seniors and the address of welcome by the Very Reverend President. The eyes of the student body were on the figure in red dominating the speakers' platform.

This was February 10, 1959, and the occasion a Student Reception for Boston's new Cardinal and Boston College's famed alumnus. Indeed, after his name, on the dignified red and white program was the figure: " '17."

At last, it was time for the Cardinal to speak. Erect and smiling, he faced that audience to whom he was a most familiar figure. Opening his hands in a typically expressive gesture, to their delight and astonishment, he began telling them in his drily humorous way of the many problems becoming a Cardinal entails. For example, the wardrobe—how do you know when to wear which pair of shoes? And how about the black trousers showing beneath the too short red cassock? Over the roar of laughter, he then proceeded to demonstrate his solution to the last problem: there beneath the cassock he lifted up a bit were the red stockings—complete with garters— over the black pants!

Oh, there might be many Cardinals in the world, but nobody in that crowd doubted that there could be just one Cardinal Cushing. And they loved him!

This was Homecoming Day—of an unusual kind! And it drew the Cardinal's mind back to his days as a B.C. student.

"I am an encouragement to the average student," he said, emphasizing the "average" with an eloquent wave of his hand. "I was a uncouth lad, non-studious. I found it hard going, not only in studies, but in deportment, too." He paused, with his characteristic ease, and then went on leisurely, but earnestly: "Well, I imbibed some principles, which I applied through my life. I've always tried to do my best every time I received an assignment, tried to do it as well as I could." Then, with the smile spreading across his face again: "The Jesuits work miracles. Here I am—a Cardinal!"

College life at B.C. began for Richard J. on Wednesday, September 17, 1913. His was the first class to start school in the new location on a beautiful plateau rising above the twin reservoirs in the fashionable Chestnut Hill section of Boston. On this splendid collegiate site, which had been renamed "University Heights," ground had been broken for the first college building on June 19, 1909. The new expansion program was the work of a convert from Anglicanism, Father Thomas I. Gasson, S.J., who had become President of the Harrison Avenue institution in January of 1907. His idea was to separate the college from the high school and give it room to grow into a great university.

Father Gasson might have had a very difficult time raising the funds he needed had not a most distinguished and devoted B.C. alumnus, William Cardinal O'Connell, become Archbishop of Boston just three months after he launched his campaign. It was the Archbishop who advised the pioneering president to inspect the Chestnut Hill site to which Richard Cushing made his way from South Boston that September day in 1913.

The Freshman news notes in *The Stylus* at this time are exuberant: "The Freshmen feel proud of their twofold distinction. They are the first class to begin their college career in the New Boston College, and their numbers are greater than any previous entering class."

The entire issue is joyous over the new building, with its Gothic towers. Eventually named Gasson Hall and made the Administration Building, it was called at its opening, the "Recitation Building." The strong influence of literary romanticism is evident in the poetry commemorating this forward step in education taken by Boston Catholics. Witness these lines from "Mater Triumphalis" by Edward A. Sullivan, '14:

". . . Not that we doubt of thee, Mother, who cry to thee here in thy second adventurous birth,

Not that we question thee—seeking thy constancy

have we not measured the wells of thy worth?

Clung to thee, sensing the might of thy tutelage,

fashioned our souls to the soul that is thine,

Does not the sun of thy new-risen glory burn with the fire of a mission Divine?"

Four hundred students walked through the arched doorways of the new building on its opening day. This was certainly the beginning of Father Gasson's expansion dream, the beginning of the rise to the present enrollment of 9,000, but what effect did the change have on the spirit of the boys, on those intimate relations between the Jesuit profes-

sors and their students which had meant so much
to Cardinal O'Connell and others of the Harrison
Avenue days? What effect did it have on a certain
freshman from South Boston?

The answer to both questions would seem to
be the same: it was still B.C. and they were still
B.C. boys. The exams would be as rough as ever, but
there would be as many good times as ever. And
witty, likeable Richard Cushing was right in the
center of them. With two other boys, he took charge
of a big freshman event: a "Smoke Talk," which
in *The Stylus* is termed the "final frolic" of the first
term. The Smoke Talk was a reception for the football team of 1913, and "a very enjoyable evening
was had." The principal speaker was "Mr. E. Mark
Sullivan, former assistant district attorney of the
U.S." Nor was that all. The enterprising committee
had also obtained a visit from one of the candidates
for mayor of Boston.

Richard Cushing was the kind of boy others
would think of when it came time to pick officers or
committees. He was a fellow who looked as though
he knew what he wanted and how to work to get it—
the type who would get things done. At the same
time, he was so unassuming and indifferent to honors, so witty and so ready for a joke, that he livened
up any gathering, and put everyone at ease. He was
a fellow you would notice in a crowd, even if he
were just standing quietly looking on. It was not
only the neat, clean-cut look to him—he was always

careful about his appearance—but rather his natural easy confidence and that indefinable quality of "approachableness." In the collegiate jargon of those days, he was a "regular fellow."

An ability to cut through old demarcation lines was another of those qualities about young Cushing that was outstanding. Then, as now, he had no patience with barriers dividing one group from another and though he had as much love for home and neighborhood as the next boy, he never could see the sense of making an issue of it. What kind of division lines could exist at a local Catholic institution like B.C.? During the daily, hour-long streetcar ride from South Boston to the Heights, one would soon notice that "lower-end" South Boston boys sat apart from the "upper-end" boys. The Cushings, now living at 910 Broadway, belonged to the "upper-end" section, but this all meant precious little to Richard. Another division existed between the B.C. High boys and the graduates of Boston's famed Latin School. The former had the advantage of having come from the college's preparatory school, but the latter had the distinction of being alumni of the first school of its kind in America. And when you are a green freshman, not too sure of your standing, you tend to be quite belligerent about your background—unless you are a Richard J. Cushing. A third basis of rivalry and one from which he was perhaps not entirely free was the distinction between the "city boys" and the "suburbanites." With mock concern, Dick often inquired of a fellow student who lived only eight miles from the heart of Boston, "Everything going well in the sticks?"

It came as a surprise to no one when in his sophomore year the results of the October elections revealed that his classmates had made him Vice-President of the class. Asked on his appointment as Archbishop of Boston to describe him as they remembered him in college, former classmates used such terms as "vigorous, energetic, full of life, facile of tongue, good company, humorous." One recalled his deep, hearty laugh (which if it changed with the years became even more hearty). "He looked pretty husky," another said, "and no one ever pushed him around."

But perhaps we can find the real clue to the secret of his effortless ability to win people in the recollection of one fellow student. It is only a small incident, to be sure, but it is worth noting because it is typical.

Father John S. Keating, sophomore professor of Greek, had been trying to extort the correct answer from one faltering young man for a few minutes. At last he gave up. Completely humiliated, the fellow sat down, not daring to look at the priest's stern face. Dick, who sat next to him, leaned over and in a roughly sympathetic whisper, urged, "Ah, forget it. Tomorrow's another day."

He himself, with his usual devotion to hard study, was doing well. "He knew the answers," recalls a man in his particular section. "He was alert in class and made good recitations." Dick was aiming at a high goal, of which he was constantly aware, and if that goal meant a steady intellectual grind, he was game. It did not matter whether it was Father John Fasy's history class, Father Miley's physics class, or Father Keating's English, Greek and Latin classes, he gave the assignments all he had, with the customary good results. Though he found college math and trig rather rough going, Richard Cushing always countered with, "But I can count money!" No day-dreamer, this boy!

When in 1938 B.C. presented its former student with an honorary doctor's degree, he turned to Father Keating and said, in his self-derogatory way, "You of all people, Father, know that I do not deserve this." Doubtless, the good priest replied, "I of all people know that you certainly do!"

His words on this occasion are typical of both the boy and the man. Whether as a student or a Prince of the Church, he never let the honors conferred on him change his opinion of himself.

Extra-curricular activities in college included, of course, his beloved debating. And international problems as topics for debate were certainly not lacking, for the year 1914 marked the beginning of World War I. In the new building on the Heights, a special room had been reserved for the Fulton De-

bating Society. On its elaborately decorated walls,
spaces had been left for the names of the society's
most distinguished orators. While watching him in
action, more than one classmate probably decided
that the name of Richard J. Cushing would appear
on those walls when he graduated. But Richard
himself had other thoughts in mind, thoughts which
did not include graduating from B.C. . . .

Despite Father Twomey's decisive action of
some years previous, Richard still took a great interest in politics and stumped South Boston on
behalf of a friend of his who was a candidate in the
state election.

Catholics were now being elected to prominent political offices in Massachusetts despite a
new anti-Catholic campaign which had begun
about 1908, probably as a result of fears over the
increasing strength and enormous growth of the
Church. The new hostile movement was nation-wide.
All over the country secret societies and anti-Catholic journals had sprung up, recalling the days of the
Know-Nothings and the American Protective Association.

However, when the anti-Catholic sentiment
died down with the nation's entrance into the War
and the resulting unity of all Americans behind the
common cause, Massachusetts Catholics could look
back over the period without much bitterness. The
majority of their fellow citizens had shown little
eagerness for hostile action, even though they might

still entertain mistaken fears. Moreover, two Catholics had been elected mayor of Boston during the movement: John F. Fitzgerald in 1910 and James M. Curley in 1914. The Honorable David I. Walsh had been elected Governor in 1913, the first Catholic to attain to that honor.

Certainly these were exciting years in many ways and young Cushing studied each event intently. He must have learned much about the older and newer elements in his state—the older Yankee stock and the new immigrant groups, among which the Irish predominated. Though he must have learned the value of patient forebearance in dispelling prejudices, he was never a passive onlooker. He believed in action and in making one's position known with wisdom and prudence but with enthusiasm and energy, too.

Richard was finding many opportunities for indulging in his flair for oratory. And since he was engaged in his political speech-making at the time he won the Vice-Presidency of his class, he naturally came in for no little teasing. His friends accused him of practicing up in South Boston in order to walk off with the honors at the Heights.

In the apartment at 910 Broadway, where Mary Cushing presided with as much vigor as ever, life was good. Elizabeth was now twenty-two; Dolly, twenty-one; Anna, fifteen, and John, eleven. Everyone still congregated in the kitchen, leaving the parlor for special occasions only. The teapot was the ever-visible sign of hospitality, and since the girls were never allowed out after dark, they invariably brought their friends home. This made the small apartment at times a buzz of talk and noise, but no one minded.

Mary Cushing taught her daughters all her domestic secrets and made them proficient in cooking, sewing, and the other household arts. The girls were very close to their parents and Anna, the youngest, recalls that all the children went to them for help and advice. Together Patrick and Mary came to their decisions and guided their sons and daughters accordingly. As far as Richard was concerned, whatever his parents said, went. He had more than one quarrel with his sisters—as one might expect—but with his parents, it was always love and respect. For his young brother, he had a special affection. John was similar to him in many ways—sturdy, quiet and sincere—and in later years, as a priest, the few moments of relaxation which Father Cushing allowed himself were usually spent with John.

As for interest in girls, Richard Cushing showed none. His sisters never remember his speaking of any girl, nor of his going out with anyone. True, the November, 1914, *Stylus* lists the name of "Richard Cushing" on the Sophomore Dance Committee, but it is more than likely that as Vice-President of the class, he was drawn into helping to plan the affair.

For Richard's mind was elsewhere. It was on the holy priesthood.

When a first cousin, John P. Kenneally, a night school law student working days as a claim adjuster, tried to persuade him to switch over to law school, he received a firm refusal.

"There's a good future for claim adjusters," urged Kenneally.

"Not for me," answered Richard in the same decided tone. "I'm going to be a priest."

This calm statement caught the other young man unawares.

"A priest!" he exclaimed. "What do you want to be a priest for?" To him it had many disadvantages, to say the least. Sure, you got three square meals a day and a roof over your head, but that was about all. The rest of the picture was dark: plenty of hard work and no money. What was more, marriage was out. John could not see it. What about all those drawbacks?

Richard knew all that, but it did not matter. He would be a priest. "That's what I've always wanted to be, ever since I was a kid."

At the end of his sophomore year, he again decided to go to the Jesuits. For years now, he had been closely associated with the good Fathers, and had always admired their religious and scholarly qualities. Their international affiliations and world missions, too, would appeal to this young man, whose interests and outlook had never known the restrictions of any form of provincialism.

Yet when Richard left home that summer, it was not to join the Jesuits; it was to join the army.

Once again he had found that he could not take the step he had been contemplating during the previous years. Perhaps he felt that a teaching career was not for him, despite his esteem for the spirit of the great Order.

Unrest and apprehension marked the American national scene in that summer when Richard Cushing left the house on Broadway for his term in the army. Only a few months before, on May 7, the country had been horrified by the sinking of the huge passenger liner, the *Lusitania*, by a German submarine. Among the 1,153 dead were 114 American citizens, and feeling was running high. A grave crisis seemed close at hand. The United States had only a small standing army at the time, but in those tense months, many young men felt the strong urgings of the patriotic spirit and joined up in order to be ready for the action which seemed to be inevitable, despite Wilson's desperate efforts to keep the country neutral.

Richard's army career, however, was very short-lived. Big and strong he was, but he suffered from asthma, and at the training camp, these attacks became so bad that he soon found himself on his way home.

What next? That was a hard question to answer. He could not think of going back to Boston College. Everyone there believed he had gone to the Jesuits. Besides, if he wanted to become a priest, why not get started? Having completed two years of college, he was now eligible for entrance into the philosophy House of St. John's Seminary in Brighton, training ground for the priests of the Archdiocese.

Richard reached a decision as that eventful summer neared a close, and thus September of 1915 found him enrolled at St. John's Seminary, a candidate for the diocesan priesthood.

Nor was he the only B.C. boy to take the step that meant just a short walking distance from the Heights, but such a great difference in a way of life. The "History of the Class of 1917" recorded in the B.C. yearbook, *Sub Turri,* of that year, has some significant words to say of what took place in the summer of 1915:

"Many of our men," it notes, with what might be styled the faintest hint of incomprehension mixed with pride, "finding that their calling was not toward the conquering of the world, entered an institution near at hand to labor in the vineyard of the Lord."

4

PRIEST

IN THE MAKING

The quiet-spoken lady in the dim, faded parlor was reminiscing on her days as a kitchen helper at St. John's Seminary. From her window she could glance every now and then at the cluster of seminary buildings on the hill opposite, prominent among which stood the old stone Norman style Theology House in sharp contrast to the newer brick buildings that have risen around it.

Turning from the peaceful scene, she pointed to a large autographed photograph of Richard

Cardinal Cushing which occupied a place of honor on her TV.

"He still remembers me," she said with quiet pride. "He writes to me once in a while." She was silent a moment, then said softly, "I never thought he'd get to be a priest, let alone what he's become!"

To her listener's startled exclamation, she answered quickly, "Oh, he was full of the devil, you know! Used to turn on the radio and pick up his cassock and start dancin', he did. He was always fooling around. And he liked my fried bread—that he did! He'd come around for it, between meals, and I'd give it to him, too."

She paused again, and then chuckled at another thought. "Riley the cook was a sour-tempered man and mean to the boys. Once I remember the Cardinal said to him, 'Riley, when I'm ordained I'm going to get a gun and come back for you!' Oh, he was full of it, that one!"

It surely was these kitchen escapades that the Cardinal had in mind when he said of his seminary days, "I was always hungry and always in trouble!"

In trouble he certainly was not, for as in high school and college, Richard Cushing soon established a reputation for being a serious and brilliant scholar and a responsible, exemplary seminarian.

From the outset, with his usual zest, he entered wholeheartedly into the life at the seminary. St. John's in 1915 had only recently entered a second stage in its development with the change of administration in 1911 from the Society of St. Sulpice to the direct and immediate supervision of Cardinal O'Connell. Erected as a much-loved project of his predecessor, Archbishop John J. Williams, in 1884, the institution had been staffed by Sulpician Fathers from Paris until 1911 when the change was made, and Father John B. Peterson, later Bishop of Manchester, New Hampshire, became the new Rector, presiding over a faculty composed entirely of priests of the Diocese.

There were only three buildings, one of which was the chapel, on the secluded wooded seminary site bordering Commonwealth Avenue and Lake Street in Brighton, when Richard Cushing trained for the priesthood. The oldest and main building was the L-shaped, turreted Theology House, built of Brighton pudding-stone quarried right on the seminary ground, and trimmed with brick and sandstone. The other building was the Philosophy House, young Cushing's first home at St. John's. Crowning an elevation near the Commonwealth Avenue side of the property, it was topped by a white tower in traditional New England style.

The stately Romanesque chapel at the Theology House was the pride of St. John's, and the heart of seminary life. There as student master of ceremonies, Richard was to take an active part in preparing for the many beautiful functions that meant so much to students and faculty alike.

Construction was going on in 1915 close by
the chapel. The north or front wing of the Theology
House was being substantially enlarged and pro-
vision made for a new library, new lecture halls and
more student's rooms to accommodate the growing
student body. In that September of 1915, the number enrolled was one hundred fifty-three, a sizable
enrollment.

It was to a family-spirited institution that Richard J. Cushing had come, for St. John's was a closely
knit unit, firmly established on the splendid tradi-
tions set up by the Sulpicians but new enough as a
diocesan-run seminary to enjoy the warm unity of
spirit and effort common to pioneers.

The head of the Philosophy House was Father
George V. Leahy, a gentle, understanding priest
who well knew how to guide newcomers in the
first strange days of adjustment to a different way
of life. Through meditation, direction and spiritual
reading, he began the work of forming the candidates for the high calling that was theirs. The
schedule to be followed was a full one, even for an
active young man like Richard. The day began at
5:50 and ended at 9:50. In between came practices
of piety—meditation, Mass, examination of con-
science, spiritual reading and prayer—classes and
study periods; meals and recreation; special lectures,
celebrations or cultural programs.

On November 1, the Feast of All Saints, he
and his classmates received their cassocks and be-

gan to feel a part of St. John's, even if they had been
there only a month and a few days. Time went by so
fast in the "Sem" and it seemed as though the two
years in the Philosophy House would be over before
they knew it. However, scholastic standards were
high and there was to be much hard study involved
in progressing from one year to the next through
the two years in Philosophy and the four in
Theology.

This fact was sharply brought home to Richard
Cushing at the end of his first term. When the
students received their marks, his name was not
among those on the honors list, the first third of the
class. He knew he could do it and he made up his
mind to concentrate harder from then on. Philosophy courses, History, English, Science-Apologetics,
Chant—to each class he applied himself wholeheartedly. When the second term marks came out,
he was on the honors list, and his name stayed there
for the rest of his days in the seminary.

The end of his first year at St. John's brought
with it another big moment for Dick: the invitation
to continue his studies at the North American College in Rome. This was a signal honor, a tribute to the
excellent impression he had made on his teachers
and Superiors by his academic performance,
seriousness of purpose and well-rounded character.

In recalling the proud moment, His Eminence
jokes: "I went home and asked my father if I could
go. Being a little shaky in his geography, he looked

puzzled, 'What are you asking me for? You will be home tomorrow night, won't you?'" In reality, his father was thrilled to think he had won this scholarship, as his sisters well remember.

A trip to the Eternal City at that time was no light matter, however. For this was 1916, and German submarines presented a serious threat to any U.S. ship. Both the Rector, Monsignor Peterson, and the winner of the scholarship were fully aware of the danger involved. Indeed, the "Great War," news of which was read every morning in the refectory during breakfast, was naturally the chief subject of conversation. Every day it seemed more certain that the United States could not remain neutral much longer. In the event of the nation's entrance into war, American boys in Rome might be called home. Was it sensible to attempt sending more over, in view of the uncertainty of the hour?

"What do you think about it?" Monsignor Peterson asked young Cushing.

"I don't think I'd last there, because of the war," he replied. "I might be over there a few months and be shipped back home. However, I don't care one way or the other, Monsignor. If you want me to go, I'll go."

The good Rector was undecided. He was an extremely prudent man, of an extraordinarily affectionate nature which he had disciplined to the point of appearing almost cold at times. Looking at the young man before him, he tried to fathom his thoughts and to come to the right decision. Again he asked him what he thought, saying, "Ships *are* going back and forth yet."

"They're going up and down, too!" was Cushing's reply, "but I'm ready to go."

So it was decided that he would go. But in the end the whole idea was deemed definitely inadvisable. Throughout the country, very few appointments were being made: only three boys went over in 1915, ten in 1916, two in 1917. The entire enrollment of the North American College after June of 1918 was, in fact, only twenty-five.

When the final decision had been reached, Monsignor Peterson told Richard, "Well, then, continue here." Thus, September of 1916 found him still at St. John's, beginning his second year in the Philosophy House.

During the scholastic year, Dick saw little of his parents, but his mother was praying for him constantly. She was a humble woman, not the type to desire praise or attention as the mother of a future priest, yet she and her husband had great faith in their Richard and were intensely proud of him. Together they would go to see him on Visitor's Sunday at the seminary and await anxiously the week vacations at Christmas and Easter. Patrick Cushing had willingly accepted the sacrifices which putting a son through the seminary entailed; what were these compared to the joy that would be his when his boy said his first Mass?

The tonsure ceremony which ended the Philosophy period was performed by Cardinal O'Connell at the end of the scholastic year of 1917. Vacation began on June twenty-fourth, but by July twenty-third, all the students had returned to the seminary for their "farm work." On Good Friday, April 6, the United States had entered the War and besides praying for the common cause, the seminarians gave much of their recreation and vacation time to potato cutting, planting and hoeing, as their contribution to the war effort. For a while, they had been anxiously concerned about the possibility of conscription, but relief had come with the news that seminarians were exempt.

When school reopened in the fall of that eventful year, the enrollment was the largest in history: one hundred sixty-eight. The members of Richard's class, now in the House of Theology, were old friends. He himself had the reputation of being a good orator and writer, particularly adept at producing striking expressions. Many of his classmates marvelled at his obvious passion for learning. Noting the long hours he devoted to intense study, more than one pleaded, "Slow up, Dick. Take it easy."

Yet he was by no means a pale bookworm. Enjoying good health, he was able to combine his studies with strenuous exercise during recreation periods and alternate his seriousness with wit and humor. On the long Thursday afternoon walks through neighboring communities, when Theology students were divided into groups of four, everyone wanted to be in his group.

"He had an all-seeing eye," recalls one fellow student, laughing. "As we walked, Dick would be examining the scenery on all sides, missing nothing. He was full of semi-sophisticated quips about what he saw—the most amusing of companions."

His never-failing charity prompted him to spend many of his recreation periods coaching, or "proning" as it was then called, less brilliant scholars of his own class and even of the class ahead of him, particularly around examination time. His natural humility made this help doubly appreciated by those who had the good fortune to receive it.

One day seminarian Richard Cushing broke a rule which could have caused him to be expelled. The rule concerned leaving the seminary grounds without permission. For some purpose which he has never disclosed but which seems to have been an errand of charity toward a fellow-seminarian, he went to downtown Boston. And whom did he run into in Park Square? None other than Monsignor Peterson, the Rector!

That evening, he went down to the Rector's office, knowing full well what he had to face. "I cannot tell you why I was downtown," he said to Monsignor Peterson, "but I take full responsibility for my action. I accept the entire blame." He spoke unhesitatingly, even though he knew this could mean deferral of ordination.

The Rector looked at him a long moment. Then he said, "You're a man!" and made a sign for him to leave. That was all. No punishment was forthcoming. The episode was over. But on his ordination day, Monsignor Peterson said to Reverend Richard J. Cushing: "You'll have a hard life, because you're original, and no one can control your thinking. But be yourself." In the new priest's opinion, that was excellent advice.

During his years at St. John's, an enduring love was born in the heart of Richard J.-the love of the foreign missions. The mission spirit was fostered at Brighton through the *Academia,* a unique branch of the Society for the Propagation of the Faith. All the Theology House students were associate members, and some were active.

Begun in 1901 by one of the professors, Father Joseph V. Tracey, who was Diocesan Director of the Society for the Propagation of the Faith, the *Academia* held regular monthly meetings, at which two papers on mission subjects were read. The papers were carefully prepared, highly informative and interesting. They were delivered to an attentive and appreciative audience. The *Academia* meetings actually composed a course in Missiology, since the papers furnished material on the Christian apostolate in action, mission methods, the history, geography and folklore of pagan lands, and means of stimulating interest in mission work.

Richard J. Cushing was made secretary of the *Academia* for the school year of 1918-19, his second year in Theology. In the minutes of the meeting of December 11, 1918, one of his own performances on behalf of his beloved missions is described:

"Mr. Cushing gave an interesting and instructive lecture in his usual eloquent way, on Abyssinia. He traced in a pleasing manner the habits of the people of Abyssinia, their manner of living, and some of the difficulties which missionaries among these people have to overcome. The instructiveness of the lecture, together with its humor, furnished the members with a half hour of real enjoyment and profit."

For his last year at St. John's, Richard was elected President of the *Mission Academia,* after an exciting campaign. He won by a very narrow margin, but as was later noted, the result "was providential for the mission spirit of the Archdiocese." It brought young Cushing very close to the work which was to be his whole life for many years.

As in the old days when he was "yelling for money" on behalf of St. Eulalia's, Richard was an amazing success in his fund-raising drives for the Society of the Propagation of the Faith—"Proppy" in the language of the students. No one's pocket money was safe with such a zealous *Academia* president. "He was marvelous!" says one who observed him in action. "He'd get a nickel here, a dime there, and a quarter from someone else. Then when we

all thought he was satisfied, he'd pop up with a new
scheme to bring in a few pennies more."

The *Academia* celebrated its twentieth anniversary in March of 1921, during Richard's term as
president. The Rector's address for the occasion left
no doubt in anyone's mind as to the real influence
of the mission organization. "The two most important factors in increasing the zeal and the piety of
the students," he declared, "have been obedience
to the decrees of Pius X on daily Communion and
the work of the *Academia*." And in an editorial, *The
Pilot* asserted: "Much of the great success of the
Propagation of the Faith Society in this diocese is
due . . . to the knowledge and the love of the missions that burns in the breasts of the priests who
were once members of the *Academia*."

It was during young Cushing's term in office,
also, that the Brighton group began sharing their
twenty years of experience with newly found units
of the Catholic Students Mission Crusade, through
a newsletter. In August of 1920, the *Academia* had
sent President Cushing and Secretary Anthony P.
Laverty to the Washington Convention of the Crusade, and much note had been taken of his address
at the meeting.

If his own tremendous enthusiasm and popularity had brought him the honor of the presidency
of the *Academia*, his high scholastic rank and con-
scientiousness brought him still another honor in
the form of his appointment as student master of

ceremonies. This responsibility of training other students for liturgical functions became his when he was a third-year theologian. He had to know perfectly all that was required for each ceremony and coach others, taking them through their parts again and again until everything proceeded smoothly. It was a real responsibility, especially since Monsignor Peterson was an expert on liturgical matters and wanted each ceremony in the chapel celebrated with all due reverence and propriety.

There were "advantages" to this duty, however, as the Cardinal likes to remember:

"You didn't get much to eat out there in those days—except for the muffins. Every morning they gave us muffins. I think I ate 6,000 of them. Well, you had to send your laundry home, and when the mothers of some of the boys sent the laundry back, they always sent some food. I was going around to the students to train them for the ceremonies, all the way up from altar boys to the priesthood, so I knew the lads who were getting the food. When I thought they had received from home, I'd go around and get something to eat from them!"

His last year, the year of his diaconate, brought another high honor to Richard: he was named second prefect. The title of prefect was awarded to the highest ranking senior theologians, and to be second prefect meant that scholastically he was the second highest in his class. The boy from South Boston was truly ending his seminary preparation in glory.

And now ordination was approaching. On May 26, 1921, the life at St. John's would end. If he had been the type to indulge in reminiscing, there was much to recall. There had been the momentous decision concerning the American College in Rome; there had been the excitement of the War and with that the dread epidemic in Boston of the "flu," which saw the seminary turned into a hospital for about three weeks. There had been his beloved *Academia* activities, which were not to end even now, and there had been long, full days at the seminary's new summer "villa" on Lake Winnepesaukee in New Hampshire. There had been duties, responsibilities, studies, good companionship, honors, and through it all, the ever growing desire for total dedication to the service of God in the priesthood.

Monsignor Peterson's best-remembered conferences were his descriptions of the natural man, the Christian man, the saintly man, and the priestly man. Full of practical wisdom and delightful humor, the intimate talks made a deep impression on the students. Richard J. Cushing left the seminary and the inspiring influence of this man, who passionately loved the priesthood, with a profound reverence for his calling and an equally profound humility.

"We are just tools!" he was to declare emphatically many a time in the years to come. "Just tools in God's hands, and pretty poor tools at that!"

He was ever convinced, too, that priests should be strong, mature men, selfless and able to "take it."

"I have always tried to be a manly man and a priestly priest," he could say after years spent as Christ's minister.

Manliness, reverence and natural humility are apt words to describe the character of the young man who presented himself for ordination to William Cardinal O'Connell on May 26, 1921, in the Cathedral of the Holy Cross. He was a fine figure of health and quiet happiness. His keenness of mind and strength of will were evident in the high, serene forehead, the steady level gaze of the blue eyes, the full, firm lips, and the square, set chin. He looked every inch a young man who meant to live to the fullest measure of generosity his chosen vocation.

When the ceremony was over, and Father Cushing found himself surrounded by friends and relatives at the reception in the apartment on Broadway, he was at his good-humored, sociable best, but he was impatient to begin doing something for souls. Receptions and congratulations were all right—his mother and father were in their glory—but he felt more at ease when he was busy working.

Friends and relatives at that reception must have made somewhat the same comments reporters would make on another great occasion in Richard Cushing's life, his episcopal consecration. With the solemn seriousness springing from his awe and respect for the office he had assumed, he could com-

bine an easy geniality and delightful humor stem-
ming from his complete forgetfulness of self. He
himself expressed this characteristic outlook in what
could almost be called his life's motto:

"From the start I resolved to take the priesthood seriously, but never myself."

5

DEDICATED TOOL

OF CHRIST

"Have you an appointment?"

"No, Your Eminence." The young priest was silent a minute and then added with his winning smile, "I thought I'd take heaven by storm!"

What William Cardinal O'Connell's inner reaction to that reply was can only be surmised, but the priest was to confess later, "He almost threw me out!"

"Well, Father Cushing, what do you want?"

This was his chance, and the earnest young priest presented his plea.

He had his answer at once in no uncertain terms. It was not the answer he wanted. . . .

"I didn't get heaven," he says, "but I got the storm!"

The first days after his ordination had been very happy ones for Richard Cushing. The following Sunday, he had said his first solemn Mass in his parish church of St. Eulalia. In the proud congregation were his father and mother, sisters and brother, innumerable relatives and friends. Her neighbors rejoiced with Mary Cushing and congratulated her on that "fine son of hers."

That son, though not much given to putting into words what he felt, yet understood the emotions overwhelming his mother's heart. "Many a Catholic mother holding her infant son for the first time," he has written, "has offered him to God's service as a priest, if such is His holy Will. The years pass, and her dearest wish and prayer are fulfilled. Her son stands at the altar, offering Mass for the first time. From his anointed hand she receives the Bread of Life."

What were his own sentiments during those first glorious days? His heart was full of gratitude to God ("To be a priest is the greatest call one could receive from Almighty God"), to his parents, and to the priests of St. John's. "To those who taught me in the seminary," he was to say upon his elevation to the Cardinalate, "I owe a great debt. They inspired me and others to become priests, to go all out for God and the priesthood."

Father Cushing and the other members of his class were not to receive their assignments for at least a couple of weeks. The Rector of the seminary, Monsignor Peterson, asked the newly ordained priest to spend those intervening days helping out a pastor in Cohasset. St. John's Seminary was, in fact, intimately connected with the parishes along the Massachusetts South Shore. In 1912, Cardinal O'Connell had announced that the churches of the Hull area, overburdened in summertime by the great numbers of Catholics vacationing at the beach, would be served by the priests of St. John's. Only two years later, Monsignor Peterson had begun construction of the Church of St. Ann in the heart of the town.

Although Father Cushing spent only two weeks there and was not officially assigned, the South Shore parish would always evoke fond memories. "I heard my first confessions there," he would recall. "I said my first Masses there, and the first baby that I baptized, I baptized there." The mention of that first baptism evoked another memory, a very significant one. "Some years later, I met that child, and the child was deaf and dumb. From that time on, I took an interest in handicapped children." A simple statement this, yet from this "interest"—a word inadequate to describe his passionate devotion to the helpless, the handicapped, the "exceptional" children—were to come monuments of loving care, such as the Kennedy Memorial Hospital and St. Coletta's School.

When the assignments were announced, Father Cushing found himself destined for study at the Catholic University of America in Washington, D.C. For the summer he was told to go to St. Patrick's Church in Roxbury, only a short distance from his home in South Boston.

Once again, his superiors had manifested their high opinion of his abilities. It is by priests assigned to Catholic University, just as by graduates of the North American College, that responsible diocesan positions are often filled. Hence this second vote of confidence in Richard Cushing was not merely a recognition of his talents and character; it was a clear indication of future honors.

The assignment brought no joy to Father Cushing, however. For the time being, he said nothing, yet his mind was troubled. Long ago, any doubt he might have had about his vocation to the priesthood had vanished, but the same was not true of his work as a priest. The old call of the mission fields seemed, if anything, stronger than ever. With such a fire inside, how could the thought of further study and perhaps a future teaching career at the seminary hold any appeal for him? And as for parish work, in his mind the spiritual needs of souls in the missions completely overshadowed those of the staunch Catholic faithful in a well-organized diocese such as Boston.

St. Patrick's, to which he had been assigned for the summer, was a typical example of a flourishing, active parish. The church itself, a large, red-brick Gothic structure located at the intersection of Dudley and Hampden Streets, was only about forty years old, and though rather plain externally, boasted of an inspiring interior. The parish was equipped with a fine girls' school, in addition to the rectory and convent. Described as a "highly prosperous" parish, St. Patrick's was to endear itself to Father Cushing particularly for the mission spirit of its parishioners. For it was the St. Patrick's Mission Club which would come to mean much to him, as a very active branch of the Society for the Propagation of the Faith.

During his short stay in Roxbury, Father Cushing served the Home for the Aged there, operated by the Little Sisters of the Poor.

"The old people all loved me," he recalls jokingly, "because I was the only one they could hear!"

The truth no doubt was that his respectful attention to their inevitable recollections of bygone days and his cheering good humor won them more than his oratorical powers. All his life this priest would know how to lift others out of the gloom that chills the lonely soul. He would always understand the suffering that comes from loneliness, because he would voluntarily choose the solitary path in order to dedicate himself completely to his life task of helping others.

"It is amazing how many people have a bowing or speaking acquaintance with Bishop Cushing," a former neighbor in South Boston would one day remark, "and how few know him intimately."

After only about two weeks, Father Cushing was transferred from St. Patrick's to St. Benedict's Church in East Somerville, a suburb on the other side of the city. The reason for the move is not known. In characteristically humorous, enigmatic language, the Cardinal described it thus: "I'm sorry to say I only lasted two weeks at St. Patrick's. The pastor didn't like me. So I was sent to St. Benedict's parish in East Somerville. I did a little better there" —(here a pause for dramatic effect)—"I lasted *four* weeks!" When his audience stopped laughing, he continued, "About two and a half months after ordination, I had been in three parishes. So I said to myself, 'Either I'm queer or these pastors are!'"

The good parishioners who watched young Father Cushing say Mass in their brick, mission-style church of St. Benedict during that summer of 1921 could not have guessed that he was struggling with a great desire which eventually became so strong that he felt impelled to lay it before Cardinal O'Connell.

It was for this purpose that he decided one fine day "to take heaven by storm."

The eminent spiritual leader of Boston's Catholics and her first Prince of the Church presented a formidable appearance, even for one to whom he was a familiar figure at the seminary. Stockily built, aristocratic in manner, he offered little encouragement at first sight to a petitioner. Unbending and inflexible by nature, a born disciplinarian, he was however a wise, far-sighted ruler, a keen judge of men. The piercing gaze rarely failed to detect true quality of character. And once made, his judgment would be acted upon, although there might be no softening of the tight mouth or relaxing of the stern, cleft chin to hint at the favorable decision reached.

Having asked the "heaven stormer" what he wanted, he studied Father Cushing closely while the younger man replied.

"I don't want anything, Your Eminence. I've been in three parishes in about two and a half months, and I've come to the conclusion that I just don't belong here. I'll never be happy in any of these parishes. The work isn't for me."

It was not that he disdained ordinary parish work. On the contrary, he fully appreciated the tremendous importance of the parish, "the Church in miniature." He would one day write movingly of that importance:

"Throughout the parish, Christ does for a limited group what He founded the Universal Church to do for all the world. Through the parish on the other hand, a group of the faithful, in a corner of the world, do for Christ what all the total Church in Heaven, in Purgatory and on earth does for Him throughout creation. Christ is adored in the parish liturgy; Christ is preached in the parish pulpit; Christ is praised by the parish choirs; Christ is meditated in the parish convent; Christ is imitated, reproduced, in all the mysteries of His life, by hidden lives of unknown parish saints."

No, it was not that he did not appreciate or esteem the vocation of the parish priest; it was simply that instead of "a limited group" of faithful, he wanted unlimited crowds of pagans to work among; instead of a sheltered "corner of the world," he wanted the horizons, the frontiers. Instead of an organizer and administrator, he wanted to be a builder and a pioneer.

Now, perhaps, his dream was nearing reality. Perhaps when he left the presence of the Cardinal today, it would be the beginning. . . .

"You're not going to be in a parish," Cardinal O'Connell was saying. "You're supposed to go to the University."

"Oh, I'm not interested in going to the University." The promptness of the reply and the tone in which it was spoken left no doubt of his aversion to this course of action.

Cardinal O'Connell shifted in his chair and leaned slightly forward. Slowly emphasizing each word with a touch of Irish brogue, he demanded, "What *do* you want?"

This was the moment!

Taking a breath, Father Cushing said, "Well, Your Eminence, I think I'd like to go to the foreign missions. I'd like to go to China or Africa or join the Marist Fathers in the Solomons—any place, I don't care where. I'm big and strong." The words were coming faster now. "I know I'll never be happy in one of these parishes. And I doubt if I would be happy in a teaching assignment following courses at the University. I think I made a mistake—I should have followed the Jesuit persuasion, because I want missionary work."

He had made his plea. He had practically begged to be sent into the mission fields. What would the Cardinal say?

"Your foreign mission will be right where I send you!" came the answer.

". . . He'd hear none of it," Cardinal Cushing concluded in relating the episode. "So I turned on my heel and came out. Within a few days, however, I was appointed to do propaganda work for the foreign missions, in the diocese's Society for the Propagation of the Faith. I was assigned to helping missionaries, and I loved it!"

True, it was a few more months before he left St. Benedict's for his new post, but by 1922, Reverend Joseph F. McGlinchey, diocesan Director of the Propagation of the Faith, had a new and very enthusiastic assistant. If he could not battle for

Christ in the front lines, Richard James Cushing resolved to be a valuable aid on the home front.

The Boston branch of the Society for the Propagation of the Faith already had a glowing record when Father Cushing became identified with it. The Society itself was founded in Lyons, France, in 1822, and had been a friend to many mission territories since its start, including Bishop Fenwick's and Bishop Fitzpatrick's Boston. Over a period of fifteen years, it had sent a total of $46,639 to Boston. In 1845, the grants were stopped because the diocese had grown sufficiently to begin contributing to the Society instead of receiving from it. The Irish immigration that swelled the Church in Boston in Bishop Fitzpatrick's day impelled him to request a further subsidy, but the parish branches of the Society which he had organized still sent contributions to the original group.

It was Bishop Fitzpatrick's successor, Archbishop John J. Williams, who was largely responsible for making the diocese "mission-minded." In 1903, he appointed Father James Anthony Walsh as the first full-time Director of the diocesan Propagation office. Its first Director, Rev. James A. Healy (later Bishop of Portland, Maine) had been Chancellor of the diocese. Father Joseph Tracy, his successor, had been a professor at St. John's Seminary while heading the Propagation work. Father Walsh, the future Founder of the Maryknoll Missioners, set the Propagation of the Faith on firm foundations and by his great missionary zeal made an unforgettable impression on all who heard him speak on his favorite subject. Father Healy, Father Tracy, Father Walsh —through the work of these zealous men, the diocese of Boston in 1904 had the honor of being the most substantial contributor to the missions in the whole Catholic world.

"Father Walsh and I were very close friends," states Cardinal Cushing, "and strangely enough, when he was first assigned in the Archdiocese, it was to St. Patrick's in Roxbury, where I was assigned."

Father Walsh's office consisted of one room in a very inconspicuous wooden building at 62 Union Park Street, near Holy Cross Cathedral in Boston's South End. The one-room office shared the second floor with "Mrs. Farrell's Laundry," and Father Walsh laughingly named it "The Rookery." When he resigned in 1911 to found Maryknoll, he was succeeded by Father Joseph McGlinchey, under whom the work went ahead vigorously. By 1922, when Father Cushing arrived on the scene, the offerings received from the faithful for the foreign missions amounted to more than $400,000 a year.

The work of the two priests consisted primarily of raising the much-needed mission help. It was, beyond any doubt, a task for which Father Cushing was singularly adapted. As a boy and a young man, he had been particularly successful at collecting money for the church. Not only did he have speaking ability, a voice that never failed him despite hours of talking, and indomitable energy, but he also possessed within himself the means of firing his listeners with enthusiasm: his deep conviction that the cause of the missioner is the cause of Christ and his ardent love for that cause.

If Father McGlinchey and his assistant worked untiringly during the week, their Sunday schedule was the heaviest of all. Each Sunday they travelled to a different parish and preached at every Mass, which might mean six or seven sermons in a morning, with perhaps a final one at Benediction in the afternoon. To keep this up week after week was no light burden, but it was an effective method. People in Dorchester and Chelsea, in Somerville and Plymouth began to make the missionaries' problems their own, with highly rewarding results.

Father Cushing was now living at the rectory of Holy Cross Cathedral, at 75 Union Park Street, and commuting each morning to the Propagation of the Faith office at 25 Granby Street in the Back Bay section of Boston, just off Commonwealth Avenue on the route to Boston College, and close to the historic Charles River. The building at 25 Granby Street had once been the residence of Cardinal O'Connell and was now known as the Diocesan House. The chancery office, to which Cardinal O'Connell came every day from his Brookline residence, was located on the third floor of this ornate mansion, and the Propagation on the second.

Because of this arrangement, the Cardinal had ample opportunity to take notice of the multiple activities and dedication of Father McGlinchey's assistant ("He said I was the noisiest man he ever had in the office!"). This latter statement is not to be taken seriously. The Cardinal undoubtedly observed, instead, his quiet deference, calm strength of character and readiness to be of service. Thus, despite his youth, Father Cushing was the man His Eminence picked to look after his residence at secluded 46 Rawson Road, Brookline, during his annual winter vacation in Nassau. Cardinal Cushing retains very vivid memories of that particular charge:

"Any time the Cardinal went away, I had to stay at his house. I was very husky then. I weighed about two hundred pounds and had a pompadour haircut. They used to call me Tunney, after the world champion prizefighter. I was responsible for the house—and the dog. I hated dogs. This one's name was Moro.

"Then there was the Irish cook. I feared her more than I did the Cardinal. She'd come up in the morning, and she wouldn't ask you what you were going to eat or what you'd like to eat. She'd have a big plate, with baloney, sausages, eggs and bacon, and she'd just put it down there in front of you, look at you and say, 'Eat it!' I used to give the sausages to Moro!

"Finally, there were the rats in the place. They were as big as cats and you'd hear them come down the stairs, patter, patter. I spent a good deal of my time throwing rocks at the rats!

"Two days before the Cardinal came back from one of his trips to Nassau, Moro died. Now, Moro meant more to the Cardinal than I did. So when Moro died, I said to myself, 'Well, I'd better pack up, because now I'll be shipped off to the foreign missions!'

"On the Cardinal's arrival, I met him with the words, 'Your Eminence, I have very sad news. Moro died.'

" 'Moro died?' he repeated.

" 'Yes, Your Eminence.'

" 'Oh.'

"I said, 'He must have pined away for his master,' but to myself, I thought, 'He pined away from those sausages!' "

Shipped out he definitely was not, however. On the contrary, when Monsignor McGlinchey, his beloved superior, was made pastor of St. Mary's in Lynn, it was he whom Cardinal O'Connell named Director of the Propagation. This was a clear indication of his high regard for the thirty-three-year-old priest.

In a more serious mood than when he told the tale of Moro, Cardinal Cushing remarked, "Somehow or other, Cardinal O'Connell liked me. He was always very kind to me." With his unerring judgment, the great leader of the Church in Boston had fathomed the worth of this subordinate who was always quick to minimize any personal achievement and turn any praise into a joke directed at himself. In natural disposition and personality, the two men were opposites, but they shared the same zeal for the glory of the Church.

During the seven full years that had intervened between ordination and this new honor, Father Cushing had taken very little time off from work. Every so often, he dropped in on his family still living in South Boston. These visits brought great joy to his mother, who was now approaching seventy and had lost her husband Patrick only three years after they had known the supreme joy of seeing their boy ordained a priest.

Patrick Cushing died of pneumonia in April of 1924, after being sick only about a week. Although in his sixties, he had always seemed the same vigorous "Pa," and his passing was a shock to the family. His priest son, conquering his emotions, said the funeral Mass. He would not be able to bring himself to officiate at his mother's funeral. She, however, was to be spared to her family for a few more years yet.

Once in a while, Father Cushing would take an afternoon off to go out to dinner and to a ballgame with his brother John. For the most part, though, he was immersed in his beloved labors for the missionaries, with whom he had been one in heart and soul all his life. As a Cardinal, he would write:

"The vicissitudes, the hardships, the sufferings of Christ's warriors, they are ours, too. Their victories as well, the glories of their triumphs, in them must we also glory. Of them, their trials and their victories, therefore, we must be a part, and if they are to be of our life and being, then shall every Catholic in his soul acclaim unto God this work of Christ. Unto this work of Christ we shall offer our minds and our hearts. Upon it we shall spend our zeal and love. Turn your eyes toward that missionary frontier which, as it were, encircles us afar upon the horizon. Visualize the missionary Fathers and Sisters in Africa and India; picture them upon the island-dotted waters of the distant Pacific; thread your way in their footsteps through the teeming towns and cities of Japan; penetrate the jungles of the Philippines as they carry to souls the knowledge of the crucified Christ, or climb with them the mountains of Latin America. On this far-flung frontier the battle of life is, in all truth, waged."

"The far-flung frontier"—this was the focal point of his outlook. When he returned from the Roman Consistory that made him a Prince of the Church, he would declare to a vast TV audience, in ringing tones:

"The happiest days of my life were spent as a simple priest with the Society for the Propagation of the Faith. I have always been a kind of missionary. I have always pictured myself on the deck of the bark of St. Peter, looking out over the Universal Church."

6

MAN OF MANY FRIENDS

Two little girls approached the Propagation of
the Faith Office and asked to see the Reverend Director, Father Cushing. Their manner, despite an
understandable timidity, betrayed a feeling of importance at having been chosen to bring the mission
money collected by their classmates to the Propagation Office.

They were shown toward a room at the back,
but upon entering the office, found themselves apparently alone with an object which held them spell-
bound. It was a large bear rug. Fascinated, they

stared at it. Suddenly a frightful sound chilled them
to the bone.

"Gr-r-r-r!"

A split second and then the two children
bolted for the door.

Father Cushing had noticed the rug's effect on
the little girls and, knowing that they had not seen
him in the back of the office, had decided to have
some fun. Hurrying after them now, he called out,

"Hey! Don't run off without giving me the
money!"

He loved a good joke, and was enjoying this
one to the fullest, but he had no intention of letting
the mission money slip away!

Visits from children, teenagers, and adults representing various mission clubs, as well as from
missionary priests and bishops were a regular part
of Father Cushing's long work day. Through the
missionaries, he became familiar with the vast mission field, from Alaska to the Solomons, from Jamaica to China. He came to know the success stories
and the disappointing setbacks in one lone mission
outpost after another. He listened sympathetically
to the problems, to the plans of those zealous men,
and while he listened, he was making his own plans
to raise the money they needed.

Although statistics and figures were an insepa-
rable part of his work, Father Cushing never allowed them to obscure the human element, the personal concern and individual approach which mean

so much to the missionary. He gave each caller his full attention, assured him of help, kept his problem in mind and as soon as possible came to the rescue. The much-needed aid would be accompanied by a warm, encouraging letter, showing that far from having forgotten the missionary's visit, Father Cushing remembered even minor points of the tale the good father had told of his mission life.

One cold winter day, Bishop Turquetil, of the Oblate missions among the Eskimos, called on him at the Cathedral rectory. Remarking on the heavy snowfall and the warmth of the rectory, the Bishop pointed to the pounding radiators and said, "I never appreciated coal until I went to the Far North. Some of my coal up there costs $125 a ton."

"That got me out of my chair in a hurry!" Father Cushing said later. Yet he had not misunderstood. $125 a ton, delivered, was the cost on the Arctic missions.

From that time on, the Oblates of the North benefited greatly from Father Cushing's efforts on their behalf.

It was such personal contacts which helped the young Director to maintain his initial enthusiasm for his work, despite the necessarily routine nature of a great part of it.

After becoming Director, Father Cushing had realized a plan to form new supporting organizations in addition to parish branches of the Society. These new groups crossed parish boundaries and joined together men and women of the same trade, of the same business building or of common interests. Thus, while continuing to count on the parish groups, particularly the Teresian Guild of St. Ann's in Neponset and St. Patrick's Mission Club in Roxbury, he now had new sources of income in the Mission Circle of the Boston Elevated Railway Employees (with whom he had worked in the Maintenance of Way Department during one summer while in high school, and as a fare collector while a college freshman); the State Public Works Building Mission Circle, composed of employees of all the departments housed in that building; the Hotel Statler mission group; and the Sen Fu Club. The latter, whose name means "spiritual father," the Chinese title for a Catholic missionary, numbered over 1500 women who raised sums of considerable size by means of various ingenious enterprises.

In Cardinal O'Connell, the zealous Director found a kindred mission spirit. A true Roman, the Cardinal's outlook was universal, and he gloried in the fact that his diocese had from the beginning of his rule been a leader in contributions to the mission cause. On February 21, 1921, he had received a glowing tribute from Cardinal Van Rossum, Prefect of the Congregation for the Propagation of the Faith. Expressing the Holy See's gratitude to Boston, the Cardinal had congratulated the Archdiocese on its "splendid success in its organization of the societies in favor of the foreign missions."

With his clear administrator's vision, Cardinal O'Connell had been instrumental in having the control of the Society for the Propagation of the Faith transferred from lay hands in France to ecclesiastical authority in Rome.

"When I became Archbishop," he wrote in his autobiography, "the management, control and distribution of these vast sums of money were still in the hands of this lay Board in France at Lyons. I was convinced that . . . while the motives were, no doubt, excellent and the success of the organization obvious, still, the preponderant influence of the whole work was that of a few laymen of France who were now the head of a great religious work. . . . In 1909, I had occasion to visit the Holy Father and, during my stay in Rome, I called on the Cardinal-Prefect of Propaganda, Cardinal Van Rossum, a Hollander, and I had a long and very frank conversation with him on the subject. . . . The work of reorganization was soon begun by the Roman authorities . . . and today is in perfect working order, thanks to the magnanimity of the Lyons Board."

The Cardinal's private charities on behalf of missionaries, though not perhaps known to many even in his own diocese, made his name blessed throughout the Catholic missionary world.

A well-known missionary from Hu-Pei Province, China, left Boston overjoyed at having received sufficient funds from the Cardinal to begin construction of an asylum for the great numbers of abandoned waifs in his huge "parish" of one hundred thousand souls. He had sought in vain through Europe and other American cities, but had met with success in Boston.

Not all the help given to missionary endeavors was of a purely financial nature, however. Father Cushing's sermons in the parishes aroused a number of young people to think of the missions not merely in terms of monetary gifts, but also as a worthy ideal to which to give themselves. Many of these high-minded boys and girls came to his office to discuss their vocations with him. He counselled them and encouraged those whom he could. When they joined one or another of the various missionary orders, he kept in contact with them and promised them remembrances in his Mass.

Father Cushing had a way with young people, it was said. He was particularly popular with the small set in the Cathedral neighborhood. They could spot his tall, lanky figure from a distance and would leave their games to fall in behind him as he walked along Washington Street. The word had gone around that here was a man who could never disappoint youngsters. He was sure to turn into a candy store and "treat" the whole crowd. The rumor was well founded and his popularity forever established.

One morning, as he left the rectory for his office, a little girl puffed by him trying desperately to beat the tardy bell at the Cathedral school.

"Will I make it?" she asked the smiling priest.

"I'll help you over the fence," he offered, although the good Sisters in charge of the school had forbidden fence climbing. "You should make it then."

He had boosted the little girl up and almost over the high fence when he heard a cool woman's voice reprimanding her on the other side. There was a note of bewilderment mixed with the indignation in the nun's tone. How had the child managed the misdemeanor?

The answer was readily forthcoming.

"Well, you see, Sister, Father Cushing's pushing me up from the other side!"

All this love toward the youngsters was not on the light side. He was ever on the lookout for worn clothing on the loyal friends he had made in the South End, and when the child in question was from a poor home in which money for new clothes or shoes was not to be had, Father Cushing provided. Since he was already contributing much of his salary to the Propagation of the Faith, and paying his board and room at the Cathedral rectory, these additional charities left him with precious little for himself. That was a matter of small concern to Father Cushing, for he had few expensive desires, anyway. As long as he had the fare to get to the office in the morning, he was satisfied.

He did not even have that one morning, however. This time it was not the children who had won his change, but rather the "ten-cents-for-a-cup-of-coffee gentry". They, too, had passed the word that it paid to be on his early morning route, and this particular day, being unable to refuse anyone, he arrived at the turnstile without a dime left. When he had sheepishly withdrawn his hand from what had proved to be an empty pocket, he explained his plight to the cashier and was permitted to pass through. "I'll be back tomorrow with two dimes," he promised.

Father Cushing was a thoroughly familiar figure in the South End. Wrote Bishop John J. Wright, former secretary to Archbishop Cushing, when speaking of his superior's installation as Archbishop of Boston:

"Everything that morning fairly sang that the Cathedral of Boston was welcoming one of her own. Father Cushing had been a priest of the Cathedral staff. The South End knew him well and loved him with good reason. The new Archbishop had a correspondingly lively knowledge and warm love for the South End. One of the most delightful and witty talks he used to give in the early months after his installation was woven hilariously around adventures involving almost every lamp post, corner and byway of the section surrounding the Cathedral."

Evenings at the Cathedral rectory were often the scene of brief but delightful moments of fraternal relaxation and conversation for Father Cushing, Father Robert Barry, and Father James Hennessy. The latter was to recall them with nostalgia from a far-off South Sea island. For Father James Gerard Hennessy, a Cambridge-born boy who had studied at the North American College and been ordained in Rome in 1930, although a curate for five years at the Cathedral, was to volunteer for missionary service and eventually lose his life in the waters north of Luzon with the sinking of a Japanese prisoner-of-war ship. Father Cushing felt very close to the zealous young priest, whose story might well have been his own, had the Cardinal given consent. In a booklet entitled *Where Is Father Hennessy?* and published in the summer of 1943, when the volunteer missionary's fate was still unknown, he tells his inspiring story:

"I first met Father James Hennessy ten years ago. As Director of the Propagation of the Faith Society in Boston, I lived with him at the rectory of the Cathedral of the Holy Cross. To know him was to love him and admire him—he radiated goodness, friendliness, devotion, apostolic zeal and exceptional ability.

"My work kept me in touch with Catholic missionaries all over the world. Frequently they would visit Boston and stay at the Cathedral rectory. Father Hennessy met many of them. He became deeply interested in their work.

"One day he came to me and said, 'The foreign missions are suffering from lack of priests. It seems to me that the problem could be solved if a number of priests on the home front volunteered to give a limited number of years to service in mission fields. I'm ready to be the first to volunteer, to try the plan. I'm ready to give the next five years of my life to the foreign missions.'"

Although no mention is made of the fact in this booklet, years later the writer would tell a newspaperman that Father Hennessy did not at first meet with much more success than he himself had when he broached the subject to Cardinal O'Connell: "The Cardinal stalled him off. Father Hennessy came to me with his woes, and I asked him where he'd like to go. 'I'd go to the diocese of the next bishop who pops in to see the Cardinal, no matter where he comes from,' Hennessy said. And then who should walk in—big as life—but Bishop Wade, head of the Marists in the Solomons. Amazing! The Cardinal weakened when he heard the story, gave Hennessy his blessing, and off he went."

The Cardinal's hesitation about granting such a permission is understandable in view of the fact that the idea of secular priests being "loaned" to missions for a determined period of time was something new. When he did acquiesce, he manifested a real fatherly interest in the heroic young priest going to one of the most primitive missions in the world. Wishing him godspeed, he assured him of a welcome back into the Archdiocese after his years of missionary service had ended.

"That is a summary of how Father Hennessy set forth as a missioner to the then unknown North Solomon Islands," continues the booklet. "I accompanied him on the first lap of his journey, bade him farewell, promised him every support and returned home wondering what the future would bring.

"That was in 1936. The world heard nothing of Father Hennessy after that, but all who are close to the foreign mission field heard of him—and knew that he was doing a great work for God as he labored, day in and day out, for five long years as a missionary priest in a country hallowed by the blood of martyrs."

Father Cushing received long letters occasionally from the younger man in which he bared his soul and revealed both the hard and satisfying aspects of his new life. In one such letter, he wrote:

"Is it lonely? I have not found it so. Nobody likes company, especially an audience, better than I, but being alone for a change is not unpleasant. I often think of home and join in spirit in the nightly gathering at the Cathedral, and see you all; but not in a lonely way. I'm glad to be here and I cannot be there, too." In another letter, he wrote: "I cannot be happy until I see some dreams realized, or rather until some necessary jobs are done. Until then, Chabai is my home." The necessary jobs included preparing native catechists, training future seminarians, and administering to the needs of his numerous "parishioners."

In spirit, Father Cushing lived all the adventures, both humorous and glorious, described by his friend. He chuckled over the latter's dry humor, which kept cropping up unexpectedly in his letters. He would, for instance, proudly describe the growth of his orchard, naming about twenty different tropical fruits it would provide, only to end the recitation with: "But between you and me, I'd trade the lot for one good apple!" This was the type of priest Father Cushing could understand: one who worked tirelessly, accomplished his duty faithfully, and laughed off the hardships, bouts of malaria, and attacks of homesickness.

When he wrote a subsequent booklet a few years later telling of Father Hennessy's fate, and calling for missionary-minded young people to take up where he and other victims of the war had left off, it contained these significant words: "Where is Father Hennessy? He is in the minds and souls of all who knew him. He is a constant and continuing inspiration to spur each and every one of us to do our part for the greater glory of God."

The thought of Father Hennessy was indeed very often with Richard Cushing as he labored unceasingly at his desk. His would never be the missionary's life, but he had long ago learned to be happy at the post he had been assigned. Not only was it a work of charity, which fact alone would have endeared it to him, but it also harmonized with his universal vision. In his characteristic optimism and charity, he saw promising, inspiring qualities in everyone and in everything. It was always his conviction that hard work and love of God could better any situation. This was the type of moral encouragement he offered to those who sought his help and advice.

"It is my firm belief that love of God will make you a better man or woman in whatever you undertake," he would write in later years. "A doctor who strives truly toward sanctity will be a better doctor because of that striving, and a street-sweeper who has an ideal of perfection will sweep cleaner. Everyone, every man, woman and child, requires something special to live for. When that something is a goal of sanctity, it will fill and enrich every moment, every action of his life." Optimism and charity stand out clearly in these concluding words: "I have found saints on every side in my contacts with my fellow men—great saints, humble saints, unexpected and often unrecognized saints. I would hate to think what the world would be like without them."

Given this attitude and affability with all, is it any wonder that many turned to him with their problems? His response to one such appeal exasperated his good mother.

It was not because she expected anything from him for herself that she objected to his liberality on this particular occasion. On the contrary, her daughters say that she never took a cent from him as a priest. In fact, on his every visit home, she had a ten dollar bill waiting for him. He knew right where it would be—in her apron pocket.

Mrs. Cushing's anger was aroused because a cousin of theirs was the recipient of the ten dollars she had just given her son. The woman, whose husband drank, had gone to the Propagation Office with a sad story, and as usual, Father Cushing had reached into his pocket. He had come up with the ten dollar bill and handed it to her. Not knowing when to leave well enough alone, the woman told his sister Dolly about her brother's generosity, and thus the news reached his mother.

What? Her gift handed out as fast as it was given? Mrs. Cushing was indignant and furiously muttered something about "the curse of the Irish!" It is doubtful if her anger lasted long, however. She must have learned long since the futility of urging her son to keep some money for himself.

In 1935, Father Cushing's office became more readily accessible to people of all walks of life with the opening of the new diocesan office building at 49 Franklin Street in the center of Boston's business district. "As a memorial of his sacerdotal Golden Jubilee of 1934," records the *History of the Archdiocese*, "the Cardinal carried to realization a long-cherished project of bringing together in one building those hitherto scattered diocesan offices which from the nature of their work needed to be located downtown." One such office was the Propagation of the Faith, the files and records of which had been stored at the Cathedral rectory for about two years. The Granby Street building had become the Boston Academy of Notre Dame, a high school for girls conducted by the Sisters of Notre Dame de Namur; and since 1929, the chancery office had had a handsome building of its own on the grounds of St. John's Seminary in Brighton. Two years previous, the Cardinal had built a beautiful episcopal residence on the Commonwealth Avenue side of the same grounds, and his former home on Rawson Road, Brookline, had become St. Francis Friary and Retreat House.

These various moves were all part of a dream cherished by William Cardinal O'Connell. When he succeeded to the Archbishopric of Boston, he was well aware of the fact that most of the diocesan property was in the run-down South End section, and that in sharp contrast to the respected position of the Church in the higher strata of Roman society, many people in Boston had little esteem for things Catholic. It was a sad situation that demanded change, and William O'Connell was the man to effect it.

In the days when Bishop Fitzpatrick and the Jesuit Father McElroy of Boston College had laid plans for the Cathedral of the Holy Cross and the new school near the Church of the Immaculate Conception, it looked as though the South End would remain the exclusive residential district of the city. It could boast of pretty little parks flanking broad streets, and there were rows of fashionable brick mansions gracing the tree-lined avenues. But the trend changed in favor of the newly filled land in the Back Bay section along the Charles, and the South End deteriorated steadily. Dilapidated tenements and saloons surrounded the great Cathedral by O'Connell's time, and the diocesan offices located in once-fine brick homes on Union Park Street were difficult to reach from the residential sections of the city. It was a rather appalling situation.

"So," writes his biographer, Dorothy Wayman, "O'Connell dreamed a dream—a magnificent, virtually incredible dream—and held fast to it and fitted each step into its plan for years. His dream was to take the Catholic Church in Boston out of the catacombs, by building on the hilltops around Boston a little Rome, such as he remembered on the seven hills of Peter's city. Hills were an integral part of his vision. Like the Psalmist he said to himself, 'I have lifted up my eyes to the mountains from whence help shall come to me.'"

The expanding seminary, the new chancery and episcopal residence, the ever-growing St. Elizabeth's Hospital, the beautiful Cenacle Retreat House, St. Gabriel's Passionist Monastery and Retreat

House—all on Brighton's hilltops—were the results of his vision, as were Boston College and the College of the Sacred Heart in Newton. Not all the moves were made toward the hill areas surrounding the city, however. Many new institutions were established within Boston's limits, but in better sections. Emmanuel College for women was situated on the wide Fenway; the League for Catholic Women had its headquarters in a dignified mansion facing the Public Garden at Arlington and Beacon Streets; and the Cathedral itself was given a new school and rectory.

Contrary to expectations in some quarters, Cardinal O'Connell had refused to consider a new Cathedral, despite the unfavorable surroundings of the South End. He had said:

"To those who ask me if I intend to build a new cathedral in Boston, decidedly no. What this rushing age, this restless atmosphere of America needs, is the beauty of a tradition, which it almost entirely lacks. To me the Cathedral of the Holy Cross, built by the sacrifice of a generation past and by a saintly bishop who has gone to his reward, is a doubly sacred thing. I love every stone in it, and I never enter it without thinking of those whose sacrifice and labors built it. What do present surroundings matter? These will change as all modern cities change, but in the midst of constant changes will be that one perpetual reminder of the faith and fidelity of a people and a bishop whose prayers and

aspirations have woven themselves into the very
fabric of the edifice. Let us keep our old churches
as we keep our old friends."

Is it any wonder, then, that although his successor would further his endeavors to expand and
improve constantly the facilities of the Church in
Boston, he would remain adamant in his refusal to
build a new Cathedral? Archbishop Cushing would
instead spare no cost to repair and beautify the
great church and thus, forge ever stronger the tra-
ditions binding his day with the past he revered.

In 1934, however, Father Cushing was involved in setting up the intown office building at
49 Franklin Street, a project which the Cardinal had
entrusted to him, although His Eminence himself
took great interest in the work of modernizing the
building and especially in the construction of the
chapel, the St. Thomas More Oratory. Father Cushing supervised the decorating of this haven of peace
and recollection in the midst of the busiest sector
of Boston.

As he observed the constant flow of people in
and out of the Oratory in the years following its
opening, Father Cushing thought time and again
of the advantages of such an intown chapel. The
Franciscans from the Friary at the Cardinal's formal
residence on Rawson Road told him that the confessions they were hearing there every afternoon
from three to five were not the confessions of devout faithful. They were the confessions of people

who had been away from the Sacraments for many years. Why not a real shrine intown, to meet such an obvious need? Thus was born the idea of the unique St. Anthony's Shrine on Arch Street today, which has made daily Mass and Communion a reality for countless numbers of working people. Nor was this the only innovation to come from Father Cushing's thoughtful reflections on the blessings of the Oratory. Years later, when he occupied a position undreamed of then, he would establish the first airport chapel, the first railway chapel, a fish pier chapel, and chapels for new suburban shopping centers. With Richard Cushing, experiences have always given rise to thought, and thought has inevitably been translated into action.

So it was with the story of Father Hennessy. Each new letter convinced him that a diocesan priest turned missionary could be a tremendous asset to needy mission areas. This conviction would one day result in his "lend-lease" plan—the loaning of his priests to other dioceses—and in the Society of St. James the Apostle—the organization of diocesan priests who volunteer to serve in Latin America for a number of years.

Another priest, Father Frank McGuiggan, made a deep impression on him during his years in the Propagation Office, and this impression, together with the memory of an older seminarian who had left his class at St. John's, eventually led to another pioneering project: an American seminary for belated vocations. In his *Pilot* column, Cardinal Cushing wrote:

"Father Frank McGuiggan had been for years a well-known Shakespearean actor, back before the First World War. He served in that war and then began his clerical studies in 1919 at the old Boston College High Special Latin Class, under the direction of a good friend of mine, Joseph A. McHugh. Father Frank was born in 1888 and ordained only in 1928, at the age of forty, after a hard challenging course at Boston College, and St. John's Seminary. He died two years later, in 1930, but who can completely tell the story of the grand work for God and the Church in those two years? Two years of priestly service, he considered, and we consider, a fitting reward for the long and difficult studies that he had made to prepare himself for the priesthood.

"I was in the Propagation of the Faith Office at the time, and I remember how inspired I used to be, whenever I would see him working in his parish, not for the applause of theatre-goers, but for the approval of the whole Court of Heaven. Now it is for men like Father Frank McGuiggan that I propose to establish this seminary."

That was Richard Cushing's way of looking at people and events—from the supernatural side out. This view explains his never-failing optimism and active charity. Not all the fruits of his vision and thoughtfulness had to wait for the future to be realized, however. Many were the unpublished activities of the indefatigable Father Cushing, which won him the gratitude of those concerned.

Early one morning, he was making his way down a Back Bay street in a heavy snowstorm when he was astonished to see two Sisters of St. Joseph plowing through the drifts ahead of him. Overtaking them, he inquired their destination. They were stationed at the headquarters for the League of Catholic Women on Arlington Street, he learned, and were on their way to the Marist Church of Notre Dame des Victoires, on Isabella Street. They found this church the most convenient for daily Mass, the Sisters said.

Father Cushing had no comment to make then, but a short time later, he appeared at the League House and offered to come every morning to celebrate Mass. His offer was of course eagerly and gratefully accepted. Eight years he served the House in this way, and as his gift to the Sisters, provided the furnishings for their tiny chapel.

Charities of all kinds increased his daily responsibilities, but he thrived on work and loved to repeat a maxim he had undoubtedly heard many times in his boyhood home: "Work never killed anyone." It was this philosophy which had sent him crusading through the Archdiocese appealing for the funds needed to build mission chapels to the number of thousands and seminaries for the training of native clergy, a program he was one of the first to champion. It was this zeal which had made the Boston Office of the Propagation of the Faith a model for others to emulate the world over.

Recognition of his untiring and highly successful labors was now forthcoming. In 1938, Boston College awarded Father Cushing the Honorary Doctor of Law degree at the June Commencement exercises. This was the first of many similar honors which would come to him from universities all over the country, and leave his opinion of himself totally unchanged.

April, 1939, brought with it an honor of a different kind. The newly elected Pope Pius XII named Father Cushing a domestic prelate, with the title of "Rt. Rev. Monsignor." It was in his downtown office that he added the red piping about his collar, and having remarked to his secretaries, "Well, that takes care of that," promptly went back to work.

The son of Patrick and Mary Cushing, at the age of forty-four, was a Monsignor, with a far greater honor just two months off. Could he have known then what the future held, he would have made the same declaration he sent to the press when elevated to the Cardinalate:

"Trying at all times to live as a simple priest, I have endeavored to fulfill whatever duties my place in the priesthood required. That program will be continued."

7

UNEXPECTED HONOR

The Right Reverend Monsignor Richard J. Cushing was disturbed. And Cardinal O'Connell was the only man who knew why.

"I don't want this thing, Your Eminence," the younger man told his superior as soon as they were alone together. "It just doesn't appeal to me. I'm perfectly happy where I am. There must be a number of priests who want to be bishops. They can have it, but I just don't want it."

113

Richard Cushing was still bewildered and over-whelmed by the word from Rome asking whether he would accept appointment as Auxiliary Bishop of Boston. To be made a monsignor was one thing—it involved little change in his way of life—but a bishop! This was quite another matter.

William Cardinal O'Connell, then eighty years of age, and despite failing eyesight, as vigorous as ever, listened to the earnest arguments set forth by this forty-four-year-old subject, so different from himself. He must surely have recalled that scene of eighteen years previous when the young priest just out of the seminary had said of an honored career beginning at Catholic University: "It doesn't appeal to me."

What *does* appeal to you, young man? Cardinal O'Connell had no need to ask that. He knew better than most that Richard Cushing wanted nothing more than the opportunity to go ahead helping others, working hard as a simple priest, without fanfare. He literally had no other "ambitions." He had been grateful for the recognition given his efforts with the new title of monsignor, but had the honor never come after fifty years of such service, it would not have occupied his thoughts once. And ever afterwards, in his mind, and indeed in his speech, too, for years to come, he would be "Father Cushing." Just that and no more.

Now, only about two months after being made a monsignor, he was telling Cardinal O'Connell in strong, sincere tones: "The mitre is going to be a crown of thorns to a man of my type. I'm downtown there, sort of a man about town. Everybody who is in trouble calls for me." He shook his head, straightening at the same time and speaking frankly and almost anxiously, "I don't know, but I don't think a bishop should be doing the things I'm doing."

O'Connell saw clearly that for Richard Cushing, steps upward held no attraction. If he could have put it down to a fearful hesitancy to assume challenging burdens, on the young Monsignor's part, he would certainly have disapproved, but he would have understood. No one knew better than he that new honors are often accompanied by new trials. His own appointment as Bishop of Portland, Maine, had come as a disappointment to that diocese desirous of a man from among their midst. His name had not been one of those submitted to Rome for the Coadjutorship of Boston, and when named to that position, he had had to face hostility not unmixed with unkind hints that his powerful contacts in the Holy City had won him the post. A leading Boston paper had not hesitated to remark: "He numbered as his personal and intimate friends many of the most influential churchmen in Rome . . . with the powerful friendship of Cardinal Satolli. . . . Bishop O'Connell was not the choice of the church authorities of the archdiocese." Yet he had faced that situation courageously, sustained by his knowledge of the saintly Pope Pius X's trust in him, and by his own fearlessness: "I went my rather lonely way," he wrote, "absolutely ignoring the annoyance of others and without either fear or rancor, indeed without bothering my head about them at all." He had reorganized the vast archdiocese, uniting it solidly behind his vigorous leadership, and his efforts, as so often in the past, had been rewarded, this time with the red hat. Honors meant hard work, yes, but were there not many rewards? If Father Cushing did not fear the work—and Cardinal O'Connell knew he did not—then why should he shun the honor?

As if in answer to an unspoken question about his "downtown activities," Father Cushing said, "I don't know how I'm going to get out of this type of work. I know everybody around the city; I am always helping people, even getting them out of jail!" He paused and then affirmed again, more decidedly than ever, "I just don't want the thing."

"Well," replied Cardinal O'Connell, "you had better think it over for two days."

A hard man to understand, this Cushing, even for an experienced judge of men. If an honor came unsolicited, why not accept it—with all due humility, yes, but with gratitude and some ordinary human satisfaction, too? O'Connell himself had found the greatest comfort in recalling the trust and confidence great Popes had placed in him. The words of Pius X: "*La mia fiducia in voi, caro O'Connell, e' assolutamente illimitata* (My faith in you, dear O'Connell, is absolutely unlimited)", had always been enough and more than enough to see him through everything. He recognized and admitted his shortcomings, but he had great confidence in the guiding power of the Holy Spirit in His Church. Moreover, he was ever driven on by a great ambition to make good. He had written concerning his elevation to the Cardinalate:

"No one in Rome . . . had ever given me the slightest indication that I would be named to the Sacred College. And indeed, why should they? I had, to be sure, given considerable satisfaction to the Holy See by my mission to Japan, and since becoming Archbishop of Boston, I had literally night and day devoted myself to the reorganization of the diocese. But to my mind, these were the merest matters of daily duty, certainly meriting no special reward except the very encouraging feeling of a hard duty done to the best of my ability.

"I am telling all this as the literal truth before God, and not, as sometimes happens, as a speciously modest evasion of a false humility. The fact is that I knew only too well that I had received from the Holy See, and especially from my dear saintly *Pio Decimo*, favors utterly and completely beyond my deserts or my merits. And if I had any temptation to be proud of my achievements, such as they were, it was in my very natural desire to rise to the opportunities given me by Almighty God and to discharge the duties of my office in such a way as not to be entirely unworthy of so many and repeated acts of the kindest benevolence from my saintly Father in God, Pius X."

This was O'Connell—straightforward, capable, independent, and confident. What he actually thought of Father Cushing's reluctance to become a bishop will never be known, but it certainly must have puzzled him, since he knew that the reluctance definitely did not come from anything approximating false humility or timidity about becoming a public figure with numerous responsibilities.

Were there any real obstacles? Surely the successful Propagation Director must have realized that he was a very able man, and as for the reaction of people and clergy, he should have recognized, too, that he would be anything but unacceptable.

In considering his priest's attitude toward the honor, Cardinal O'Connell might have recalled his own hesitation in accepting the rectorship of the North American College in Rome and his decision to reject, if the Holy See agreed, the invitation to become Archbishop of Manila and Metropolitan of the Philippine Islands. But in both cases, he had had grave reasons. The offer of the rectorship was linked to the ticklish matter of the "Americanism" controversy. His suitability for the Manila post could be called into question because at that time when the

United States had just bought the Philippines, the Administration of Theodore Roosevelt favored another man as Archbishop. Moreover, as he wrote to Rome in declining the appointment, "Inasmuch as he had not concealed, from the beginning of the Spanish-American War, his sympathy for Spain and had openly stated the war was unjust, he had been openly criticized as lacking in patriotism. As a result, his nomination to Manila would without doubt give rise to considerable comment and would arouse suspicion on the part of the civil officials, and this would certainly sooner or later be the cause of grave difficulties." These had been serious reasons for declining, and the Vatican had appreciated his candor, an appreciation it showed by later naming him Coadjutor of Boston with right of succession to the Archbishopric on Archbishop Williams' death.

What reasons could Cushing have? In his complete openness, he would surely have manifested any real impediment had he known any. The man had no enemies; on the contrary, his work had made him benefactor to many abroad, and his own love of giving had made him innumerable friends at home.

Yet when at the end of the two-day period, Father Cushing returned to his Archbishop, his reply was the same: "I don't want it."

Why? Perhaps in addition to his humble opinion of himself, the answer might be that he could not reconcile the image of a bishop as it was presented to him in Cardinal O'Connell with his own image of himself. "I don't think a bishop should be doing the work I am doing," he had said. By work he probably meant not so much the position of Propagation Director as the way in which he fulfilled that charge—his endless round of fund-raising appeals, his constant appearances at meetings of the supporting clubs, and his whole way of life, which to his mind was unconventional, to say the least. How reconcile this with the picture of a bishop he had in Cardinal O'Connell? Genial and kind the Cardinal certainly was, but he was also a stickler for protocol and the soul of dignity. Another bishop he had known well, Bishop Peterson, his former Rector, also was of a temperament quite different from his own. He simply could not see himself as a bishop.

He had too high an estimation of obedience to refuse, however. He would leave the final decision to his superior. The outcome is best heard in his own words:

"I went back in two days, and I said, 'I don't want it; it doesn't appeal. I'll only take this if Your Eminence commands me to do so.'

"He shook his head and said, *'You take it.'*

"So—I took it!"

On June 12, 1939, it was announced that Pope Pius XII had appointed Monsignor Richard J. Cushing as Auxiliary Bishop of Boston and Titular Bishop of Mela (once a diocese in Asia Minor).

The happiest at the news was undoubtedly eighty-year-old Mary Cushing. When her son had telephoned to tell her of his appointment, she had rejoiced as only a mother can in such moments. Was she surprised? No, she was not. "I always knew he'd be a bishop," she declared.

The ceremony of consecration took place on Thursday, June 29th, in the Cathedral of the Holy Cross. Consecrating prelate was His Eminence, Cardinal O'Connell, and the two co-consecrators were Monsignor Cushing's beloved Rector of seminary days, Bishop Peterson, and Bishop Addis Emmett, S.J., of Jamaica, a land whose missionaries had known the generosity of the Boston Director. Archbishop Spellman, whom he was succeeding as auxiliary bishop, looked on from the sanctuary, where sat also eleven monsignori.

Nine o'clock was the hour set for the ceremony to begin, but the crowd began to gather before eight o'clock. Several thousand persons filled the great Cathedral. Newspapers maintained that it was one of the largest congregations ever assembled there. Fittingly, two Bishops from other lands, Bishop Michael D. Miranda of Mexico City and Bishop John Byrne of Africa, were on hand for the ceremony. In addition to more than three hundred monsignori and priests, there was a large number of Sisters representing the orders in the Archdiocese. Only a few pews were reserved for those closest to the Bishop-elect: his mother, brother John, sisters Elizabeth, Dolly and Anna, aunts, nieces, and others.

The ceremony opened with the reading of the papal mandate from Pope Pius XII naming the new Bishop, whom one Boston newspaper called "probably the most widely known priest of the diocese." Then a hush fell over the immense congregation as the Bishop-elect advanced to the center of the main altar to reply in the affirmative to the prescribed questions which regard, among other things, readiness to teach the people, to exhibit fidelity to the Holy Father, to practice humility and patience, to be merciful to all in need. Afterwards, assisted by the two co-consecrators, he said Mass on a small side altar, while Cardinal O'Connell celebrated at the main altar.

At the Offertory, the Bishop-elect walked to the center of the sanctuary where he prostrated himself. His steps were slow and deliberate, betokening the calm and quiet serenity that at sacred functions always characterizes this otherwise active, dynamic worker. A soft murmer rose as he prostrated himself while the strong, reverent voices of the priests' choir were lifted in the chanting of the Litany of the Saints. At its conclusion, the Cardinal silently placed the open book of the Gospels on the neck and shoulders of the Bishop-elect. The Cardinal and his co-consecrators then touched his head, and the Cardinal, voice strong and clear though trembling somewhat with emotion, pronounced the words, "Receive the Holy Ghost," and went on to pray that the Lord might pour out grace and blessing upon

His servant, Richard Cushing. The anointing followed, and the Mass was resumed. As he walked down the five steps to the sanctuary, the new Bishop's gaze, which had been directed straight ahead, wavered a moment and came to rest on his mother seated in the front pew. On this great day, Mary Cushing found herself unable to check the tears of joy now streaming down her cheeks.

The Mass finished and the investiture completed, Bishop Cushing, arrayed for the first time in full episcopal dress, seated himself on the stool at the center of the altar and looked out over the Congregation. It was a solemn moment. At his right was the aged Cardinal, erect as ever, despite the heat and the length of the ceremony. The new Bishop's face was marked by a reflective, almost somber expression.

The ceremony was over. With steady step, he descended the altar steps and walked to the front pew where his mother awaited her son's first individual episcopal blessing. The tears still there, she knelt joyously for this blessing, and then watched him walk down the middle aisle of the church, blessing the kneeling congregation. The aged Cardinal remained standing at attention while the new Bishop made his way slowly down the aisle. When Bishop Cushing returned to the main altar, the monsignori and priests proceeded to the sacristy. There they received his blessing and when he had removed his vestments, he returned to the crowds waiting to congratulate him.

Reminiscing about that solemnly beautiful occasion, one of his friends has written, "I attended that consecration. After everyone left the altar and most of the people had departed from the Cathedral, his family was still in their places. I stayed, as did a few others, because I felt something was to be added. Bishop Cushing came out on the altar and with visible emotion, he addressed the people. He said only a few words, but among them, "Please, please don't forget the missions." Then he left the altar and went outside between the Cathedral and the rectory building. We went out with everyone else."

Hundreds of South Boston and South End well-wishers, former neighbors, and friends pressed forward to receive his blessing. Press photographers snapped him in an informal moment of light-hearted laughter with the two former auxiliaries, Archbishop Spellman and Bishop Peterson. Gone now was the somewhat awed, pensive expression, to be replaced by the ready smile and customary relaxed manner. Finally someone asked everyone to leave, saying that Bishop Cushing had been fasting for a long time and needed to take some food.

All this took place in the morning. The afternoon found Bishop Cushing back at work.

"I think it was the quickest ceremony in history," laughs the Cardinal today. "There were no invitations, there was no sermon, and there was no luncheon. I took the morning off, was consecrated a bishop, and went back to work in the afternoon."

At the Propagation of the Faith office, he began the difficult task of saying goodbye to his co-workers. He was sure that he would no longer be head of the 'Prop.' Everyone was moved, not only in his own office, but in the *Pilot* newspaper offices, the Catholic charities—throughout the building.

"Where will you live?" Cardinal O'Connell had asked the young Monsignor whom he had ordered to accept the bishopric.

"I don't know, Your Eminence."

No comment had been forthcoming then, but a short while later, he had been told to go to the Sacred Heart Church in Newton Centre, as pastor, the post vacated by Bishop Spellman on his appointment to the See of New York. The naming of Bishop Cushing to the Sacred Heart pastorate was announced on the eve of his consecration.

A few days later, it was also announced that he would continue as Director of the Propagation of the Faith, to the delight of all.

So now he was a bishop! If he read one Boston newspaper's quasi-explanation of his appointment, just prior to the consecration, it must have prompted a variety of thoughts. It declared that Bishop-elect Cushing was well qualified for the high office to which he had been advenced by Pope Pius XII, having had executive work of all kinds. It spoke of Cardinal O'Connell's interest in him, mentioning that the Cardinal had frequently spoken publicly and privately of Bishop-elect Cushing's remarkable zeal and success.

That he had been successful at his own post could not be denied, but as to the "executive work of all kinds," he was to declare later, "I never had anything to do with the running of the diocese (before Cardinal O'Connell's death). I was always on the outside, never involved in the internal affairs. I never wanted to be!" Had not his first reaction to the appointment been: "Oh, don't do that! I don't know anything about these things!"

As for Cardinal O'Connell's feelings about him, he was to say, "Whether he wanted me or not, I don't know. I think he had others in mind, although he was always very good to me, like a father."

In reality, the aged Cardinal must certainly have rejoiced at having in his new auxiliary a willing, docile collaborator, a man of whom he knew he could ask anything without being disappointed.

Bishop Cushing's choice of a coat of arms revealed his deep attachment to his "home town." The right half of the shield, the personal half, contains symbols for St. Richard of Chichester (book and crozier), and St. James the Greater (three scallop shells), his two name saints. A cross in the background echoes the Holy Cross Cathedral, while the XP, or chi rho, symbolizes Christ. The left side of the shield represents the Archdiocese, with a cross again standing for the Cathedral of the

Holy Cross poised above the three historic hills of Boston and the blue waves of her harbor. (The waves were added by the Bishop at the time of his elevation to the Archbishopric.) Fleur-de-lis tips on the cross recall the French missionary priests who labored to establish the Faith in New England in the 18th Century.

Beneath the shield appears the episcopal motto: *Ut Cognoscant Te*, That They May Know Thee. No words could better express his life, his love, his aim. The full text is: "That they may know Thee, as we also have known Thee, that there is no God beside Thee, O Lord" (Ecc. 36:5), and it is taken from the Epistle of the Mass for the Propagation of the Faith. To spread the Faith, to deepen it in men's hearts, to cherish it ever dearer, to translate it into works of charity—for this he lives. But he has never thought of himself as accomplishing anything alone. Always he has seen himself as merely uniting and directing the generous efforts of the "humble, unknown saints" among whom he feels it a privilege to labor.

"Twenty years ago today," he wrote to a Sister Superior, on June 29, 1959, "I was consecrated a Bishop. Whatever I have accomplished since that time, or since my ordination in 1921, has been due to good friends and co-workers like you. I thank God today especially, and indeed every day, for your friendship, good will, cooperation and charity."

8

NO TIME

FOR HIMSELF

It was about one o'clock in the morning at the Boston City Hospital. Behind the old brick walls facing Massachusetts Avenue in the South End, a young Jesuit chaplain was serving the night shift.

As he passed from one room to another, his eye was suddenly caught by a flash of gold and something purple. He turned back, curious, and stopped in surprise. The gold was a pectoral cross, the purple was a bishop's biretta. There by the bedside of a patient unable to sleep was Bishop Cushing, saying the Rosary with the sufferer.

Quietly the priest stood there taking in that scene. Outside, the city was sleeping, but the Bishop was sleepless and mindful. Strong and vibrant, though hushed, his voice rose and fell in the age-old prayer to the Mother of God. It seemed at that moment as though he had no other care or thought but to bring comfort and peace to that patient.

He must be on his way home from some fund-raising affair or parish celebration, thought the priest.

The young Jesuit saw the same scene repeated again and again during the times when he had the night shift at the city hospital. Speaking of these inspiring memories, he said, "I have never been more edified in my life."

Press photographers often snapped the dynamic Bishop Cushing at Confirmation ceremonies and Propagation of the Faith gatherings; newsmen recorded his speeches and praised his oratory. But in his amazingly full days, there were many acts witnessed only by the most needy and recorded only in grateful hearts.

Such an intense interest in individuals, particularly in forgotten, lonely, suffering souls, coupled with an equally intense interest in children found adequate opportunity for expression in Bishop Cushing's position as pastor of Sacred Heart parish in Newton Centre.

Speaking of his pastorate at Sacred Heart, the Cardinal today says, "I was there about five years, but I only lived there. I went intown to the Propagation office every morning at eight o'clock and I came back every night at eight o'clock." This characteristically brief understatement gives no hint of his dedicated performance of parish duties and his complete immersion in the life of the parish. Indeed, whenever possible, he himself brought Holy Communion to the parish sick, and even "chaperoned" school dances.

Sacred Heart in Newton enjoyed a spirit of close cooperation and good will among the clergy, the teaching Sisters of St. Joseph, and the people. Something was always going on in this active parish. It might be a Holy Hour in the red-brick, square-towered church that defies architectural classification, or a lawn fete, or a play put on by the school children, or perhaps the High School prom.

Founded in 1890, Sacred Heart parish was justly proud of the fact that it had had two bishops appointed as pastors, Bishop Francis J. Spellman, from 1933 to 1939, and now Bishop Cushing. In 1936, the parish had been honored by the three-day visit of Eugene Cardinal Pacelli, then Secretary of State to Pope Pius XI, whom he was to succeed in 1939. To commemorate the event of his visit, Bishop Spellman had erected a plaque bearing an affectionate quotation by the distinguished visitor, recalling the pleasant experience of his stay. Bishop Cushing, who had met Pius XII on that same visit to Boston, hung a portrait of him over the memorial tablet.

Distinguished visitors, in fact, were no rarity at Sacred Heart. Combining the two spheres of his activity, Bishop Cushing often showed up unexpectedly at Sacred Heart High School with a missionary Bishop or an Army chaplain just back from the theatres of war. From such guest speakers, the boys and girls of the parish learned first hand about both the spiritual and physical combats being fought in those agonizing years between December 7, 1941, and August 14, 1945.

The major part of Bishop Cushing's stay at Sacred Heart was shadowed by the horrors of World War II. Perhaps no one knew better than this "Bishop of the Missions" the great devastation wrought by the war in the Pacific and the tragic losses to the mission effort. From the missionaries he learned of the terrors of night bombings and the sufferings of concentration camps. It was Bishop Cushing who comforted heart-broken parishioners when telegrams arrived from the War Department with the ominous beginning: "We regret to inform you. . . . " It was he who would celebrate the pro-burial Mass in Sacred Heart for the beloved son dead in the foxhole or off coral shores. Whenever Newton servicemen or women visited him, he gave them silver rosaries and promised them prayers. Their families brought their letters to him, knowing that he was always anxious to share their news.

To his "favorites," the children of the parish, he urged prayers for peace, along with their sacrifices and zeal for the war effort. He had great faith in the power of their prayers and encouraged them in every way to storm heaven for peace. It was his custom to send each child in the parish a letter a few days before the First Friday of every month, urging him to receive Holy Communion on that day, so as to gain the blessings promised by the Sacred Heart to those who receive Holy Communion on nine consecutive First Fridays. These letters were warm and enjoyable notes which the children cherished and often answered with sincere expressions of love for "you, Bishop," and assurances of reception of Holy Communion. In some of these monthly letters, Bishop Cushing impressed the little ones with the gravity of the war situation and the great need for prayer.

"Next to the prayers that the priest offers at the Holy Sacrifice of the Mass, there are no prayers more powerful than those that fall from the lips of God's little ones," he told them in one letter. "Surely Mary will answer your prayers. You have been doing everything that little children could do to help your country in its present crisis. You have been performing your duties at home, at school and at church. You have given your 'mighty mites' for stamps and bonds. At your Communion on Friday and at daily Mass, pray, pray, pray for peace."

Not all the letters were totally serious, however. There were often little humorous stories or poems that brought gales of laughter from the young readers. His letter for May, 1944, for example, which reminded the children of Mother's Day and what it should mean to them, contained the following poem to give them "a general rule by which to judge yourself in accordance with the ideals of your mother":

"Whilst walking down a crowded street the other day
I heard a little urchin to a comrade turn and say:
'Hi Chimmie, lemme tell youse, I'd be happy as a clam
If only I was de feller dat me mudder t'inks I am.
She t'inks I am a wonder, and she knows her little lad
Could never mix wit' nuttin' dat was ugly, mean or bad;
O, lots of times I sit and t'ink how nice 'twould be, gee whiz,
If a feller was de feller dat his mudder t'inks he is.' "

Bishop Cushing's love for the children was never more in evidence than at parish fetes. He had the gift of making boys and girls feel right at home with him, especially the shyest ones hanging back on the outside of the circle around him. These he would pull tight within his arms, clap his biretta on their heads and feed them lollipops and ice cream until they were beaming up at him with full confidence and delight. He seemed to be everywhere at once and actually did manage to meet just about everyone at such affairs, as movies taken of them proved later.

With the teen-agers at Sacred Heart, he was extremely popular, too, especially after he bought a juke box and had it installed in the school. The "nickelodeon," as he insisted on calling it, was stacked with records of the students' own choosing.

One afternoon a Sister's late class was disturbed by a sudden crash of music from the direction of the juke box.

"Tell that boy to leave the thing alone," the Sister immediately charged two girls. Obediently they hurried to dispatch the offender, but stopped short when they saw who it was.

"What was the Bishop playing—swing?" someone asked one of the girls later.

"Well," replied she, with admirable restraint, "it wasn't Bach."

The truth of the matter was that the Bishop loved music and could enjoy the popular brand as well as the classical. In years to come, he would form the habit of putting on a stack of records given him as gifts and read the newspaper for a short while after supper to a variety of music that ranged from Mozart to a number by Bing Crosby or a hilarious Irish recording telling in bouncing rhythms of the antics at somebody-or-other's wake.

Bishop Cushing was a part of every big moment at Sacred Heart High School. He handed out the report cards. He sat resignedly in a Dutch garden at the Junior prom. He listened over and over again to the school's representative in the diocesan oratorical contest for girls, testing her voice from several vantage points and suggesting minor changes for effectiveness. He planned the schedule for the yearly retreat during Holy Week and was on hand for it. Occasionally he took the senior class on excursions. In 1943, the trip was to the lecture of the Passionist Missionary, Bishop Cuthbert O'Gara. After the lecture, Bishop Cushing took the group to the League House, where he had served as chaplain to the Sisters of St. Joseph for eight years. There he was host at a supper for the girls and boys, who did credit to the meal the Sisters prepared for them.

"You have made this a delightful evening," he told the Sisters as he and the group made ready to leave. "I wouldn't know how to thank you," he went on, "unless it is to tell you that *he* alone"—pointing suddenly to the chubby senior class president—"ate five helpings of your good chicken salad!"

With his young parishioners, Bishop Cushing showed marvellous understanding on various occasions. In giving the Sacred Heart High students their Christmas present in 1943, a copy each of "Archbishop Spellman's Letters to His Father," of which everyone was talking at the time, he pointed

out that he had written no message on them so that
in a pinch, they could use them as gifts.

"I know how it is," he said with an eloquent
wave of the hand. "Sometimes you run short of
presents, sometimes you need to lay hands on a gift
in a hurry—well, there you are!"

Such evidence of his ability to think on their
level convinced young people that he meant it when
he told them they could count on him for help. And
because he treated them without a trace of conde-
scension, they gave serious thought to his "pep
talks," such as the one with which he ended a letter
to the outgoing seniors at Sacred Heart in June
of 1944:

"Stay in glowing health; keep close to God;
study, work, pray. Keep your mind clean and your
heart a worthy tabernacle of God. Never get discouraged. Turn every failure into success. Know
yourself, act against yourself. Aspire to be a man
modelled after the Perfect Man, Christ; to be a
woman modelled after the Perfect Woman, the
Mother of Christ. It is a high pinnacle to reach, but
you were trained in the Sacred Heart High School
to aspire to the heights.

"God be with you. There is always a welcome
for you wherever I am. Knock and the door will
open."

The boys and girls whose first contact with
Bishop Cushing was at their Confirmation were also
impressed by his way of getting to the heart of the

matter without any formalities. Once they had gotten over the momentary fright caused by his "cathedral voice" and had relaxed at his first humorous remark, with which he invariably opened his talk after the ceremony, they found themselves thrilling to the challenge of high ideals, particularly the sublime ideal of the priestly and religious vocation, which he would present with tremendous earnestness.

Bishop Cushing looked upon his episcopal duty of administering the Sacrament of Confirmation in parish after parish every spring as a potent means of performing a real mission to youth. Confirmation, through which the baptized Christian comes to the fulness of spiritual strength that he may be able to profess and defend his Faith courageously, is ordinarily administered only by a bishop, and the ceremony is an important milestone in the lives of young boys and girls. Bishop Cushing rendered it even more meaningful and memorable. He saw the great event as a perfect opportunity to encourage religious vocations. Some might protest that being only of grammar school age, these boys and girls could not know whether they were called to God's service or not. Was it not a waste of time to talk vocation to them? Bishop Cushing did not agree.

In December, 1959, he was to write:

"For over twenty years I have been serving as the Ordinary Minister of the Sacrament of Confirmation. Unworthy though I am, I have signed many,

many thousands of children with the Holy Chrism as I pronounced the form of this Sacrament. After every ceremony of this kind I have never failed to ask the boys and then the girls, 'How many of you boys desire to become priests or brothers? How many of you girls desire to become Sisters?' Up go the hands. 'Too young,' some say, 'to know their minds.' Not at all, I maintain, for experience has convinced me that the average boy or girl receives the call—Sequere Me (Follow Me)—toward the end of elementary school or specifically about the time of Confirmation. That does not mean that some, indeed many, do not receive the call in high school, college or later. But I contend that the majority of those children who have raised their hands in answer to the above questions after they had received the Holy Ghost in Confirmation have reached or one day will reach their goal unless their vocations are lost."

In view of his "Confirmation apostolate," it is easy to understand why on the death of Cardinal O'Connell in 1944 he is said to have declined an offer by two missionary bishops to stay on after the funeral in order to take over his heavy Confirmation schedule and leave him free for his pressing duties as administrator of the Archdiocese. Bishop Cushing wanted to keep planting the good seed of vocation in those generous young hearts, no matter what the personal cost in terms of sacrifice and fatigue.

The genial, kindly Bishop, who never gave the
impression of being in a hurry despite his many oc-
cupations, endeared himself to the older members
of the congregations gathered to witness the Confirmation ceremonies, as well as to the young people.
His ready humor, which flashed out at unexpected
moments, gave parishioners little anecdotes to chuc-
kle over for days to come.

Once, when he had finished speaking on the
priesthood, following the solemn ceremony, and had
asked the usual question as to how many boys
wished to be priests, a startling reply came from a
very "early vocation"—a tiny infant boy who had
decided to sound off with a shrill cry at that precise
moment.

Instantly a delighted grin lit the Bishop's face.
"Why, that's wonderful!" he quipped. "And I'm
sure that you'll make a fine priest some day, too!"

There is always some trepidation on the part of
both children and parents at Confirmation time
over the examination which the bishop may conduct
on the Sacrament and the teachings of the Faith.
Although study and drill by the good Sisters of the
parish precede reception of Confirmation, there is
still the natural fear that in the excitement of the
moment the memory may slip. Of course, often the
questioning is omitted, since adequate preparation
is assured, but with Bishop Cushing, nothing was
omitted. Yet the examination "ordeal" proved both
pleasurable and profitable.

The Bishop walked up and down as he questioned, stopping in front of first one child and then another. His height and his voice were apt to overwhelm the child to whom he addressed a question, but to the relief of all, he soon showed himself an easily pleased examiner. If someone in the throes of stage fright forgot the formula, Bishop Cushing would joke about the $64 question, re-word his query, and beam delightedly when the now relaxed youngster came up with the right answer.

In every public function the children had first claim to his attention, and he would pose for pictures unwearyingly with one group after another, often singling out the most bashful child on whom to shower particular attention. He was never too engrossed in the affair of the moment to fail to notice a child trying to take his picture. Once in a small town, the pastor and his flock had planned a special tribute to the Bishop. After the Confirmation ceremony, the parishioners filed out in procession behind the boys and girls, and the pastor brought up the rear, with the Bishop at the end in the place of honor. It had been prearranged that once outside, the procession would stop and the people divide to form two lines facing the Bishop, whom they would greet and speak to as he passed along. But when they had formed the two lines and turned back expectantly in the Bishop's direction, they found that the prelate had left the line to pose for a little lad who had been trying unsuccessfully to keep up with his big strides so as to snap him. Forgetful of all else, Bishop Cushing had stopped, picked a spot where the light was better, asked the boy how he wanted him to pose, and then complied exactly with the little fellow's wishes.

Returning to face the admiring smiles of the people, he apologized with no trace of embarrassment and said, "He's only a little shaver now, but he'll remember this day when he grows up!"

For Bishop Cushing, crowds were never simply crowds. They were groups of individuals, and his sermons, his whole manner evidenced this outlook of his. He would remember the parents of a certain boy who had come to him with study problems and on meeting them he would at once ask about the boy, to their wonder and pleasure. He would stop in the middle of a church aisle to speak a few words to someone he had recognized, inquiring after a sick relative or a son in college.

"It's amazing how he can remember people," one woman remarked. "I had met the Bishop once in my parish and some time later attended a ceremony at his church in Newton. Afterwards, I stood on the steps watching him coming out and speaking with various people. Certain that he would never remember me, I simply observed from the sidelines. Suddenly his eyes fell on me, and to my surprise, he greeted me warmly. Not only that, he talked on the very subject we had spoken of on the first occasion. For him, it was as though we had met only the day before—imagine! with all he has on his mind!"

A certain convert met him when she attended Mass at Sacred Heart. Bishop Cushing celebrated, and since it was a low Mass, it was brief and unaccompanied by ceremony. Ten months later, this woman went to a Confirmation ceremony in a church quite distant from Newton. Seeing her and recognizing her at once, the Bishop held out his ring for her to kiss and said with a smile, "You're getting the trimmings now that you missed the first time!"

How could someone so busy give himself so fully to so many people on such a personal, individual basis? "How does he do it?" That was the question no one could answer.

Bishop Cushing knew how he did it. He found time for everyone because he left no time for himself. He could remember other people's interests and needs, because he had forgotten his own.

In the needs of others, he saw the will of God. No demands upon him were too great. A tool could never tell its user when it had done enough. His time, his thoughts, his energies were his only to give. In every request, in every appeal, he saw the will of God and complied unhesitatingly. Refusal was out of the question.

"Sometimes God encourages us to do something which is good without actually commanding it," he has written. "In these things also we should be ready and glad to do God's will, and we must not allow our own convenience or laziness to prevent us from doing it. The saints always took care to do God's will generously and cheerfully even in the smallest things."

Cheerfulness—it seemed to come natural to him, and he communicated it with ease to everyone he met. No fatigue or worry ever downed it, because it was the result of effort and charity, not mere natural disposition. The war and its accompanying death and destruction caused him suffering, as did the moral evil of a growing secularism which he saw clearly in the world about him. Yet he was optimistic, and this buoyant optimism of his, based on confidence in God, made him the avowed enemy of discouragement and defeatism.

When his responsibilities had increased with the years and his higher position permitted him to see even more clearly the ills besetting the world, he would still preach a resounding message of optimism. To worried parents, disheartened students, or lonely old people, to the sick and helpless as well as to confused youth seeking a high ideal though surrounded by temptations, he has always stressed the positive side. With God's grace and will power, every failure can be turned into success. This is the philosophy to which he has clung all his life. This is the explanation of that life.

"Sometimes you think that total night has overtaken us," he has said. "Lift up your heads. Countless golden points pierce the darkness: the night is alive with stars."

9

BISHOP OF

THE MISSIONS

From time to time, the stenographer glanced at the Bishop across the desk from her in the office of Sacred Heart Rectory. Bent slightly forward and holding a letter in his hands, he was frowning in concentration as he dictated rapidly. She had noticed that he looked drawn and tired. His broad shoulders seemed to sag a bit and his usual high color was missing. Now and then he passed a weary hand over his eyes.

I wonder how much sleep he got last night, she thought, and how much he has had to eat today.

Suddenly he said, "I don't feel well."

The stenographer put down her pencil at once, but to her surprise the Bishop continued dictating. Writing quickly to catch up, she wondered whether she had heard right. After a moment, she glanced in his direction and stared in amazement. His head was going down slowly, but he was still dictating!

What to do? She wanted to rise and help him, but was held back by the fact that he had not stopped speaking. How could someone who was obviously very close to unconsciousness keep on giving dictation? It was as though the will had refused to submit to the demands of the body.

At last, however, he slumped down onto the desk. The stenographer sprang to her feet to help him onto a couch, but after laying still only a moment, he murmured, "It's nothing. If you'll just put a cold cloth on my forehead, I'll be all right."

It was evident from his manner that such an occurrence was not rare with him. The stenographer had been employed by the Bishop only a short while, but she had already seen enough of his daily schedule to realize that this collapse was from sheer exhaustion.

Had Bishop Cushing been only Director of the Propagation Office or only Pastor at Sacred Heart, his days would have been full ones, but to the duties connected with both these positions, there were added the Confirmation ceremonies, an endless round of speaking engagements and official functions, visits to numerous diocesan charitable institutions, various drives and appeals on behalf of religious orders, conferences with every missionary stopping in Boston, and a tremendous daily mail traffic estimated to average 3,000 to 3,500 letters a month.

Four full-time and two part-time office workers were required to handle this staggering amount of mail, every piece of which the Bishop personally answered. A partial explanation of the heavy mail was his correspondence with missionaries and with the supporting organizations of the Propagation Society. Other letters were responses to his appeals or requests for his presence at ceremonies. A great number, however, were addressed not so much to Bishop Cushing in any official capacity as simply to Bishop Cushing, the man who could and would help. Some of these "little people" were shut-ins he had visited to comfort; some were prospective religious vocations whom he encouraged and guided; some were men and women with problems they had found too big to handle alone. All had one thing in common: the certainty that Bishop Cushing would take a personal interest in them.

"The greater the need of a person, the more eager is he to respond to a plea for assistance," said a nun of him when he was appointed Archbishop of Boston. "He is impartial, but if he favors any particular groups, they are the needy and those in sor-

row. He never has refused help to anyone, if the
need was an honest one. When it is in his power to
say 'yes' to a request, he does so and spares no
effort to provide what is needed, at once. He never
says 'no' if the cause is a worthy one."

People spoke this way of him with complete
assurance because they had been given ample evidence of his response to appeals. Yet few if any of
his admirers realized the full number of his activities on behalf of others.

"People ask him if he is free at such-and-such
a time, say two o'clock, on a certain day," said a
member of his office staff. "He checks in his appointment book, and if that hour is open, he accepts
the invitation to speak or preside, even if he has
another appointment scheduled for four o'clock. He
barely leaves himself time to hurry from one place
to the next."

Despite his crowded days, Bishop Cushing
earned the reputation of being very punctual. Without seeming to cut short any gathering, he timed
everything so precisely as to arrive promptly at
each affair.

Likewise, whenever this prodigious worker
made a promise, he kept it. Even when the promise
was one he had made only to himself, it was maintained. If an idea seemed good to him, he would go
through with it although it proved to involve a
greater demand on him than he had anticipated.
To cite one example, he had begun to send a Christ-

mas card to all the servicemen and women who manifested a desire to hear from him. With the passing of time and the ever-growing fame of his charity, the mailing list for the Bishop's Christmas greetings grew to vast proportions. The project became a major enterprise. Yet he neither dropped it or allowed it to become impersonal. Moreover, he did not limit his thoughtfulness of servicemen to the Christmas season. His daily morning Mass at seven o'clock was celebrated for their welfare.

"Be with me in spirit at that hour," he told them in his 1943 Christmas card. "I will certainly be with you."

So great an involvement in the lives of others made of the Bishop's own life what one would be tempted to term an impossible existence. He took his meals at all hours and frequently missed lunch or supper entirely, in order to meet his schedule. At his downtown office he would have sandwiches and a glass of ginger ale right at his desk, only once in a while allowing himself the luxury of brewing a cup of hot tea in the office's little kitchenette. Even then, he had no patience to sip slowly, but would pour the tea from cup to saucer, saucer to cup, so that it would cool quickly. When arriving home long after the supper hour, he would eat his meal on a tray in the study while going over the parish mail.

"He does the work of four or five men," was a frequent comment. "How can he keep going?

Doesn't he ever take a vacation?" Bishop Cushing had, in fact, no desire whatever for a vacation. It is said that in 1943 he went away for less than a week with two priest friends. After the first day, however, he grew restless and anxious to get back to his duties. He was happiest when he was hard at work.

On holidays, such as Thanksgiving, Christmas and Easter, he would send the three Sacred Heart curates, Fathers Bernard J. Winn, James T. Cotter and Francis X. Murray, home for family reunions. He himself would handle the sick calls, meet visitors and answer telephone inquiries. Left alone at the rectory table at noon, he would forego the traditional feast and settle for a lamb chop. He grew to dread these lonely holidays more and more as the years passed.

Because he had so little time to call his own throughout the year, he saw his family only rarely. When they gathered together for holiday celebrations, his absence was conspicuous, yet they understood that he felt it his duty to remain at his post.

On Christmas day, 1943, the curates worked out a plan to remedy the Bishop's loneliness at dinner. In their devoted love for him, they had sensed what he took great care never to show: his dread of that solitary meal. Father Cotter arranged with his family to delay their gathering so that he could keep the Bishop company at noon. This thoughtfulness moved the Bishop greatly, and although he protested, he appreciated the little plan his curates had made on his behalf.

Those who noted how seldom Bishop Cushing saw members of his family might have concluded that they were not close. Such was not the case, however. "They would do anything for one another," remarked a friend, "but they are not given to showing their feelings. That is their way." Actually the Bishop had had his mother out to the Newton rectory as much as possible until her death. Mary Cushing had passed away on September 27, 1940, while her son was preaching a sermon at a special Mass of the Holy Spirit, opening the academic year at Boston College. So deeply had he felt her loss that he could not conquer his sorrow sufficiently to celebrate the funeral Mass. Yet in later years, he kept no framed pictures of her or his father or any member of his family on his desk or on the walls of his room. Indeed, there is such an absence of things personal in the Cardinal's residence today that it would be difficult to tell just by glancing about the rooms who resides there. Likewise, although pictures of him with children have appeared innumerable times in newspapers, it would be a hard task to find one of him with his sister Anna's two sons, the oldest of whom was named for him. Love and devotion were always there, but Bishop Cushing rigidly adhered to his idea of the priest: the man who belongs to others, not to himself or his own.

That he considered himself completely at the disposal of everyone was obvious from his eagerness to please. If a visitor called unexpectedly while he was dictating, he would get up at once and go to the parlor. If the phone rang, he would pick it up himself, to the amazement of the caller who expected to have to explain the purpose of the call to one or two secretaries before speaking with the Bishop. Once the visitor was gone or the phone call ended, he would pick up the dictation at the point at which he had left off, thus reducing the time lost to the minimum by his power of intense concentration.

Far from protecting himself against requests that might well have been handled by others with more time to spare, he would offer to preside at this function or that, to appear at children's parties, to visit someone's sick mother, or to take groups of underprivileged children on an outing. On all such occasions he meant to please in whatever way he could and would follow any suggestion made to him. If the old folks wanted a close view of a bishop "all dressed up," he would appear in full array. If the collegians hinted that the best gift to them would be a few days vacation, he would obtain that. So famous did he become for announcing an extra few days off that after inviting him to speak to the student body, school administrators invariably sat down to figure out when they might best schedule the free time he was certain to give.

Any hour, moreover, was agreeable to Bishop Cushing when it came to making people happy. One evening he received a strange call: could he please consecrate a chalice right away? The story was that friends of Father John S. Keating, the Bishop's professor of English, Greek and Latin back in Boston College days, had given him a gold chalice for his sacerdotal golden jubilee. They had brought it to him on the eve of this fiftieth anniversary of ordination to the priesthood, but had forgotten that he could not use it the following day at the Mass unless it were first consecrated. Hence the call to Bishop Cushing. The man who made the request did not know the Bishop personally, but had heard that he never refused people.

He was not disappointed. The Bishop would be glad to do this favor for Father Keating, to whom he had already sent his own congratulations as pupil to revered teacher. When the men reached the Newton rectory, they saw the Bishop waiting on the doorstep for them. More than that kind of service, what could one ask?

Bishop Cushing's casual visits to various Boston charitable institutions were often the beginning of a deep interest on his part, followed by effective aid. The powerful attraction he has always felt for unfortunates led him one day to drop into the House of the Good Shepherd, a home for wayward or endangered women and girls, to suggest a Christmas entertainment. He wanted to bring joy and evidence of interest to those girls whom he called "more sinned against than sinning." The initial encounter with the Sisters of the Good Shepherd and the girls themselves started him thinking of ways to improve the school operated at the Home. Eventually he broadened its curriculum, adding, for example, courses in shorthand and even hairdressing, so that the young women would have greater job opportunities on leaving. Learning of a beauty shop for sale, he bought it and sent all its equipment to the Good Shepherd School for the hairdressing course.

The needs of the Good Shepherd nuns and their charges were constantly on his mind. One day he decided it would be a fine thing if three "nickelodeons," as he still called juke boxes, were installed to liven up recreation periods. The three were duly sent, to the great delight of the girls. On a much more serious level, the Bishop raised the funds to build new quarters for the Sisters Magdalens, a branch of the Good Shepherd Community composed of penitents who, instead of leaving the Home after receiving a whole new outlook on life, had expressed a desire to become religious and to assist the Sisters of the Good Shepherd.

To assure the institution of continued financial assistance, Bishop Cushing started a Good Shepherd Guild, borrowing the idea from his Propagation work, in which it had been so successful. He also publicized the activities of the Home, its program of rehabilitation and the dedicated labors of the Sisters, particularly through attractive illustrated brochures.

As with every other interest of his, Bishop Cushing's personal concern never decreased, even when new honors made it more difficult to give of his time and attention. As a Cardinal engaged in planning a modern home and school for the institution, he instructed the Superior to assure the girls that "I love them and want to do this for them."

Another institution which Bishop Cushing visited regularly was the Blessed Sacrament Mission in Roxbury, at which the Sisters of the Blessed Sacrament conduct a school for Negro children. He loved nothing better than to hand out ice cream to the little ones crowding around him in the garden of the school. Needless to say, the Guild of the Blessed Sacrament received his strong support.

The Bishop showed his love for the Negro in still another concrete way. As director of the Boston Propagation Office, he sent funds southward to build at Bay St. Louis, Mississippi, a seminary for Negro aspirants to the priesthood. He also paid the tuition of a great many Negro seminarians.

It was to be said one day of Bishop Cushing that he was interested in those at both extremes of life, the very young and the very old. His interest in two Roxbury institutions illustrates this fact. One was the Blessed Sacrament School, the other the Home for the Aged, run by the Little Sisters of the Poor, which he had visited as a very new priest.

March 19th, the Feast of St. Joseph, found him
spending the afternoon there just to chat with the
old folks and tell them funny stories from his apparently inexhaustible store. So entranced were
they by this "wonderful young Bishop" that they decided to cultivate a "Bishop's Garden" in which they
would grow their finest flowers for him.

He was always touched by such expressions of
appreciation. Letters from children in the institutions he visited particularly delighted him. From
the Peabody Home for Crippled Children in West
Roxbury, for example, he was apt to receive a little
note which read thus: "Dear Bishop Cushing: I am
not a Catholic, but I asked my minister if I could
write to you and he said I could. What I want to
know is when you are coming again to give us
another movie show."

Particularly warm expressions of gratitude were
continually coming to him from the religious women
of the Archdiocese, whom he helped in every way
he could.

Admiring their works of charity, he offered his
services in their behalf time and time again. For the
Grey Nuns at Holy Ghost Hospital for Incurables in
Cambridge, he wrote a booklet on the Order to at-
tract vocations. He attended almost every meeting
of the lay organization supporting the works of the
Franciscan Missionaries of Mary, who among other
charitable activities were very effectively operating the Mission Salvage Bureau, shipping needed

supplies to missionaries. He raised funds for the renovation of the Bedford convent of the Marist Sisters, and felt himself more than amply rewarded when they responded immediately to the request of Bishop Emmet of Jamaica for Sisters to conduct a new leper colony on that island.

Bishop Cushing's chief means of publicizing his fund-raising projects for the various institutions and Orders as well as for the missions was by speaking at gatherings of every kind. He had by this time become well known as a very able speaker. People who came from considerable distances to hear him were not disappointed in their expectations. Nor did they usually disappoint the Bishop regarding the purpose of the talk.

The speeches invariably began with a jest, a humorous anecdote or a personal experience. Very often he would pin the joke on the one nearest him at the table or on his host. Once, after apologizing for being late for the Communion breakfast of a certain women's club, he went on to say, "You see, the committee member whom you sent to call for me wore such a large hat that it blew out the car window and I had to walk back to pick it up!"

At a dinner given by the Boston Irish Charitable Society in March of 1944, the Bishop shared the oratorical honors with Massachusetts Governor Saltonstall and Senator Taft of Ohio. When he rose to speak, he looked long at his audience without a word. Then he said, "Taft!" and paused. "Saltonstall!" Another pause. "And Cushing!" He waited a moment and exclaimed with a broad grin, "What a ticket!" This last was met by a delighted roar, the usual reaction to the Bishop's brand of mild shock humor.

At times his first words to groups for whom he was a most familiar figure were simply, "My name's Cushing!"

Assured thus of an attentive, sympathetic audience, the Bishop would deliver his message and make his appeal. Despite the size of the gathering, no one, even those in the last seats, had any reason to worry about being unable to hear. It is said that once when he was preaching in the Cathedral, with the Cardinal presiding from the episcopal throne in the sanctuary, His Eminence sent a cleric to ask him to turn down the microphone.

The cleric walked to the pulpit and then returned to Cardinal O'Connell with the message: "He hasn't got it on at all!"

So successfully did Bishop Cushing present the projects dear to his heart that other fund-raising groups and public relations leaders urged their speakers to attend his talks in order to study his techniques. When they asked the Bishop, however, to elaborate on his methods of dramatizing a cause and persuading audiences to give, he received them courteously, but could be of little help. Whereas he carefully wrote and rewrote his speeches on solemn occasions and his sermons at Holy Hours, his fund-

raising appeals were more a matter of personal enthusiasm, well-chosen examples and striking facts.
At such times Bishop Cushing the speaker was
simply the Bishop Cushing Boston had grown to
know and love. That was sufficient. It was not technique, it was personality.

The Bishop could be a very fearless, forthright
speaker when his topic was not a needy mission or
charity but rather a stirring call to Catholic action
or a defense of right thinking. At such times Bishop
Cushing made his point in no uncertain terms.
Speaking at a memorial Mass to two thousand employees of the Boston Elevated on the theme that
religion in the United States is subject to severe intellectual persecution, he said,

"The violent attack on religion in other lands
is a manifestation of persecution in its most brutal
form. Persecution, however, need not be physically
violent to be effective. It is frequently more disas-
trous when it is a matter of cunning rather than of
brutality. . . . An index of the fierceness of this moral
attack can be found in the 500,000 abortions performed each year in the United States. It can be
found in the thousands of birth-prevention clinics.
It can be found in the fact that one marriage out
of six now performed ends in a divorce court, and
that divorces tripled in Suffolk County (in which
Boston is located) during the past three years. It
can be found in 70,000,000 people in our country

who are identified with no form of Christianity, Catholic or non-Catholic."

Genial and humble Bishop Cushing was, but he was also a man of great moral courage. Both aspects of his nature would continue to shine forth as the years passed. Speaking as a Cardinal on the need for the generous mission spirit, he would one day declare with fiery conviction: "Unless we think of every ordained priest as part of the universal Church, we shall have a flock of spiritual millionaires who will rot from within. We cannot keep the faith unless we propagate it." No fear of sounding too strong in this man of ardent principles.

On April 21, 1943, the Mission Church in Roxbury, the beloved Redemptorist Basilica of Our Lady of Perpetual Help, witnessed an extraordinary speaking effort on the part of the Bishop, this time in behalf of the missions. That day he delivered eleven talks, speaking at every Novena service in both the upper and lower churches of the Basilica. From twenty to twenty-five thousand heard him. The fifteen thousand dollars collected went into his Solomon Islands Mission Fund, a campaign he had launched in the early part of that year.

The War would continue for many more months, but ever since the Fall of 1942 had seen the start of the slow, bloody advance from one Pacific island after another toward Japan, Bishop Cushing had begun to plan for the post-war years. He felt himself bound to see to it that the tremendous labors of the heroic "soldiers of the Cross," like Bishop Wade and Father Hennessey, would not be lost. As he read of the bombing of mission territories, the capture and imprisonment of missionaries, the bayoneting of Father Arthur C. Duhamel, S.M., a native of the Archdiocese, he suffered intensely. But with the American advance and the rescue of Bishop Wade, as well as other priests and sisters, his heart lifted again. He determined to raise the needed funds for reconstruction of those missions bought at such a price.

The goal he set in 1943 was fifty thousand dollars. The funds actually collected were double that amount, thanks to his own tireless preaching and the publicity given the project in Catholic newspapers throughout the country. When troops in the Solomons learned of the campaign, men of all faiths sent substantial contributions through their chaplains. Many of these men had first heard of the "Boston Bishop of the Missions" from the natives of the islands. In a large leaflet entitled, *What Our Fighting Men on Guadalcanal Think of Catholic Missions,* Bishop Cushing published a letter from an army chaplain giving the actual comments of the men and the amount they contributed. The leaflet undoubtedly brought in more contributions for what he termed the "resurrection" of the Solomons.

Over and over again in the latter days of the war, Bishop Cushing urged consideration of the possibilities for mission growth in the postwar period. In one of his pamphlets, he wrote: "What of the foreign missions tomorrow, when the clash of arms shall be stilled? What will be their prospects in the years to come? The possibilities of that future are almost breathtaking. It may well be that the end of this war can usher in an era of Catholic growth, unprecedented in magnitude and grace."

This was the substance of many talks all through the closing period of the war, particularly his monthly conference to the Catholic priests in training at the Chaplains' School at Harvard and later at Fort Devens. His words made a deep impression on the members of each class.

Just as Marines on Guadalcanal preserved the belt of the first man among them to be killed, and wrote beneath it: Lest We Forget, so also Bishop Cushing reverently kept the shreds of the garments worn by the first missionaries to fall victims to the invaders of the island. Sent to him by those who knew his love for the pioneers of Christ, the shreds were placed in a special receptacle, upon which the Bishop revealed that he had written: Lest I Forget.

His special way of remembering the supreme sacrifice of those missionaries was to encourage generous young men and women to take their places. At the close of the absorbing pamphlet entitled, *Where Is Father Hennessey?* he wrote:

When this war is over, there will be a great need for more and more priests, brothers and sisters. They will be needed here at home and in the countries of the Far East, throughout Oceania and Africa, in European lands and in the missionary outposts of our own country.

Where will they come from? Probably some of the young men in their teens who have seen service on the battle zones of the Global War and who have witnessed the great work of the missionaries may be called by God to serve as officers in His Apostolic Army. Many missionaries of today served in World War One.

But the greatest supply of future Soldiers of the Cross must come from the young men now in high school or at the beginning of college careers. They are the hope of the future. May this account of a Boston priest who dared to do the extraordinary for God and for souls prompt many of them to imitate his example.

There can be little doubt that this and other booklets being published and distributed widely by Bishop Cushing did much to help the mission cause. Each one showed his taste for good printing, for appealing covers, attractive art work and distinctive page layouts. To make the faraway lands become actual realities to readers, several booklets featured colorful maps pinpointing the mission stations and the trips of the missionaries, after the manner of biblical maps tracing the Apostle Paul's journeys. For human interest appeal, as much as possible the Bishop let the missionaries speak for themselves, through letters. He would provide an introduction, background history of the particular religious order or mission area, and conclude with a moving appeal for action, suggesting practical ways of helping. Through this method, readers were able to think in terms of a specific leper colony, mission school, dispensary, or orphanage, staffed by priests, brothers or sisters whom they had come to "know," whose vision and hopes had become their own.

In all his publications, whether for diocesan or mission projects, Bishop Cushing wrote in a personal vein, identifying himself closely with the needy institution. He introduced his reader to it by showing it through his own eyes, as he had first seen it. It is noteworthy that he who had always refused to speak of himself, his life and doings, never hesitated to include the personal element in the interests of others, for he had long ago realized that people would strongly support a cause if they felt that they had been let in on the "inside" story and were being treated as the Bishop's partners. Hence in the booklet on the House of the Good Shepherd, he wrote, "I find it easier to get money for a chapel in Timbuctoo than for the House of the Good Shepherd on Huntington Avenue. It is the aim of this pamphlet to bring into the spotlight for a moment a work which has been going on quietly and unnoticed—a work as heroic, as close to the heart of Christ, with needs as compelling as those of any work on the frontiers of Christianity."

In another booklet, on the cover of which the
flaming word, CHINA, stands out from a mysterious
blue-green background picture of an oriental temple
rising into a mountain-pierced sky, he begins a story
of "flood, famine, war and bandits—the triumph of
modern missionary methods and modern missionary
martyrs" by telling of his meeting with the priest
whose tale it is. This opening chapter is an excellent
example of the Bishop's use of suspense. Starting to
tell of the missionary's journey to the U.S., he suddenly stops short: "But let him tell the story, as he
told it to me in the Propagation of the Faith Office."
Beneath this enticing close is a photograph of a
coolie caravan threading its way along a narrow, sun-
lit path—a well-calculated inducement to read on.

The element of suspense in telling a fascinating
story was coupled with highly descriptive language
to become a regular feature of Bishop Cushing's
writings at this time, both in the pamphlets and in
his weekly column on Propagation work in the Archdiocesan paper, *The Pilot.* The booklet, *Horizons,
A Call from the Missions of the World to Catholic
Women,* which was an appeal for vocations to the
Maryknoll Sisters, offers a striking example of this
colorful language:

> A few frightened fishermen crouching in an upper
> room in Jerusalem. . . . "And there appeared to them parted
> tongues as it were of fire, and it sat upon everyone of
> them." In the twinkling of an eye had begun the fierce

and tumultuous struggle which was to cast forth that fire unto the uttermost corners of the globe. That very day were added to the Catholic Church three thousand souls. That very day started the great missionary "trek" which has wound its way all around the globe. The casting of that fire has been a work hot, fierce and arduous, full of struggle and strain and defeat, full of failures and new beginnings. But it has been a pageant full of life and brilliance and glory—of color and movement. The forward missionary surge of the Catholic Church catches up in every age the richest contributions of chosen souls and carries them along in its eager march.

This particular passage reveals his propensity for stirring action verbs and for the inverted order of noun followed by adjective, e.g., "a work hot, fierce and arduous." At times he used the Shakespearean adjective-noun-adjective order, as "a big man and gentle," in his description of his father already quoted.

A good example of Bishop Cushing's ability to combine suspense and vivid description for effective beginnings may be found in the opening paragraphs of a leaflet entitled, *Missionary Co-operation.* (1940):

On a bright April morning in the year 1541, the royal fleet of the King of Portugal sailed into the open sea and began a memorable journey. Bound for India it carried a small army of soldiers, fortune-seekers and adventurers. One passenger stood out amidst that noisy, carefree army. He was young, dark-eyed, dark-skinned, with a mop of luxuriant black hair tumbling across his brow. He was just thirty-five. Garbed in the habit of a priest, his expressive face glowed with emotion as he bade farewell to the friends who flocked about him. . . . Who was he? The question dominated the fleet. Was he a chaplain? A missionary? An ambassador? Or was he a plain adventurer like themselves? Who was he? The secret came out at last. He was all his fellow passengers thought he was. He was a nobleman, a chaplain, a missionary, an ambassador invested with royal orders. He was even an adventurer, seeking not gold, nor lands, nor power, but souls; an adventurer of God, dreaming about vast multitudes, the benighted hordes of the Orient, sunken in paganism, degraded, starved for the bread of God. His name was Francis Xavier, the greatest missionary since apostolic times.

This same leaflet affords a sample of another mark of the Bishop's writing: frequent use of brilliant contrasts. He took real delight in presenting together two figures, two concepts, or two facts seemingly radically opposed to one another, only to point out their basic similarity or compatibility in the unifying bond of faith. The paragraph following the description of Xavier in the leaflet reads:

> In striking contrast to this portrait, consider that of another missionary. On a bright April morning in the year 1888, a tall, straight man and his beautiful daughter of sixteen mounted the steps of a Carmelite convent in Lisieux,

France. For a moment they knelt together in the chapel. Then the old father took his daughter in his arms and kissed her an affectionate farewell. . . . Months passed by and with their passing this childlike nun climbed the heights of sanctity. Delicately nurtured, sensitively framed, she threw herself into the daily routine of a Carmelite's life, asking no privilege, accepting no exemption, performing a work of perfection that taxes the stoutest of souls. Who was she? Who was this burning candle of love? Teresa Martin, popularly known and universally loved as St. Therese of the Child Jesus—the Little Flower. And why did she cast herself into this hidden, arduous life of prayer, sacrifice, and mortification? For the same reason that Xavier accompanied that unruly mob to India: to save souls.

Whereas the initial pages of these pamphlets "with a purpose" were written in a colorfully descriptive language and consisted of a thrilling story or anecdote, the closing chapters were invariably very down to earth in language and practical in content. Even the long adjective-strewn sentences were missing, replaced by short, arrestingly terse remarks appealing to the more cautious side of human nature. Witness the description of the Good Shepherd Guild near the end of the booklet on that Home: "In many respects it is a unique Guild. There are no officers and no social activities. There is no check on who attends or who does not attend the meetings. In fact there are not meetings as commonly recognized. . . . A monthly Holy Hour is held in the convent chapels. Attendance is voluntary."

Everything in the Bishop's publications was aimed at furthering the goals close to his heart. He found time to write pamphlets, to collect and edit letters, to put out prayer leaflets, beautiful Propagation membership certificates and poem or quotation cards because all such literature made good works better known.

Some of these little leaflets half revealed the secrets of his own way of living. They provided some sort of explanation for his never-failing cheerfulness and zest, which so perplexed those who saw the arduous life he led but not the driving force beneath it, the driving force of the missionary which he truly was at heart.

Writing of missionary nuns, he said, "*Why* is a missionary nun? Always the missionary, man or woman, is the apostle, thirsting for more and ever more souls. The missionary nun has given her life, and her whole being is absorbed in the salvation of souls. . . . She knows peace, awe, lightness of heart. She is, at last, alone with her God."

Alone with God in the midst of ceaseless activity—that was his goal. He made no secret of his great admiration for St. Francis of Assisi. In fact, he gloried in his membership in the Third Order of St. Francis, by which non-religious followers of the Poor Man of Assisi may spread his spirit of Christian peace and joy in the world. In a pamphlet on the Third Order, Bishop Cushing wrote:

The earth revolves about the sun at a tremendous
rate of speed, yet all the objects on it remain undisturbed.
Why? Because it carries with it its own atmosphere. That
was St. Francis of Assisi. Wherever he went, whenever he
spoke, the sweet atmosphere of his intense spiritual life
hovered about him, enveloped his audience and scattered
the aroma of heaven. . . . Wherever adherents of the Third
Order of St. Francis may live, they have the strength and
the spirit to live beyond the things of the earth and to
grasp the hand of God, singing all the while like their
singing Patron, that happy minstrel, that troubador of God,
everybody's saint: Francis of Assisi.

Bishop Cushing wrote those lines in 1943. The
following year, 1944, was to bring another big
change in his life, a change which would mean far
greater burdens than he had ever known before. Yet
these very responsibilities would provide new opportunities to give of himself and thus, paradoxically,
the burdens would mean more happiness.

"It has been proved over and over again," he
has said, "that if you set out simply to find happiness, you never find it. Just as you think you have it
in your grasp, it eludes you. It is only when you
abandon the idea and set out to make other people
happy, to do good unselfishly, that you suddenly
discover you are really happy at last."

10

"THAT THEY

MAY KNOW THEE"

The great Cathedral of the Holy Cross was filled on the morning of April 28, 1944. Priests, religious and laity knelt in silent prayer, awaiting the commencement of the pontifical funeral Mass, to be sung by the Apostolic Delegate, Archbishop Amleto Cicognani, in the presence of Cardinal Dougherty of Philadelphia, the only Cardinal in the United States.

The man who had ruled over Boston Catholics for thirty-six years was dead. William Cardinal

O'Connell lay in state before the altar, his red *galero*, the distinctive possession of the Prince of the Church, at the foot of the bier. Soon it would be suspended from the ceiling high over the main altar, and left to disintegrate.

To the crowds who had come to the Cathedral during the days of obsequies, since his death on Saturday evening, April 22, it seemed impossible that Cardinal O'Connell was no more. He had been Archbishop of Boston for as long as many could remember. As they stood outside the crowded church on those rainy days, waiting a chance to enter, they could not help but wonder who would succeed him as leader of the Archdiocese's 1,133,000 Catholics.

On that morning of April 28, Bishop Cushing had no such thoughts in mind. Since the Cardinal had requested that he deliver his eulogy, much to the Bishop's surprise, he was intent on carrying out this sacred charge to the best of his ability.

During the four days of obsequies, the Bishop had presided at Masses attended by adults and children from all the parishes and had celebrated the pontifical requiem Mass at which Archdiocesan priests and nuns had assisted. Now the moment for the final act of homage had come.

Beginning his eulogy with the text: "Behold a great priest who in his days pleased God, and was found just; and in the time of wrath was made a reconciliation," he developed it around the theme of

the "great priest" and a second theme drawn from
the quote with which Cardinal O'Connell had closed
his autobiography: "The life of the Spirit, unquench-
able, can never be completely content until the soul
has found repose in the possession of God." On both
themes, Bishop Cushing could speak movingly, because they echoed the dominating ideals of his
own life.

Cardinal O'Connell's dedication to the Church,
his tremendous accomplishments, his strength of
character, his piety, his universal spirit—all these
virtues the Bishop traced with ardor and conviction.
He spoke of his death, calling it an inspiring testimony of faith: "He passed from this life blessing
his priests and people and kissing a crucifix that he
had cherished from his student days in Rome. The
prayers of his flock were generously answered: God
gave to our Good Shepherd a beautiful Christian
death."

He could speak from first-hand knowledge, for
he had been close to him when his life was drawing
to an end. It had been a truly Christian death, yes,
but one aspect of it had impressed the Bishop
greatly. He had given expression to this aspect in
an earlier passage of the eulogy:

"Any man exalted above his fellowmen, most of
all in ecclesiastical life, can have few intimates. In
an extraordinary degree, Cardinal O'Connell succeeded in combining a genuine love of his priests
and people with a detachment which kept him from

the softening consolation of their friendships; but he paid the price for this magnificent service to God and country with a lonely life and a no less lonely death."

The close of every day prior to Cardinal O'Connell's death had found Bishop Cushing at his bedside leading the members of the household in the Rosary: "I used to go in there every night on the way home from the office in town and say the beads. He was more or less unconscious then."

Once as a Cardinal he would speak thus of his predecessor: "I always like to say a kind word for Cardinal O'Connell. He was a brilliant man, and he was always good to me. Nobody really understood him. I saw him at his best and at his worst—towards his death he was very lonely." (And, as an afterthought: "He died in that room I sleep in.")

Cardinal O'Connell had made no secret of the sufferings he felt a man in his position must undergo, but with this revelation he had also disclosed the source of his tranquillity. He wrote thus in his *Recollections of Seventy Years*:

> It may be considered a platitude to say that, in such circumstances and conditions similar to my own, one entrusted with the proper care and administration of a diocese can expect to find help and consolation from God alone, by Whose Divine Will he is placed as a Bishop to rule the Church and care for the flock committed to him by the Vicar of Christ. That, I repeat, may seem but a platitude, but it is and will always remain the absolutely literal truth.

As he goes along his lonely and oftentimes weary way, he will find again and again that in times of difficulty even those upon whom he thought he could rely, prove to be only broken reeds, friends in the sunshine; and, judging by my own experience, he will pass through many dark days with a heart on the verge of breaking and yet no glimmer of light, no ray of help, will penetrate into the cell of his loneliness until, encompassed from without by false friends and bitter enemies, he will be forced to cry out as Christ did on the Cross, "*Deus meus, Deus meus, ut quid dereliquisti me?* (My God, my God, why hast Thou forsaken Me?)" Then, if his faith is still firm as a rock, he will hear God's voice and His answer will be, "Behold, I am with you all days even to the consummation of the world."

Bishop Cushing saw both the loneliness and the peaceful serenity of the great Churchman during those sad days toward the end of April.

When the obsequies were over and the Cardinal laid to rest in the mausoleum at the little Shrine of the Immaculate Conception, on the Seminary grounds—the site he had chosen—Bishop Cushing found himself Administrator of the Archdiocese until such time as a new Archbishop would be appointed. He had been elected by the priests serving as diocesan consultors.

The spring and summer months that followed were understandably busy ones. There were all his previous preoccupations—his Solomon Island Fund, his Confirmation schedule, his Newton parish, his usual round of speeches at meetings, benefit affairs and graduations, plus new duties as administrator of the second largest diocese in the country. Moreover, he had begun a major renovation on Holy Cross Cathedral in May and was closely supervising the operation.

As that summer of 1944 gave way to fall, the Archdiocese of Boston was still without a Shepherd. But on the morning of September 29th, Boston's newspapers bore the jubilant headlines: *Bishop Cushing Named Boston's Archbishop.*

He had not wanted the position, just as he had not wanted to be a bishop. When he had received a notice from Rome asking him whether he would accept the appointment as Archbishop, he had replied in words echoing the sentiments expressed to Cardinal O'Connell five years previous. Yet, characteristically, he accepted when he realized that such was the earnest desire of his Superiors.

"I do not deserve the recognition that has come to me," he was to say in an informal talk to students of Emmanuel College ten days later. "God knows full well that I did not desire it. I accepted it only because I felt that it was a tribute to the priests of the Archdiocese."

Bishop Cushing was officially notified of his appointment at about eight o'clock in the evening of September 28th, through a phone call from Archbishop Cicognani in Washington. The news had just come to the Apostolic Delegate from Rome. The local newspapers received the word at 11:44 from the Associated Press. That very night, at one in the morning, in fact, the Bishop called his home in South Boston. Mary Cushing was no longer there to hear the news that would have once again filled her heart with overwhelming happiness and pride, but her daughter, Elizabeth, rejoiced as only an "older sister" can at the new honor.

The next day, the Archbishop-elect, for that was now his official title, went about his usual duties. He cancelled none of his appointments and announced that he intended to continue his daily routine. At 6:30 that morning, he celebrated Mass for the Sisters of St. Joseph in the Sacred Heart Parish Convent. Later in the morning he went to St. Bridget's in Framingham, a town west of Newton, where he officiated at the solemn rites for a World War I Chaplain of the famed Yankee Division. At five o'clock of that afternoon he was at St. Elizabeth's Hospital in Brighton blessing ill priests, nuns and lay persons. He had brought them flowers and had also sent floral greetings to convents throughout Boston and to his little friends at the Peabody Home for Crippled Children. That evening, he was back in his own Sacred Heart administering the Sacrament of Confirmation to two adult converts. Such was his first day as Archbishop-elect of the great Metropolitan See of Boston.

He had made no official public appearance, but he had issued a statement which expressed perfectly his feelings, his outlook, his loves, and his faith. The first sentence, picked up and marked for special stress by many newspapers, was a sincere revelation of his state of mind: "It is with feelings of profound humility and reverential gratitude that I received the news that His Holiness, Pope Pius XII, has designated me to be the successor of our late beloved Cardinal Archbishop as spiritual leader of the priests, religious and laity of the Archdiocese of Boston." Then, turning from the honor that had come to him to the God for Whom he had accepted it, he said: "My first act is to ask all to join with me in fervent prayers to Almighty God. May He inspire and strengthen me. May He grant me light to know His Will, guidance to do His work, grace to spread His holy message of faith and love and salvation everywhere, at home and throughout the sorely tried mission fields."

"At home and in the missions"—he knew well the mission field, but he was also very familiar with matters closer to home, although he had had little to do with diocesan administration work. "I knew the conditions of the diocese," he has said. "I knew the problems because I had been all over, in every parish at least three times, preaching." Problems there were bound to be in such a large archdiocese embracing so many institutions, yet the Archbishop-designate had unlimited confidence in his people. The following week he was to say at Emmanuel College: "There are fine priests in the Boston Archdiocese and wonderful people. God knows I should know because the people made me." His first official statement showed that confidence:

"As priest, auxiliary Bishop and administrator, I have come close to the Catholic people of the Archdiocese—the zealous clergy, the devoted religious, the loyal laity. Their deep and abiding faith, their generous response to many noble and charitable causes, have stirred my gratitude and affection. I know that I can count on them for whole-hearted cooperation."

From those of his own flock, his thoughts turned at once to his fellow Americans of other faiths. Among them he counted many friends; for them he had great respect. Stories of his charity toward Catholic missionaries calling at his Franklin Street office were manifold, particularly the story of his having given his own overcoat to one who had come unprepared for Boston weather. But not everyone was aware of his kindness to clergymen of other faiths, such as the minister who came to him with a problem of too few chairs to seat his embarrassingly large congregation. He had a good-sized hall and very good attendance at meetings, but few chairs and no money to buy more.

"How many do you have in the congregation?" asked the Bishop. The minister told him. The next question was, "How many can you seat now?" Receiving that answer, Bishop Cushing figured out just how many chairs were needed, thought a moment, and said, "If you can have some men waiting at the hall at about six-thirty this evening to help unload, a truck will drive up with the chairs you need."

They say that when the minister left the Bishop, there were tears in his eyes.

No wonder, then, that among the many expressions of joy when the appointment was made known, there was this word from the Episcopal Bishop of Boston, Rt. Rev. Henry Knox Sherrill: "I am delighted at hearing of Bishop Cushing's appointment to head the Boston Archdiocese. He is a friend of mine and I am sure his ministry will grow with the opportunity that now is his."

Non-Catholics who, like Bishop Sherrill, admired and loved the Archbishop-elect were not disappointed if they looked for references to themselves in his official statement. "To them (Catholics) and to all our non-Catholic brethren," he said, "I give assurance that I shall labor always in a spirit of love." He then went on to define that love:

"... in love of God, the Source of all good, Whose moral law gives to men the only charter under which life has a meaning and a purpose.

"... in love of country, our great and beloved country, whose basic ideals are those for which the Church has stood since her founding, ideals of the dignity and inalienable rights of the individual.

"... in love of mankind, of all men as children of God and brothers in Christ."

The final thought of the Archbishop-elect's message was on the war and the reconstruction that must follow it. He was still the Bishop of the servicemen, the Bishop of the bombed mission posts and impoverished missionaries. His words were:

"I ask therefore the prayers and assistance of all, both in these trying days when sorrow weighs heavily upon so many families, and in the difficult days to come after the war ends, when, with God's help, mankind may build an enduring peace, a peace which can be achieved only if the teachings of Christ, the 'Prince of Peace,' are heard in the hearts of men.

"My love and blessing and prayerful greetings go forth under the goodness of God to the priests and religious at home, to those serving as chaplains in the training camps or battlefields of the war, to all the faithful, to our young men and women serving in the armed forces, and to my missionary friends throughout the world."

Much labor lay ahead, as no one knew better than he. One day, years later, he would look back over his life and remark, "All I have done is work, work, work." He had no illusions about the future, but he knew he was not alone.

"Trusting in God and desiring only His Will," he concluded his statement, "I answer the call of the Vicar of Christ on earth. May God and His Blessed Mother be with us in all our ways. In His Will and under her protection we shall pray and work."

The appointment of Bishop Cushing was hailed with great enthusiasm. People of every faith were delighted that a Boston-born Bishop, consecrated right in the city's own Cathedral, had been named Archbishop. The general opinion was that no better choice could have been made. All day Friday and Saturday, the 29th and 30th, the congratulations poured in from heads of state, organization leaders, and the thousands throughout the Archdiocese who considered themselves his personal friends. On Saturday morning, when he was able to return to his desk at Franklin Street, the felicitations began arriving from his missionary associates jubilant over the elevation of him whom they counted as their "own." One came from the Bishop, priests and Sisters of Honolulu, another from the missionaries at the leper colony on the Island of Molokai, of Father Damien fame, and still another from the Negro Seminarians at Bay St. Louis, Mississippi.

The editorial in the Saturday, September 30th, issue of *The Pilot* summed up the general delight reigning in Boston: "The news comes as the answer to uncounted prayers of petition voiced by priests and faithful."

The comments in other Boston newspapers at this time echoed the same thoughts. The *Boston Traveler* wrote:

"The Most Reverend Richard J. Cushing, the newly appointed Archbishop of Boston . . . brings to the exalted office . . . the love, respect and complete good will of every clergyman and layman of his own creed and every Bostonian of every other creed. This is true because he is pre-eminent in equal measure as a spiritual servant of God and a fellow citizen among his fellow men. Along with the profound humility and reverential gratitude with which Bishop Cushing accepts the stern demands and heavy cares of this high office, there must be in the back of his thoughts a reserve of confidence and comfort. He must know that he has received the news every Boston Catholic has been hoping for."

The *Boston Herald* was particularly concerned with attempting to get at the facts behind the appointment and with the Archbishop-elect's social outlook:

"He was not altogether unknown in Rome, although he has never been out of the United States and is not aquainted personally with the prelates of the Vatican. But it is recalled now that the present Pope was familiar with his achievements in the missionary field, for he once referred to him after he became Auxiliary Bishop of Boston, as 'the unparalleled Auxiliary.'

"Usually it is the American students sent to Rome for a period who go higher here in the Catholic Church. That was true of William Henry O'Connell, for example. Not so in the case of Archbishop Cushing, and not so in the instance of the new Catholic Primate of England, the Archbishop of Westminster, who succeeded Cardinal Hinsley.

Neither had visited Rome. Neither appointment was foreseen by either the Catholic laity or the Catholic clergy. The know-it-all gossipers had named a dozen men as successors to Cardinal O'Connell, but Bishop Cushing was hardly mentioned. . . .

"He leads a simple, almost austere life and an acquaintance has characterized him as "almost terrifying in his austerity." He loves human beings as human beings, and especially those at the extremes, the young and the ailing old. His statement after he learned of the elevation indicates clearly enough that his general outlook on the Boston community will be identical with that of the broadminded Cardinal."

A real understanding of his make-up was shown by a comment in the *Boston Globe*: "To a man of character and valor a trial of strength and courage is a challenge and a delight. Archbishop Cushing has accepted the challenge; his heart will be gladdened by the size and the diversity of the labors he must undertake."

The appointment elicited remarks from at least two papers regarding the nature of the Catholic Church itself and its policy—remarks which probably pleased the Archbishop-elect more than all the others in praise of his life and deeds. The *Globe's* comment was: "It is true in the Catholic Church, as in life, that the man who performs one task well is rewarded by assignment to another yet more arduous. The Church's acknowledgment of merit is an invitation to prove it once again. Woodrow Wilson may have had this custom in mind when he announced his discovery that the strength of the Church was, largely, its basic democracy. For, as one Catholic writer has pointed out, while this Church has its princes, they earn their rank."

On the same theme, the *Boston Post* noted: "One of the great fundamentals of the Catholic Church has been given its most graphic demonstration in the selection of Archbishop Cushing. The Catholic Church is, perhaps, the greatest exponent of the democratic principle. A man of humble beginnings and of extraordinary gifts may rise to become a prince of the Church."

"I come from the poor, I have lived poor, I will not change," declared the Archbishop-elect the third day after his notification. The occasion was an informal talk to the priests and parishioners of St. Michael's Church, Lowell, which was observing its sixtieth anniversary. "Under God," he affirmed, "the people, the poor especially, made me, and it is my delight to be with them."

The impressive installation ceremony took place in the newly renovated Holy Cross Cathedral on November 8th, with the Apostolic Delegate, Most Reverend Amleto G. Cicognani, officiating. Nine Archbishops and about forty Bishops from all over the United States and Canada attended. Approximately one thousand priests, two hundred nuns and two hundred seminarians were in the congregation,

the remaining seats being filled by officials of city,
state, and nation. The gathering of prelates exceeded
anything the Catholic Church in Boston had known
before. When, attired in their bright robes, they assembled in the Cathedral for the ceremony, the
sight was a thrilling one. Yet the man who occupied
the central role in that splendid pageantry was the
same one who the day before had begged leave of
his distinguished guest, Archbishop Cicognani, to
officiate at funeral services for a retired schoolteach-
er out of gratitude for the time she had given to
Propagation work.

The high point of the installation ceremony was
the moment when Archbishop Cicognani escorted
the new Archbishop to the throne of authority, a
raised and canopied seat, at the left side of the altar
as the people face it. Seated on this throne, Archbishop Cushing received the crozier (the shepherd's
staff). He was now the spiritual leader of all Catholics in the Metropolitan See of Boston.

Scenes of Bishop Cushing blessing little children, comforting sick and neglected old folks,
earnestly pleading for aid to missions, firing youth
with high ideals, booming a heartening "yes" when a
"no" was feared—these and similar memories must
have come to many of the people in that Cathedral
as the new Archbishop of Boston rose to address
them.

The world's youngest residential Archbishop,
he looked younger than his forty-nine years. His

stocky build, full face and energetic movements evidenced a strength and vigor that seemed to defy the strain of his daily work schedule.

The address Richard James Cushing gave on that day which marked a tremendous turning point in his life epitomized the man. His opening words were: "To Almighty God I consecrate anew all that I have and all that I am, for His glory, for my own sanctification, and for the welfare of the souls entrusted to my care." He obviously felt called upon to give even more generously of himself, if that were possible. This was the only aspect under which personal references entered the address. His mind was wholly taken up with the great office of Archbishop itself. He saw it in its historical perspective and in its present role; he saw it in its spiritual and temporal influence; he saw it as it had been filled by the men before him.

"My thoughts," he said, "are drawn in two directions as I stand in this holy place—toward the hallowed past and toward the hidden future. The past humbles and yet challenges me with the thought of what our predecessors did toward building the heritage that is ours; the future bids us augment that heritage and transmit it to others."

This was no mere perfunctory nod of deference toward a little-remembered past. Richard Cushing lived and moved in constant awareness of a debt toward those who had gone before. His reverence for the past, however, would not put a check on his pioneer spirit of initiative; rather it would challenge him to meet the needs of his day as effectively as his predecessors had risen to the demands of their times.

"Both past and future meet in the text from which I have presumed to take the motto for the present: 'That they may know Thee, as we have also known Thee, that there is no God beside Thee, O Lord.'"

Beginning with the life of the first Bishop of Boston, John de Cheverus, he devoted the major part of his address to a tribute of praise for each of the men who had ruled over the diocese, ending with Cardinal O'Connell.

His thoughts thereupon turned to the task ahead of him, and in accents of deepest sincerity, almost as though from a desire to affirm over and over again his intentions, he declared: "... I give myself this morning to the priests, the religious, and the Catholic laity of the Archdiocese of Boston, and to others to whom I can be of help."

The desire to serve having manifested itself, the characteristic humility appeared next in the form of a plea for prayer—not that he might successfully carry out many projects for expansion and development, but rather that he might promote the spiritual values which give life and meaning to everything else. The new Archbishop of Boston visualized goals of a height and extension far surpassing the temporal aims he would announce through the years to come.

"Pray for me, please," he concluded, "not that I may attain the heights of learning nor the pinnacles of visible success, but that I may be saturated with, and help others achieve, that spirituality which flows from the knowledge and love of God."

That They May Know Thee—for this goal, the selfless devotion to duty in the past; for this, the restless drive of the future toward ever wider horizons of activity born of love.

11

THE NEW ARCHBISHOP

The new Archbishop of Boston strode to the center of the makeshift platform and gazed out over the strange audience. No sign of uneasiness marked that tall, erect figure nor did he hesitate before beginning to speak. Spreading wide his hands in a gesture of familiarity, almost as though he were addressing a group of intimates and co-workers, he boomed out a hearty "My dear friends."

And the three hundred men in identical shapeless grey uniforms relaxed—in a single, rhythmic movement.

189

It was New Year's Day, 1945. Archbishop
Cushing might have spent it at many a festive hall,
at many a welcoming home, where hearts were rejoicing in hopeful expectation.

Instead, he went to those to whom New Year's
Day meant new bitterness, the beginning of another
year behind bars. He went to the old State Prison
of Charlestown, a forbidding granite structure to
which only an apostolic heart could feel itself drawn
on such a day. In all the one hundred fifty years
that convicts had climbed to the third floor auditorium, this was the first time that an Archbishop had
come to mingle with them, to join them as a friend.

His Christmas had been one of charity with the
innocent and the little ones of his flock. His New
Year's Day was for those who had erred.

"Life is like a baseball game," he declared. "We
may make errors in the early innings, but the thing
that really counts is the score when the game ends.

"We all make mistakes. That is only human. The
things that count now are the innings still before
you. Forget the errors of the past—start the ball
game all over again."

The hearty voice, the ringing confidence in the
inmates' goodness, the buoyant optimism of the man
were infectious. The prisoners sensed that day what
many a despairing soul was to experience in the
years to come: Archbishop Cushing believed in his
fellow man and lived to help others.

That day he administered the Sacrament of Confirmation to twenty-two convicts before the altar which they had decorated with seasonal greens. Every man in that assembly, whether Catholic or not, was impressed by the solemn ceremony. The Superintendent of the prison school acted as sponsor, standing behind each kneeling figure, his hand on each shoulder, as the Archbishop anointed foreheads with the holy oils and laid his hands on bowed heads.

Afterwards he said, "I have come here to be an instrument of God in bringing you His help. Your hearts and souls are just as precious in the eyes of God as my own or any man's—for God made us all." Earnestly he urged, "Speak to God in your own language—He will hear and understand you. When all others fail you, speak to Him."

Then as though sensing what many might be thinking—"*He* can say that, but what about *us*?"— the Archbishop emphasized, "It makes no difference what you're here for. The important thing is being repentant and beginning all over again."

How could one indifferently shrug off such an appeal to hope and confidence? None could; and so, before the eyes of prison guards lining the overhead gallery, many an inmate wiped away a tear that had caught him by surprise.

Two months had not yet passed since November 8th when the nation had welcomed F.D.R. back to a fourth term as President, and the episcopal

throne of the Boston Cathedral had welcomed a
new occupant; but newspapermen had already discovered that the new Archbishop seemed very likely
to keep them well supplied with stories. And though
he desired no glory for himself, he had at once made
it clear that reporters and photographers would not
have to "crash" any affair he planned—he was too
well aware of the value of publicity in promoting
causes. Hence they had not missed this unprecedented prison visit. Men who had made the news
for one crime or another were again in the limelight,
but this time as kneeling penitents before a man who
radiated warmth, blessed them in God's name, and
had an encouraging word or friendly tap for each.

Always most strongly drawn by the most hap-
less of any group, the prelate did not leave the
prison without visiting the death house. Two men in
the "condemned row" received his blessing that day.
The pair were awaiting execution for murder.

As he moved among the groups of prisoners,
Archbishop Cushing resolved to repeat the visit. It
was plain even to one as modest as he that it had
meant much to these men. Why not come for Christmas next year?

This was to be his way: make an initial attempt
in some area of charity, and then repeat it again and
again if it proved successful. However, he was not
one to stop at the level of occasional personal efforts.
Thus, later, during his Christmas Eve, 1946, visit to
the Charlestown State Prison, he formed the idea

Birthplace: 806 East Third Street, South Boston

Eighth
grade
graduate

The Oliver
Hazard
Perry
School,
South Boston

With
senior
classmates,
Boston
College
High School,
1913
(TOP RIGHT)

Part of the same class fifty years later

Seminarian Richard J. Cushing (RIGHT)

At work on the seminary farm (RIGHT)

With members of his class, 1921

At ordination, May 26, 1921

First Mass in the seminary chapel

As Archdiocesan Director of the
Society for the Propagation of the Faith,
with visiting Chinese priest, 1937

Before Episcopal Consecration, June 29, 1939

Mary Cushing, mother of
Rt. Rev. Msgr. Richard J. Cushing,
shown as she left
her home on Farragut Street,
South Boston, to go to the
Holy Cross Cathedral to see the
consecration of her son.

Mrs. Cushing holding the picture of her son, now a Bishop.

Archbishop-elect Cushing preaching on the
Feast of St. Therese, Patroness of the Missions—October 3, 1944

Installed as Archbishop of Boston, November 8, 1944

50,000 symbolic candlelights, Holy Name Rally, October, 1947

Time out in the mammoth Holy Name Parade, October, 1947

Service and entertainment for the old folks
on St. Joseph's Day

With President Harry Truman, 1948

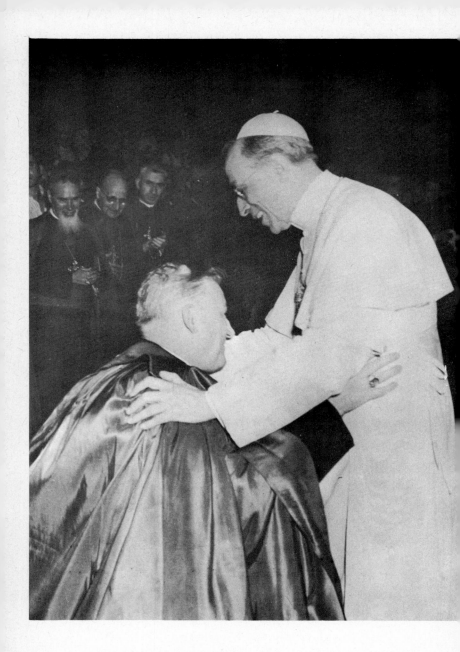

Meeting with Pope Pius XII, Holy Year Pilgrimage, 1950

Leader of Boston pilgrimage to Ireland posing for souvenir photo

"The best part of pilgrimages is coming home"—Archbishop Cushing

Chapel at the Archbishop's residence

In typical greeting

With Chinese-American friends of a Sunday School Class

Batter up! At a Catholic girls camp run by the
Sisters of Divine Providence

Rare moments of leisure

Official portrait, 1954

Personal service for 97-year-old Mary Kelly
at the annual party for the aged

"A man never stands so straight as when he stoops
to help a needy child"—Archbishop Cushing

Six-year-old singer, Phillip Phillips,
wins praise from the Archbishop
at the Mayor's Field Day, 1954

A steel-helmeted Archbishop
is right at home with shipyard workers

"Almighty Father, invest this Thy servant
with the dignity of the priesthood"

Applying the trowel with skill to the cornerstone
of the new Novitiate for the Daughters of St. Paul, 1955

Entering Holy Cross Cathedral with His Beatitude, Maximos IV for Mass in the Byzantine-Melkite Rite

A visit to President Eisenhower with members
of the National Council of Catholic Nurses

Receiving the Variety Club's Great Heart Award,
May 26, 1956, his thirty-fifth anniversary of ordination

Congratulations from Ted Williams to the winner of the
Great Heart award, given to "the one who has done
the greatest amount of good to the greatest number of people"

"God love you all!"

An afternoon at the ball game with delighted orphans
and the Sisters in charge of their Home

Leaving on a pilgrimage to the shrines of Europe, 1956

A chat with the painter in a school
being converted into a monastery

Outdoor Mass
and blessings
for the sick
on the grounds
of the
Archbishop's
residence

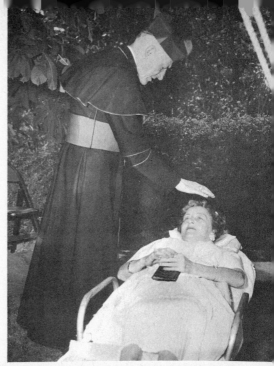

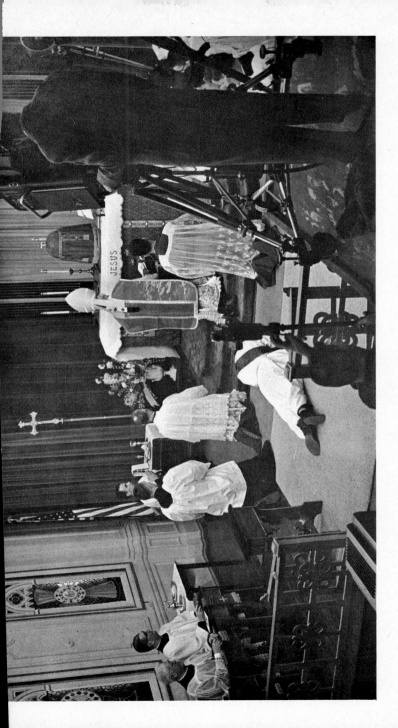

The solemn ordination ceremony on television
at the Archdiocesan TV Center

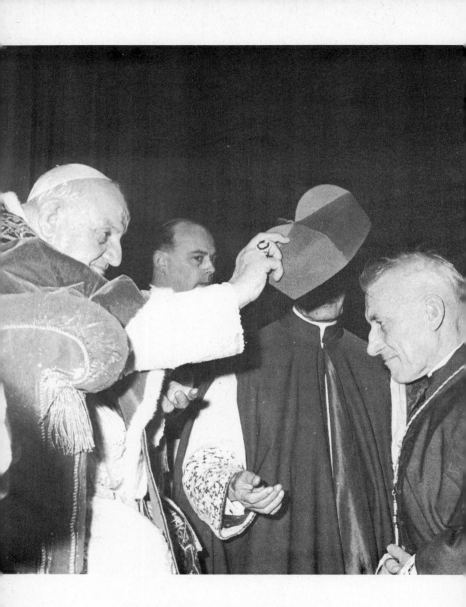

A Papal Consistory in December, 1958,
and Boston's Archbishop receives the red biretta
of a Cardinal from Pope John XXIII

In the splendor of St. Peter's Basilica,
the new Cardinal approaches the papal throne
for the placing of the "galero" or "red hat"

Portrait with Good Pope John

On arrival home from Rome, December 21, 1958

"This honor belongs not alone to me but especially
to all those for whom and with whom I have worked,
in whatever position was entrusted to me"

Bearing a precious burden on
Exceptional Children's Pilgrimage to Lourdes

With Bishop Cornelius Lucey of Cork, Bishop John J. Aherne of Cloyne
and Canon Michael Hurley, parish priest at Glanworth at
the Marian shrine on Cardinal Cushing's father's birthplace,
Glanworth, County Cork, Ireland

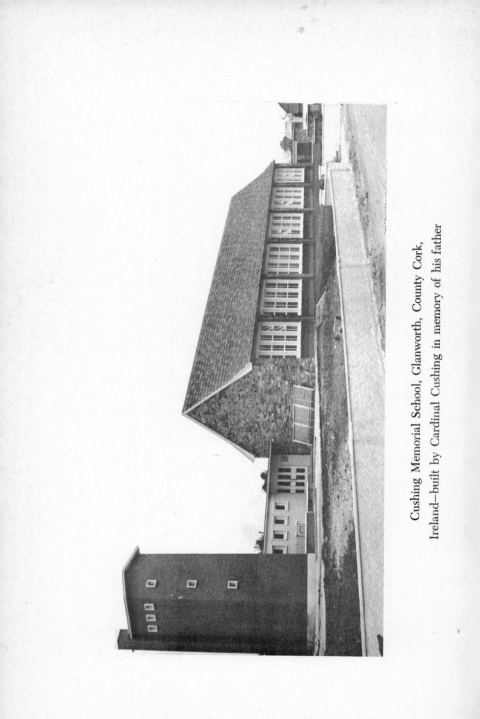

Cushing Memorial School, Glanworth, County Cork, Ireland—built by Cardinal Cushing in memory of his father

With J. Edgar Hoover, Director of the F.B.I.

Congratulations from President Pusey, after receiving
an honorary degree at Harvard University, June, 1959

Two great men in conversation at Harvard

An embrace for the Cardinal from the French Ambassador
after being elevated to grand officer in the Legion of Honor

A Cardinal's salute to the Mission Drum and
Bugle Corps Competition, Boston, June, 1959

Delivering a stirring challenge to the
1959 National Catholic Youth Organization Convention
right after recovering from a sudden collapse
during the banquet

A warm greeting for Gregory Peter Cardinal Agagianian
at Boston airport

East and West meet: "The Catholic Eastern Churches
are the living proof of the Church's universality"—
Cardinal Cushing

World Sodality Day, 1960, and with a crowd of 20,000 before the ancient "Vladimir Mother of God," prayers for the Ecumenical Council are said in various languages

Four American Princes of the Church—
James Francis Cardinal McIntyre, Richard Cardinal Cushing,
Francis Cardinal Spellman and Albert Cardinal Meyer—
in front of the National Shrine of the Immaculate Conception

With an Arctic missionary and his canine companion

With Polish-American children in native costumes
before Mass in honor of Polish pianist Paderewski

A captain and his crew

"Never thought I'd get such a close look
at a Prince of the Church!"

A friendly handshake before a Prelate
who has always shown keen interest in athletics and athletes

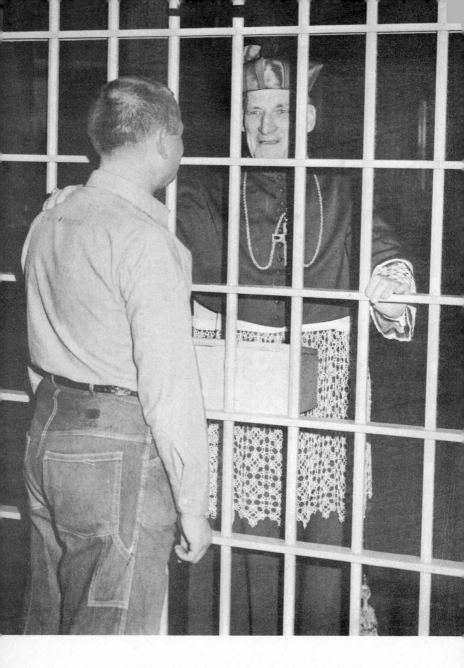

"I was in prison . . . and you visited Me"

From the prison gift shop—an unusual mark of distinction

A characteristic gesture during an address

Papal Legate to the Peruvian National Eucharistic
Congress, 1960, kisses the Peruvian flag on arrival

In adoration of the Blessed Sacrament
during the solemn Eucharistic procession

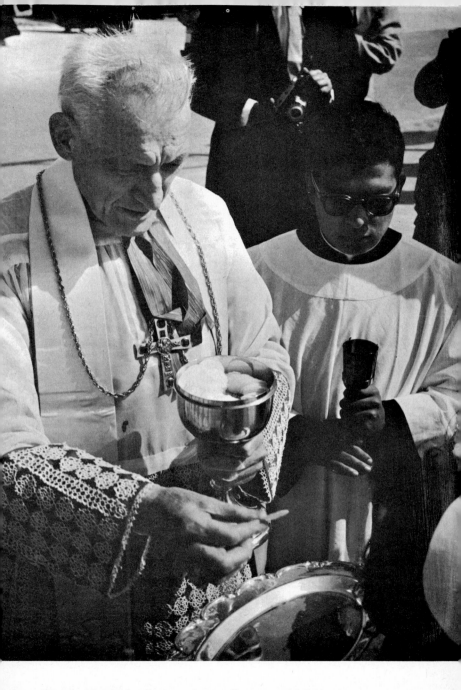

Distributing Holy Communion to Congress participants

Crowning the Peruvian Army's Patroness, Our Lady of Ransom

Act of homage to new Peruvian priests—
hope of Latin America's future

A fair exchange

Breakfast for God's children

Blessings on thee, little man . . .

"Let the little children come to Me"

With a crowd of South American admirers;
nephew Father William Francis, missioner
of the Society of St. James, looks on

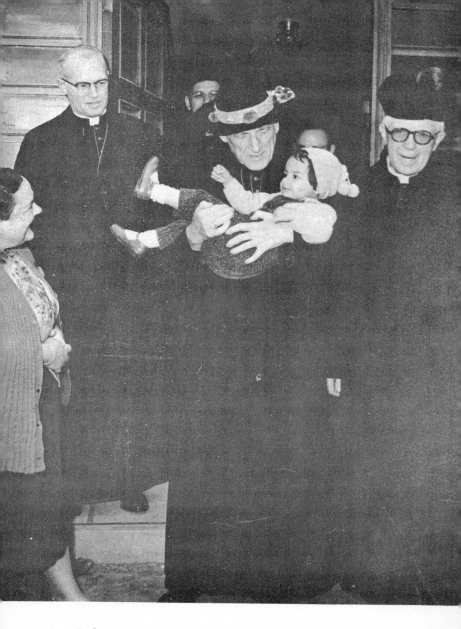

In his arms, a tiny member of Christ's Mystical Body;
at his side, a heroic missionary, Archdeacon Thomas Duggan,
who at seventy gave up his parish in Ireland to go to Peru

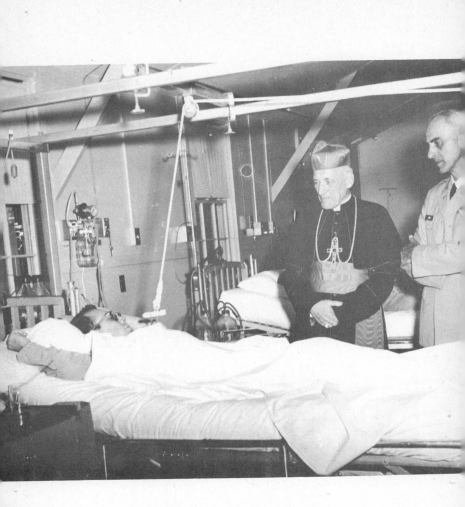

Words of sympathy for a soldier-patient
at Fort Devens, Massachusetts

Mass on the main deck of the
guided-missile cruiser, USS Boston

Receiving an honorary degree from Boston University, 1962

Between friends—
at Boston's birthday celebration for President John F. Kennedy

Speaking in the robes of the
Eastern Rite Basilian-Salvatorian monks

The washing of the feet in accordance
with the Holy Thursday liturgy

Nazareth, haven for homeless children—
fulfillment of a dream

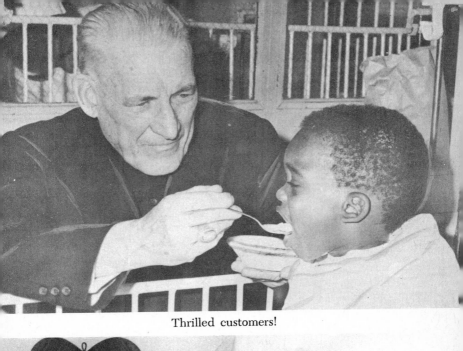

Thrilled customers!

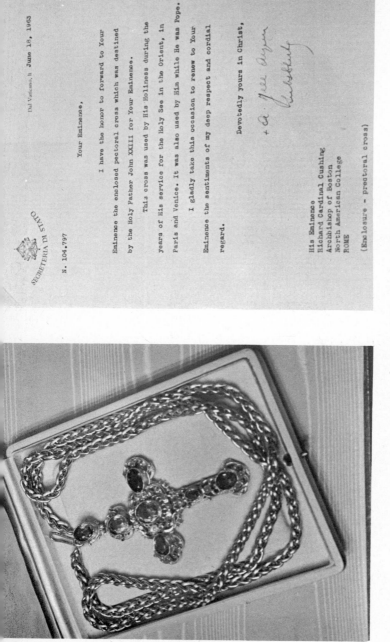

SEGRETERIA DI STATO

N. 104.797

Dal Vaticano, lì June 12, 1963

Your Eminence,

I have the honor to forward to Your
Eminence the enclosed pectoral cross which was destined
by the Holy Father John XXIII for Your Eminence.

This cross was used by His Holiness during the
years of His service for the Holy See in the Orient, in
Paris and Venice. It was also used by Him while He was Pope.

I gladly take this occasion to renew to Your
Eminence the sentiments of my deep respect and cordial
regard.

Devotedly yours in Christ,

+ A. Dell Acqua
Sostituto

His Eminence
Richard Cardinal Cushing
Archbishop of Boston
North American College
ROME

(Enclosure - pectoral cross)

Pectoral cross of Pope John XXIII
destined by the beloved Pontiff for Cardinal Cushing
and presented to him two weeks after
Good Pope John's death, June, 1963

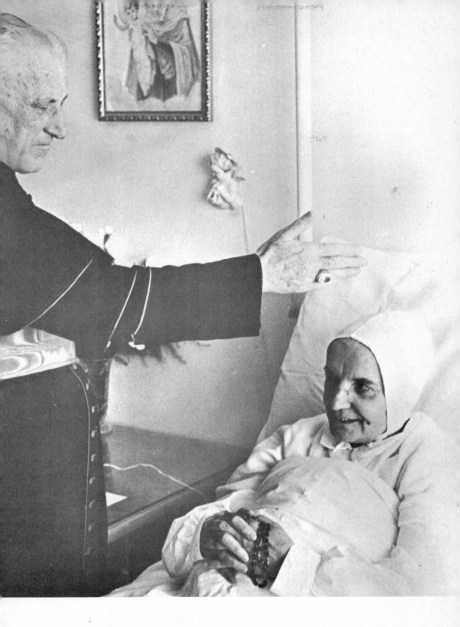

A blessing for Mother Thecla, Co-Foundress of the
Daughters of St. Paul, who staff "Regina Apostolorum"
Hospital for Sisters only, in Rome

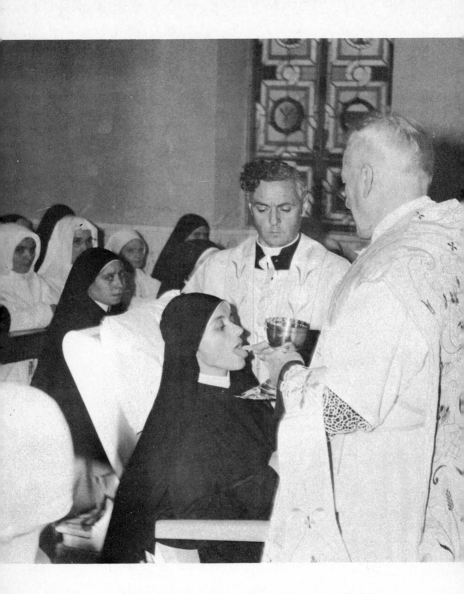

Communion to Sister Mary Domenica, D.S.P.,
incurably ill with cancer, at the "Regina Apostolorum" Hospital

With the Very Rev. James Alberione,
Founder of the Daughters of St. Paul,
and workers at the large new extension to the Hospital for Sisters
to which the Cardinal is making substantial contributions.
For each of the workers,. too,
he had a bottle of wine and a gift package.

Portrait with Pope Paul VI

Requiem Mass for a fallen President and friend,
John F. Kennedy, November 25, 1963

Solace for a valiant woman,
Mrs. Jacqueline Kennedy

The World's Cardinal

"Command me if I can be of service to you"

Dinner with Episcopal Bishop Anson Phelps Stokes, Jr.,
of Massachusetts

for a permanent source of help to his "friends." That
source of help was Our Lady of Ransom Guild,
which was to give aid, both moral and material, to
released prisoners. Many a paroled man was to make
good because of the devoted efforts of the Guild
workers.

The 1946 visit was a memorable one. The top-
floor auditorium was filled with double the number
of men that had been there the year before. About
six hundred watched as twenty-one of their number
were confirmed, having completed instructions in
the Faith under their chaplain, Father Joseph A.
Robinson.

It was the last two candidates, however, who
drew every eye—for they were handcuffed to prison guards. An audible gasp from the inmates
marked their approach to the altar. The two men
were convicted murderers, soon to face the electric
chair. One was a lapsed Catholic, the other had been
converted in the "death house." Both received the
Sacrament of Confirmation from Archbishop Cushing, who rounded out that unforgettable evening by
speaking to the convicts of St. Dismas, the good thief
to whom Christ said: "This day you shall be with Me
in Paradise."

Visits of the Archbishop to penal institutions on
the great holidays were to become a custom, but on
January 2nd, 1945, when Boston learned that its
new Archbishop, after spending his Christmas with
the little tots, had gone to celebrate New Year's with

prisoners—there was wonder on many faces. Newsmen, among others, were convinced that Archbishop
Cushing was unpredictable—but newsworthy.

It is a tribute to the Archbishop's personal appeal that his picture so frequently appeared on the
pages of the Boston papers, for the world situation
provided an abundance of headline material. The
very day he was installed as Archbishop of Boston
was election day, November eighth. Side by side
with news of the colorful ceremony and reprints of
his address were voting results, as Franklin Delano
Roosevelt defeated Thomas Dewey for the Presidency, and Maurice Tobin became governor of
Massachusetts.

Every issue of the papers in that excitement-
filled period at the close of 1944 and the first half
of '45 bristled with stories of American war gains,
of lives lost, and heroes being made: the stand at
Bastogne; the liberation of the Philippines. While
one section appealed for salvage paper and another
dealt with rationing, excited prophets of the post-
war world filled up another page with speculations
about whether Americans would all be owning their
private planes as soon as the war was over. There
was even news that several cities were planning to
lay out "air parks" for the thousands of expected
private plane owners! Then there were the usual
touching stories of wounded veterans, such as one
armless, legless soldier for whom a fund of $65,000
had been raised. The stars of Hollywood, as al-

ways, came in for top notice side by side with local
girls off to join the Waves. There was the usual
spattering of grim crime reports, and a sobering reflection on what the moral standards of post-war
young America would be like. And always, the reports of the steady military drive toward victory.

Into this almost unreal climate of tension and
the terrain of everyday drama walked Archbishop
Richard James Cushing—asking nothing for himself,
except the chance to give and help. "He is the
answer to prayers, to prayers which successfully
countered his own," said the Archdiocesan newspaper, *The Pilot*. "The eminence was no desire of his.
But from the monasteries and convents petitions
ascended. Priests, especially the priests of the
diocese, made this the intention of their Masses.
United with them in this plea were many outside the
Church's fold. Perhaps the most ardent prayers of
all came from the hearts of the very poor and hope-
lessly sick."

Bishop Cushing had been known to so many
as an extraordinarily approachable shepherd that
they could think of no better man to become their
spiritual leader at a time when everything seemed
unstable and abnormal. And their hopes were not
disappointed by the initial events of his reign as
Archbishop.

Certainly, those of his many friends who saw
the November 19, 1944, *Boston Sunday Post*, with
its two-page spread of photos taken inside Cardinal

O'Connell's Commonwealth Avenue residence must have found it hard to picture Archbishop Cushing amid those surroundings. There had been many legends about this mansion, some even holding that it was some kind of museum containing priceless treasures—for very few Bostonians, as the *Post* observed, had ever seen its interior. The photos purported to be the first ever published, and they revealed that though not full of priceless treasures, it certainly was ornately furnished. One room was done in the spirit of the Italian Renaissance, another in baroque, and the dining room in late Victorian. Marble chests, paintings in massive frames, oriental rugs, carved oak furniture; a Cuban mahogany clock with Westminster chimes—all of these made the residence anything but cozy. Yet even Cardinal O'Connell had often closed off rooms and lived only in a few—nor had he employed a large staff of servants as had often been thought. Still, it was not a home in which one could picture the new Archbishop, with his mountainous correspondence, files of Guild workers' names, and above all, his own simple living habits.

"When he moves in," observed the same article, "he will probably carry all his worldly possessions in two traveling bags. For the new occupant of the big Italian-style house is by nature a man of humility and simple tastes, little interested in material things." Yet the writer erred when he went on to prophecy that because of the need to meet the requirements of his post, the Archbishop would leave the mansion essentially the same.

The Archbishop, instead, disposed of the antique furniture, brought in his files, secretaries' desks and mimeograph equipment. In addition, he made plans to turn the third floor over to priests studying at various universities in Boston. The mansion opened its doors to anyone who wanted to see the Archbishop. For the first time its telephone number was listed, (although the Archbishop later found it wiser to keep it unlisted: "I didn't mind it so much in the daytime, but I found out the hard way how a fireman feels at three o'clock in the morning!")

Priests and laity found it easy to meet the Archbishop. In fact, he himself would go out of his way to talk to anyone who seemed bashful about approaching him. "Archbishop Cushing does not consciously put people at their ease," *The Pilot* had observed at his installation. "He simply succeeds in being himself. The cynosure these past months of many eyes, he remains his genial, unspoiled, spontaneous self."

Only about two months after his installation, a non-Catholic woman followed a wild impulse and mailed a note telling the Archbishop, about whom she had read so much, that she would very much like to meet him. She really expected nothing to come of this whim, but to her great surprise a reply arrived in which the Archbishop said he would be glad

to have her come. She not only met him, but he took
her on a grand tour of the residence himself. Plainly
he had meant exactly what he said when he declared
that he was giving himself to his people. . . .

That the new leader of Boston's Catholics had
amazing plans for the Archdiocese also became apparent at once. While there were many institutions
already, he knew there was a need for more and
newer ones. Moreover, even some of those in existence awaited help to start a new life. Soon, the
Archbishop's office at 2101 Commonwealth Avenue
was filled with blueprints and plans.

There were those who viewed this unprecedented activity with a dubious eye. Where were the
funds to come from? But Archbishop Cushing was
not worried. "Great Plans for Boston Diocese Out-
lined" ran the headline of a January, 1945, *Boston
Post* article. "Hospitals, religious houses, and new
regional high schools are part of Archbishop Cushing's program." This was just the beginning. Perhaps no one but Richard James Cushing—who had
pledged: "I was born in Boston, I was bred in Boston, I love Boston, I'm for everything that will
promote Boston's welfare"—knew just how much he
intended to do for his people, without for a moment
forgetting the missions of the world.

Nor was all his activity of the material type, to
be measured in architects' designs and deeds. The
Post article was quick to note that the new Archbishop had revived the ancient custom of singing

Vespers in the Cathedral on Sunday afternoon, and it observed: "Much of how the Archbishop feels about this service has communicated itself to the people who come to worship, for there is a warmth and an intimate friendly glow in the participation that is seldom found at any religious service. Here the shepherd and his flock are in complete unison, of one mind and desire in their adoration of the Lord. So impressive are these services, so inspiring, that enthusiastic crowds have braved some of the worst storms of the season to crowd the Cathedral and catch a glimpse of their beloved Archbishop."

A few months later, he was to open a Perpetual Adoration Shrine at St. Clement's Church in the Back Bay section of the city. There his many "good people," as he loved to call them, might take turns at prayer before the Blessed Sacrament perpetually exposed for adoration.

Nor had he forgotten his House of the Good Shepherd. He was still engaged in raising funds for a chapel for the Magdalens.

The Archbishop had so strongly and cordially encouraged religious communities to come into the Boston Archdiocese that only a few months after he had taken over, a number of orders were already moving in. He himself made sure they became known by personally publicizing their work and "preparing the ground" in his innumerable public appearances.

As early as January of 1945, people were asking: "How does the new Archbishop do it?" His activity earned him the title of "powerhouse of energy." Over the years, his daily schedule was to become even more "impossible." But, for the time being, his dynamism had everyone amazed. As one reporter expressed it, "The Boston Archdiocese of over a million people is gradually recovering from the surprise of having a streamlined spiritual leadership."

* * *

The old man had prepared for days for this speech. The Little Sisters of the Poor and all the old folks at the Home in Roxbury had heard him rehearse it until they knew it by heart. Now, at last, St. Joseph's Day, March 19th, had arrived. As for the past twenty-one years, so in 1945, too, Archbishop Richard Cushing had come to spend the great day with them. Donning a huge, baker's apron, with red ribbons, he had served the soup as always, calling out: "Soup's on! Come and get it!" Everything had gone wonderfully, and now it was time for old Jerry's speech.

"Mere words cannot, however grouped, convey to you the gladness, the real jubilation which your visits to our home occasion," began the high quivering voice. "Just to see you, hear your voice, and watch your stereotyped smile—" *Stereotyped smile!* Heavens, that wasn't what he meant to say! A stunned silence followed. What a boner!

But with a laugh and a sly wink, the guest of
honor saved the day. "How about that one!" he cried,
with glee, and Jerry took courage to go on, ending
with a song of tribute he had written to the tune of
"God Bless America." But it was the Archbishop who
had to get the song started. And he did so with gusto.
"God bless him, ain't he the good one, though!"
sighed the old ladies, most of whom he could call
by name.

In the infirmary, he bent over a frail little woman whose appetite had left her. "Just a bit more,"
he urged as he carefully fed her spoon after spoon,
to the happy surprise of the Sisters watching. No
wonder the little garden in back of the home was
named "Cushing Park." "They named it for me,"
the Archbishop announced to visitors, as though
it were his greatest honor.

The Archbishop seemed to be everywhere—and
to notice every need. At a military Mass, when a
wave of hysteria swept over Gold Star mothers at
the sound of a gun salute and taps, it was Archbishop
Cushing who first sensed the situation and rushed to
aid two who, overcome by emotion, had fainted.
Human suffering, in any form, drew him like a mag-
net. For this reason, he prayed, and begged the
prayers of his people, for a quick end to the war.

April 1st of that initial year of his reign marked
the beginning of the last land battle of the war in
the Pacific, the battle on Okinawa, which was to
cost so many thousands of lives. On April 12th,

President Franklin Delano Roosevelt died, and Harry S. Truman succeeded to the office of President. Such great crowds came to the memorial services conducted by the Archbishop in the Cathedral of the Holy Cross that people sat even within the sanctuary and along the altar rail. To the new President, Archbishop Cushing cabled:

"Today, in all the churches of the Archdiocese of Boston, more than a million faithful united with me in fervent prayers that Almighty God may be your constant strength and guide in the exalted office which is now yours. In their name I pledge you the loving loyalty of the Catholic people of this province, and in my own I offer you whatever aid you may wish to ask of me in the spiritual service of the beloved nation of which Divine Providence has made you the Chief Executive and the First Citizen.

"With all my heart I wish you the blessing of God in leading this war to its conclusion and in laying the foundations of enduring peace."

There was certainly a need for prayers, even after America and her Allies jubilantly celebrated V-E Day—Victory in Europe—on May 7th. Already, the newspapers had made sharp comments on Russian action in Poland. Hence allied relations were far from ideal. The outcome of the United Nations Conference held in San Francisco from April 25th to June 26th, was the object of fervent prayer.

Yet the works of charity, the enduring efforts of the Archbishop to build for a better world inasmuch

as lay in his power, went steadily on. The papers at
this time show him accepting a check for $10,000
from former Ambassador Joseph F. Kennedy for the
charities of the Guild of dentists, called the Guild
of St. Apollonia. The father of the future President
explained his gift by saying that twenty-five years
previously, when he and Mrs. Kennedy had four
children and not much money, their second child,
Jack, was seriously ill with scarlet fever.

"I decided that if this boy got well, I would
donate half of what I owned to charity. Well, he
got well." In keeping his promise twenty-five years
earlier, he had not stopped there.

Joseph P. Kennedy that evening spoke of the
common wish that the war might soon end, that
the boys might come home. And everyone there
thought of this man's loss of his eldest son, Joe Kennedy, Jr., on whom his fondest hopes had been
placed. In the years to come, many a building, the
object of Archbishop Cushing's hopes and dreams,
would bear the name, "Joseph P. Kennedy, Jr.
Memorial."

The Archbishop saw a goal dear to his heart
reached when he purchased two excellent buildings
on Boston's The Fenway for a Catholic Boys Guidance Center. It was to provide splendid facilities for
housing the group of boys in whom the Archbishop
had shown a very deep and sincere interest. The
front-page *Pilot* article on that occasion stated: "In
this Center there will be adequate sleeping arrange-

ments and recreational facilities for housing the group of boys, who will receive personal guidance and treatment to insure them a more healthful and wholesome outlook on life. Never has there been a greater need for this unique type of activity (the most modern methods of social service combined with emphasis on the spiritual), which presents a well-defined program of assistance to boys in trouble."

The same issue of the *Pilot* contained Archbishop Cushing's moving words on the anniversary of his predecessor's death. He wrote in part: "A year ago, utterly spent, his right hand tracing the cross over those who knelt by his bed, Cardinal O'Connell died. A superb soldier, he had fought the good fight. A peerless athlete of Christ, he had finished his course. . . . On the anniversary of his death, let us all pray with a particular fervor for the repose of his soul. And I implore you, as you remember my illustrious predecessor before the altar, pray also that God may bless the humble efforts of Cardinal O'Connell's successor."

The Pilot, indeed, presented many facets of the Archbishop's personality, for again in this April 21st issue, it showed him in an unprecedented ceremony blessing fishermen and their rods at the opening of the season! No wonder more people were buying and reading the paper than ever before. Moreover, as one of the dailies had pointed out, its editorials had become highly quotable, not a few of them being strong protests or observations on current problems.

One day in June, Bostonians enjoyed another unusual view of their Archbishop. . . . All the Boston papers carried the picture of their spiritual leader entertaining thirty excited youngsters at—the Circus! Ringling Brothers and Barnum and Bailey was at Boston Garden, and His Excellency played host to children from four to eight from various Boston homes and orphanages. According to him, it was the first time he'd been to a circus since he had crawled under the tents at the old Andrew's Square circus in South Boston.

Special seats right in the front awaited the jubilant youngsters, for whom the clowns performed their best acts. When the king of the clowns brought his trained pig to them for a close-up, the children squealed with delight and the Archbishop smiled with pleasure.

Crackerjacks, popcorn, ice cream, soda pop, spun sugar sticks, colored bird whistles, riding whips— everything the circus had to offer, the Archbishop bought for the youngsters. Their excitement was at a fever pitch. One little fellow, who had somehow thought he was being taken to the dentist, was overjoyed at finding himself at the circus. Another four-year-old clung tightly to the Archbishop's hand, in fear of all the commotion, but before long, he was yelling delightedly with the others. It was a six-year-old Negro girl who best showed her joy, however. At every new act, she would fling herself gleefully into the Archbishop's arms!

Rev. Edward S. Sullivan, the circus chaplain, had arranged the unusual party and must have been very pleased at the great joy he had thus procured for less fortunate children—and perhaps also for the Archbishop himself. These, indeed, were just about the only moments of relaxation the Archbishop allowed himself, the kind that brought happiness to others.

On August 14th, the Japanese surrendered, and the rejoicing for this V-J Day, the final end of the war, was tremendous. The crowds on Boston streets went wild with joy. But there was a more sober form of celebrating the event, too. The following day, the Feast of the Assumption of Mary into Heaven, Archbishop Cushing led his faithful in thanksgiving prayers at the Mission Church, while crowds flocked to special services concluding with Benediction of the Blessed Sacrament in every church of the Archdiocese.

It was the long-awaited hour of victory, the return of peace. No one better than Archbishop Cushing knew what a toll the war had taken and what this peace meant, not only in terms of Boston, of America, but in the missions, so hard hit in the Pacific. Not for a moment had his thoughts strayed from the brave priests and nuns at the scene of battle.

"Our first thought in this hour of relief must be of God," he wrote in his message on the victory. "In Him we have trusted, by Him we have not been confounded. May He save His people and bless His heritage! May He govern them and lift them up forever! May He keep us this day without sin!

"Together with our thought of God, closely linked with it, must be our thought of those who have suffered to bring the peace. May their greathearted sacrifices help us to remember the terrible cost of war. God grant His eternal rest to all who have died, His consolation to all who have been bereaved, His courage and wisdom to those who must now bind up the wounds of war and guide our world into a lasting peace."

Sobering words, those last. There were many V-J Day pictures—in every paper—of wildly celebrating crowds, of Japanese prisoners weeping unashamedly at news of the surrender, of people at prayer—but this message made an impression all its own. Into the minds of readers came the picture of the Archbishop whose love was universal, who stooped to help the needy of every age, race and condition, whose concern was for all.

As the war clouds lifted, and life was on its way to becoming normal again, people of every creed took hope and direction from the words, and even more, the example of this truly spiritual man whose strong figure was sharply etched in their minds against a background of all-embracing charity.

12

WITNESS IN MOTION

"Peace will not drop from heaven ready made. Peace must be built. . . . The process must start somewhere, and it can start here as well as anywhere else. Indeed, here in St. Anne de Beaupre better than in most places, a great start can be made in the building of peace."

The place was the famous Canadian Shrine of St. Anne, the grandmother of Christ. It was July 26, 1946, almost one year since the first Atom bomb had been dropped on Hiroshima, killing over 78,000

persons. In the great throng listening to Archbishop
Cushing's plea for the building of the peace were
about 1,200 Bostonians come with their Shepherd
to pray at the Shrine and help confirm good relations between Canada and the U.S.

"We may not be able to settle the differences
between peoples of nations hundreds or thousands
of miles away. . . . But we can resolve that we will
permit no differences to arise between the neighbor
nations of whom the pilgrims here at St. Anne de
Beaupre are the representatives. . . . May the peace
between our peoples be a model and an inspiration
to the world!"

Archbishop Cushing's goodwill pilgrimages had
begun.

It had often been said of him that though he
had never set foot on foreign soil, his name was
known all over the globe. He himself liked to quip
that he had never been outside Boston, or, "no further east than City Point!" But he who had never
had time for vacation trips was to begin travelling
in earnest.

The pilgrimage to St. Anne's was such a success
that the Archbishop announced plans for an international pilgrimage the following year. As with
everything he directed, this first pilgrimage was skill-
fully organized and handled, so that the enthusiastic
pilgrims received their fill of the spiritual benefits
sought, while also enjoying the trip considerably.
Papers all over the East and Canada carried the story

of Archbishop Cushing's latest undertaking. As was ever his custom, he included all his people in it, whether they were actually making the pilgrimage or not. In fact, before leaving Boston, he had prepared and addressed several thousand penny postcards, which he mailed back to his people at home from St. Anne's. (The inexperienced traveler made one error, however: all the cards bore American stamps!) Proof of his intent to make the pilgrimage truly a mission of prayer on behalf of all his people is contained in these words to his fellow pilgrims: "I ask you to be mindful of the needs and works of our own Archdiocese whenever you pray and to remember with special affection our sick, our worried, our benefactors, our priests and religious, and all our friends at home."

"May God bless us all on this first pilgrimage we have attempted," he concluded. That the Lord did so is evident in the joyful spirit of the returning pilgrims and the new gloss the event gave to the religious tone and activities of the people of Boston.

Though Archbishop Cushing personally was a humble soul for whom fanfare held no appeal, his attitude was quite the opposite when it came to the works of God. Evil and purely secular activities, to his mind, should not be allowed to monopolize the limelight; the spiritual yearnings and goals of good people deserve recognition and publicity. For this reason he was to give whole-hearted, public support to every attempt to promote true spirituality, brotherhood and works of charity, along with leaders of all faiths. And he began soon enough to present the world with the spectacle of huge assemblies of men and women gathered together to bear witness to their belief in God.

The first of these was in June of 1945, less than a year after his installation. Thirty thousand Holy Name members and other Catholic men gathered in Boston's Fenway Park for an unforgettable ceremony. "We are banded together to revive a world that almost died by its own hand," the Archbishop declared, charging in no cushioned terms that secularism had made of religion a one-day-a-week concern.

The impressive ceremonies commemorating the 3,912 war dead of the Archdiocese, were, in the words of the Archbishop, a wartime substitute for a Eucharistic Congress. The *Boston Post* reporter of the event described in awed tones the sight of the service men forming a cross before the immense altar; the sound of 30,000 voices rising and falling in the recitation of the Rosary; the solemn moment when they renewed their Holy Name Pledge. Rain had fallen earlier in the day but stopped at the outset of the services. Then, at their conclusion, it began again; yet despite the downpour, Archbishop Cushing strode across the field to give a special blessing to wounded service men, to whom he had already had rosaries distributed during the service. Going among them to shake hands and talk with them, he seemed totally unmindful, as did they, of the slashing rain.

"These are the real heroes," he murmured. "Men who dare to become saints." While the thousands streamed out of the ball park, he stayed there among the wounded, adding the personal touch that was always to characterize even the most monumental of his projects. The following June, 1946, saw an even more spectacular event. This time, 40,000 Holy Name men filled Braves' Field for an Archdiocesan Holy Hour, at which the Armed Forces Chaplains of the Archdiocese were given citations by the Archbishop. To the right of the great outdoor altar, beneath a gold star, was the number 4,317, the total of Catholics in the Boston Archdiocese who had made the supreme sacrifice for their country.

In his address, which was aptly described as stirring, Archbishop Cushing urged that Catholic Action be generated by Faith. "Catholicism is a form of life: live it!" he concluded. "Grow in it! Become strong with it! Reflect your living Faith by positive, constructive works. Confirm your living Hope by joyful perseverance through whatever tribulations the living of a Catholic life may entail. Render immortal your lively Charity by identifying it, in its source and in its object, with that Eternal God, Who is your beginning, your end, and all your life."

Vibrant the voice, vibrant the whole tempo of the gathering—significant of the new vigor of spirit communicated by the Archbishop to the thousands who were responding to his call for action.

"Perhaps the most impressive of all these great gatherings in Boston," wrote Most Rev. John J. Wright, formerly the Archbishop's secretary and then Auxiliary Bishop of Boston, "and the one which still gives us proud memories, was the famed national convention of the Confraternity of Christian Doctrine at which our Archbishop made his historic plea for prayers for the canonization of Pope Pius X (October 27, 1946). Listening as he spoke to the hushed thousands in the Boston Garden, an audience which included a devout princess, renowned prelates from many parts of the world, and hosts of humble folk who had never before seen the like, one reflected on the place to which Boston has come among the great dioceses of the world, and one was proud of the Holy Church."

In addressing that Congress by radio from Castel Gandolfo, Pope Pius XII began: "What wonder that you have responded with such loyal and holy enthusiasm to the invitation of Boston's zealous and large-hearted Archbishop, and from the widespread sections of the three Americas have flocked to this national Congress!" Indeed, that Congress was the largest ever held by the C.C.D., and it included seventy prelates from all parts of the U.S., Canada, Central and South America, making it one of the greatest assemblies of prelates ever witnessed in the United States. It was precisely this occasion that Archbishop Cushing chose to urge the speedy introduction of Pope Pius X's Cause for Beatification. Humble, gentle Pius X, who had said: "I was born poor, I have lived poor, and I want to die poor," was the Archbishop's personal model of the ideal Christian Shepherd, and nothing gave him greater pleasure than when he saw his efforts crowned by the Saint's canonization in 1954.

October, 1947, marked another monumental religious event: the national convention of the Holy Name Society, held for the first time in Boston. The final evening of the convention saw fifty thousand pack Braves' Field in a dramatic candlelight scene unparalleled in the city's history. The ballfield was darkened just before the men recited the Holy Name pledge, only one light remaining on the tall, glittering altar. Then myriads of lights from 50,000 candles in blue shades lit up the whole field that frosty October evening, and the Redeemer of the world was honored by devout hearts promising anew their loyalty to God and country, in the famous pledge that ends: "I promise to give good example by the regular practice of my faith. In honor of His Divine Name, I pledge myself against perjury, blasphemy, profanity and obscene speech. I pledge my loyalty to the flag of my country and to the God-given principles of freedom, justice, and happiness for which it stands. I pledge my support to all lawful authority, both civil and religious. I dedicate my manhood to the honor of the sacred name of Jesus

Christ and beg that He will keep me faithful to these pledges until death."

In what the newspapers called a deeply spiritual sermon, Archbishop Cushing spoke that evening on the powerful and transforming motive which religion can give to the ordinary, mediocre life. "The word 'Christian'," he said, "should mean that Christ is as much a part of us as we are part of ourselves. It should mean that self and class and family and nation and every other interest which may hold a man's heart hold second place to Jesus Christ in our lives—we are renewed in Him. If we are, though the renewal may be on the hidden level of the soul and of sanctifying grace, its effects will be visible to all; the whole world will be able to witness the change Christ makes in us. . . .

"The supremacy of Christ in our purposes will give meaning both to adversity and to the good things of life. Remembering Christ, we will not be scandalized or discouraged, fearful or ashamed, when the very things of Christ seem endangered or defeated."

To show forth the supremacy of Christ in human life may well have been the goal of the spectacular parade staged the next day, October 5th, to close the convention. Three and a half million men, women and children of all faiths witnessed the greatest civilian parade in New England history. It lasted from mid-morning until dark and travelled a packed route more than two miles long. Over that entire route Archbishop Cushing walked twice, displaying what one reporter, in an understatement, called remarkable vigor. Again and again, he raised his biretta to acknowledge the cheers of the multitudes.

About a year to the day, on October 3, 1948, it was youth's turn to capture the interest of the city. From the time of his installation, the Archbishop had begun to manifest his tremendous concern for the welfare of teenagers and his resulting interest in the spiritual, cultural and social aspects of the Catholic Youth Organization. The young folks came into their own when a mammoth CYO parade of somewhere between sixty and eighty thousand marchers formed what papers called "the Hub's greatest demonstration of faith in God and country."

Spectators, who numbered more than a million, received many an inspiring message from the colorful floats picturing a tremendous variety of scenes, from the Holy Family in their home at Nazareth to the four freedoms of American democracy.

The Archbishop was everywhere that day—shaking hands with the notables in the reviewing stands; receiving flowers from a nun and stooping to the level of a diminutive, four-year-old drum majorette to present her with the bouquet; mobbed by youngsters who broke from the crowd past police lines to kiss his ring; and responding to the enthusiastic crowds hailing him all along the route. It was a memorable day, for its overwhelming evidence of youthful loyalty to all that forms Catholic and American tradition.

Greater devotion and stronger attachment to the highest values were what the Archbishop hoped to promote in all his endeavors. Nothing new was ever undertaken until he felt it would prove truly useful for God's glory. Once he had ascertained the worth of the goal and the suitability of the methods proposed, he spared nothing to achieve it. The fact that it had never been done before did not check him at all.

His "lend-lease program" was one new plan which attracted widespread attention and proved a godsend. The plan consisted of loaning priests from Boston to other U.S. dioceses which were severely handicapped by a shortage of priests. Many a grateful bishop blessed the Boston Archbishop for this unique inspiration, which he put into effect comparatively soon after assuming the reins of office.

Archbishop Cushing now had so many projects going that reporters were despairing of ever achieving a full perspective of his total activity. "To attempt a scoring of his accomplishments in chronological order," observed one journalist, "only leads to confusion, for he has so many operating at once—in various stages of progress—that the sideline chronicler quickly runs into a series of overlaps. Adding twenty new parishes to the Archdiocese (as of January, 1946), launching drives for a new million-dollar hospital at Lawrence and a new million-dollar

Boston College High School, handling one speaking engagement after another in rapid succession—that's the sort of thing that has made Archbishop Cushing the busiest man in the state and easily one of the busiest in the nation."

That the Archbishop thrived on work, work that brought so many blessings to others, was evident in his own definition of labor: "It is not merely an activity to produce external commodities. It was intended by Divine Providence to become a means of personal development. Unless you can build your life around some form of congenial work, you cannot live a full human life." By all standards, his own life, then, was extraordinarily full.

And it was a happy life. Archbishop Cushing's buoyant good spirits were in evidence at all times. As often as not, his jokes were toward none other than himself. A good example was the one about the quarter:

The little girl had somehow swallowed a quarter, and every effort to dislodge it from her windpipe had proven vain. At last, one of the good Sister-nurses had an inspiration.

"Send for the Archbishop!" she said. "He'll get that quarter, if anybody can!"

He also had a genius for poking fun at the foibles of the city he dearly loved. Once, in addressing a group of taxi drivers who had gathered at the invitation of the Chamber of Commerce to hear themselves appointed public relations men for Boston, the Archbishop inserted the following yarn between more serious remarks:

"They tell about the Boston lady who had to go out to California to see a friend. It was a matter of life and death, or of course, she would never have left Boston. One day, as she sat with her friend on a beach, looking at the waves of the Pacific rolling into shore, she suddenly sneezed. 'I beg your pardon,' she said. 'It must be the air. I'll never get used to being 3,000 miles from the ocean!'

"When the good woman finally got back to Boston, an acquaintance asked her how she had travelled to California. 'By car,' was the reply. 'I know,' said her friend, 'but what route did you follow?'

" 'Oh,' said the Bostonian, 'we just drove out to Wellesley and then turned left!' "

The Archbishop gave concrete proof of his love for his city in another address, which was an impassioned appeal to the Boston Chamber of Commerce, delivered two months after his installation, for jobs for returning handicapped veterans. Many, indeed, were his words on social problems. There was his hard-hitting article in *The American Weekly*, entitled "The Evils of Divorce," in which he urged conscientious lawmakers and judges to step in to halt the unprecedented divorce craze. There was his address to five hundred labor representatives at a conference sponsored by the Massachusetts branch of the Jewish Labor Committee, in which he emphasized that a man's right to work "must not be contingent on such irrelevant or accidental factors as race, creed, or color." There was a Christmas Eve TV talk which included these memorable words: "No man could have my faith concerning Christ, His life and His death, without loving Him and loving the people who produced Him, the Jews. No man could have my faith concerning Christ, His life and death, without desiring to be more like He was and seeking always to serve, help, and befriend all men without exception—white, black, gentile, Jew."

Contrary to the opinion of some who could not comprehend his unfailing energy, the Archbishop often labored long over many of his speeches, rewriting them until they suited him. As in the days at the Propagation of the Faith, he concentrated on making the need real to his listeners, if the speech were an appeal. As only one who loves can, he portrayed the responsibility he felt for his "exceptional children," the mongoloids and retarded; the homeless, the physically handicapped, the unwanted, emotionally disturbed problem cases. Because his own concern communicated itself to others, people gave. Things did not stop there, however. The Archbishop felt himself obligated to let it be known exactly how his projects were progressing and where the money was going. Any newsman wishing to write about the Archbishop might find himself up against it, but let him request material on the

Archbishop's charities and he would be over-whelmed with it.

It would seem that a man so busy at home would not give even a passing nod to the proposition of international pilgrimages, but no, Archbishop Cushing had told his 1946 St. Anne pilgrims that there would be another pilgrimage, next time overseas; and in 1948, that promise was fulfilled.

On August 13th, the Archbishop left Boston to sail on the Queen Mary out of New York the following day. With him went four hundred pilgrims en route to Lourdes and Rome. One paper declared that he broke down and wept at the display of affection shown by 10,000 well-wishers who gathered at Boston's South Station to see him off to New York. The highlight of this pilgrimage of the Confraternity of Christian Doctrine was to be an audience with His Holiness, Pope Pius XII. For Archbishop Richard J. Cushing, it was to be his first meeting with the Holy Father.

In Paris, the Archbishop preached in the world-famous Cathedral of Notre Dame, the first Boston prelate to do so, at a solemn pontifical Mass. In a moving sermon, he brought greetings from American Catholics to the people of France.

"It was thrilling," wrote Bishop Wright, "to see the Archbishop of Boston in the pulpit of Notre Dame and to hear the walls of a temple once defiled by an irreligious revolution, now echo the accents of a corner of the world where another kind of revolution had eventually resulted in that privileged freedom for the Faith of which the Catholic Metropolitan of New England had become a living symbol."

Archbishop Cushing received the Legion of Honor Award from Foreign Minister Robert Schuman, in the presence of other American prelates: Auxiliary Bishop John J. Wright, Bishop Edward F. Ryan of Burlington, Vermont, Bishop Edwin O'Hara of Kansas City, Missouri, and Bishop Matthew Brady of Manchester, New Hampshire. Two days later, the pilgrims were at Lourdes, the great shrine of the Immaculate Conception and the scene of many proven cures. The Archbishop was to return again and again to this site hallowed by the appearance of the Blessed Virgin Mary to little Bernadette Soubirous. One day he would come back with a flock of his "exceptional children," that they might be blessed by the special benefits of Mary's maternal love, felt so deeply at Lourdes.

After a last early morning Mass at the great Basilica there, the Archbishop and pilgrims left for the Eternal City on August 25th. Their route took them through historical Nice, where church and city dignitaries turned out to greet them. The Archbishop's remarks were perfect for the moment and for the good will purpose of the trip: "My hope," he said, "is that the present suffering of France will be followed by the glorious resurrection that France deserves."

Sunday, August 29th, found the Archbishop celebrating Mass in the Church of St. Susanna, staffed by the Paulist Fathers for Americans living in Rome. Little did he think that ten years later, this would be his own titular church, when his name would be changed to Richard Cardinal Cushing.

The following Wednesday, the Archbishop had a special audience with Pope Pius XII. Photographs of this meeting show a pleased fatherly expression on the Holy Father's thin face, and a humble, almost timid joy reflected in the expression of the Archbishop. In his long address to all the pilgrims, the Pope thanked them and all Americans for their generosity in helping him aid the war-stricken countries, and he greatly encouraged them in their efforts to give all Catholic children the necessary instruction in their Faith. Though visibly weak from a recent illness, Pope Pius moved all the pilgrims with the warmth of his address.

After this memorable audience, the climax of the trip, the pilgrimage split up into various groups with different routes planned for each. The Archbishop set out for Assisi, drawn by his great love for St. Francis. Indeed, what but this devotion to the "Poverello of Assisi" could explain the well-known fact that he was forever giving away not only money, gifts, and food from his kitchen, but even the coat he had on or the suits in his closet? "I know what it is to be poor," he once said, "because I give everything away."

When he arrived back in New York with about a hundred of the original group, he was surprised to find a detail of Boston's distinguished Monsignors on hand to greet him. Looking rested despite the strenuous schedule which had included countless speeches and his usual thoughtful efforts to keep everyone happy, the Archbishop remarked, in a phrase that was to become familiar: "Coming home is the best part of it!" He also spoke of the deep gratitude shown by citizens of France and Italy for American help in the face of poverty and suffering. Finally and characteristically, he paid tribute to the pilgrims for having borne up cheerfully under inconveniences and having acted as ambassadors of good will and apostles of the Faith.

"I hate to travel," the Archbishop was to admit many a time. "I'm happiest at my work." Yet travel he did, his next pilgrimage being just one year later, this time to Ireland. Called the "Come Back to Erin" pilgrimage, and composed of over five hundred, it was the largest ever to leave the U.S. for Ireland.

"I'm happy to be going to the land of my ancestors," the Archbishop said in a lull between the clamorous cheers of the crowds come to see them off. "The great glory of Ireland is that from it emanated a spiritual empire which has carried the name of Christ to the ends of the earth. Even in our own day, Ireland's greatest 'export' is her missionaries. Centuries ago, these holy men went to all parts of Europe and in our own day, they have gone to every

country in the world. I hope we can catch some of
the enthusiasm of the missionary spirit, so that many
of our young men and women may feel called to the
religious life and bring Christianity to the barren
sections of the world.

"We plan a Mass each morning for the people
of Boston and for those of Ireland, especially for the
loved ones of Irish immigrants, including my own
folks, who helped build up the Church in America."

It became known that it had been the Archbishop who had prevailed on officials of the Cunard
White Star Line to send the Britannic up to Boston,
so that the pilgrims could sail from their home port
and so that Boston Harbor might see the 27,000-ton
liner once again. What was more, he announced that
the Holy Year pilgrimage coming up in 1950 would
also sail from Boston.

"When he undertook the apostolate of pilgrimages, he gave us new reasons to be proud," wrote
Bishop Wright. "For one thing, he gave an example
of the kind of temporal influence a spiritual shepherd should seek to exercise in the political and
economic community within which he does his work
of religion. The Archbishop insisted that the hundreds of pilgrims who signed up to travel with him
should be enabled to sail from Boston, and thus our
beautiful harbor, so long almost merely beautiful,
welcomed once again great trans-Atlantic liners at
least once each summer. It made one proud of the
Archbishop when Commonwealth Pier, whence

thousands of our boys had sailed in melancholy silence during the recent war years, was loud again with the laughter of embarking pilgrims and alive with all the merry business of the departure of great ships."

The welcome given the American pilgrims was truly phenomenal, even for hospitable Ireland. The Britannic landed in Cobb, and there the Archbishop and Massachusetts Governor Paul Dever were given the traditional freedom of the city, after they were met by Ireland's President Sean O'Kelly, Premier John Costello, ex-Premier Eamon De Valera, and other notables. But the welcome in Cobb, warm as it was, gave no clue to the overwhelming reception awaiting Archbishop Cushing in Dublin, the capital. The Archbishop concluded a pontifical Mass in the Chapel at Holy Cross College and walked out to be nearly crushed by admiring thousands, who tried to touch his hand or coat sleeve. Everyone wanted to see and greet the man they knew from innumerable stories and photos as a paragon of charity. It was an overwhelming tribute to one who was to say later in Cork, after encountering similar enthusiasm all over Ireland: "We are all the sons of working men, and you have given us a reception fit for royalty!"

In greeting him, Archbishop John C. Mc-Quaid expressed Ireland's deep affection for "a man of God whose chief anxiety is for the protection, faith and care of the people." The Boston Archbishop replied by saying that his Archdiocese would attempt to duplicate what Ireland had done for many years in furnishing missionaries to the world.

The pilgrims prayed in St. Patrick's Cathedral, visited Trinity College, Dublin Castle, and the ancient Kells Monastery, and prayed at the grave of Matt Talbot, the converted alcoholic who may one day be raised to the altars. Everywhere the Archbishop and his pilgrims went, they were greeted with waves from smiling Irish well-wishers. After a thousand-mile tour through countless towns, and a great many speeches, the Archbishop arrived in Cork for the last stop before going home. On the way to Cork, he spent a short while in the towns where his father and mother were born. What were his feelings at those sites? The papers reporting the news make no comment and record no remark of his. True, later there was to be a commemorative statue erected on the site of his father's birthplace, but as was always the case when his own family was concerned, the Archbishop was reticent and kept his feelings mostly to himself.

In his speech at Cork, he declared that the young men of Ireland should stay home, marry the country's beautiful colleens, and build up its unity, rather than emigrate: "All must work to bring economic success and all must work and pray for a united Ireland."

Were he one to keep all the gifts given him instead of keeping nothing at all, among what would certainly be an unparalleled collection, might be viewed Cork's gift to him: a silver replica of St. Patrick's bell, inscribed in Gaelic: "Padraig ro naomtha do chun gloire de agus onora na heireann" —"St. Patrick, to the glory of God and the honor of Ireland." On the reverse side of this bell with a personality was written: "I was presented to His Excellency, Dr. Cushing, Archbishop of Boston, U.S.A., by the Rt. Hon. Sean MacCarthy, Lord Mayor of Cork."

The following day, the Archbishop and some of the pilgrims boarded the Britannic at Cobb for the homeward journey. With him were fourteen Trappistine nuns coming to open the first American house of their cloistered Order. Their prayers, he had told them, would bring success to his efforts to increase and extend the Faith.

Good will pilgrimages—there were many more to come. In August of 1950, the Holy Year, the Archbishop led his faithful to Rome and Fatima; in July of 1951, to Spain; in June of 1954, to Rome and Lourdes; in August of 1956, to Germany, and so it went. By daily cables, he shared with those at home the enriching spiritual experiences of the pilgrimages and gave readers of the Boston papers a good insight into the apostolate of encouragement he was carrying on in Europe.

"It goes without saying," concluded Bishop Wright in writing of this phase of the Archbishop's activity, "that these religious pilgrimages in lands still bearing the tragic evidences of war had their intended effect in helping bring together the peoples of divided nations. In due course, the governments of France, Italy, Germany, Portugal and Ireland were to pay their tribute to the work of international friendship by which the Archbishop had already made his own people so proud."

In the years since his installation, Bostonians had grown accustomed to seeing photos of or reading articles on their Archbishop in the press almost every day. He had become a familiar figure on the national and international scene, for, as from his days in the Propagation of the Faith, he was always "a bishop of the Universal Church." That outlook had been present in everything he did. When he had received his pallium, the sacred symbol of his office, (an event which because of wartime conditions was delayed until over a year after his installation), sharing honors with Francis Cardinal Spellman of New York, was Thomas Cardinal Tien, beloved Chinese prelate. And shortly after becoming Archbishop, he had personally given a warm reception to French sailors who had expressed a desire to meet him. He had conducted moving ceremonies honoring the heroic people of Poland, and on another occasion, for the Lithuanians. He had brought the Maryknoll Sisters to Boston to provide a social and instructional center for the Chinese portion of his flock.

Nothing that could benefit anyone seemed to escape his notice. And he gave no thought to the cost in his own health or even "in his dignity," if he could make others happy. Many Bostonians clipped out the newsphoto showing the Archbishop arriving in a jeep at the Home for the Aged Poor when a fierce New England snow storm made any other means impossible. Then there was the picture of him up to bat in a softball game at a Catholic summer camp for girls. The caption under the half-page spread read: "Hard Hitter—His Excellency gave the ball a good clout, but when he headed for first, he found that his base running days are over!"

The photo stories were a good indication, too, of the Archbishop's endless round of activities and accomplishments. They tell of the new Orders he was constantly bringing into the Archdiocese to take care of one or another educational or charitable need; they describe the property he was buying for a new hospital or social center; they show him with Italian-American children at a new Oratory in the North End to be served by the Salesians of St. John Bosco; or in a memorable embrace with Archbishop Athenagoras of the Greek Orthodox Church, or speaking out for one good cause or another at the meetings of his many Guilds.

It was a grueling schedule, even for a strong constitution, for it was hardly ever broken by a minute's real relaxation. Outside the Archbishop's door a never-ending stream of engagements waited;

inside were appointments to fill every available hour, consultations, tiring paper work on his many projects, and the ever increasing pile of mail to be answered.

"When I assumed the office of Archbishop," he once said, "I had two choices. I could either adopt an easy, calm and beautiful way of life, or go to work. I chose to do the latter. I do it the hard way, and I know, as well as the doctors do, that I have paid the price. But I want to continue until my program of charitable, missionary and educational work is accomplished."

In December of 1953, Archbishop Cushing was forced to break his schedule, like it or not, when he was admitted to St. Elizabeth's Hospital for two major operations, one on December 8th, and the second on the 22nd. Throughout the Archdiocese, there was general concern. Fifty thousand Holy Name men offered Holy Communion and a Spiritual Bouquet for his recovery. Somehow, the rumor had spread that the beloved Archbishop was suffering from an incurable ailment.

Yet before long, though thin and wan, he was back to his desk and back on his round of activities. People tried to give him advice, urging him to take a long overdue vacation, or at least to slow down, but it was all in vain. Then came March 17th, 1954, St. Patrick's Day. With Bishop Cornelius Lucey of Cork, Ireland, the Archbishop went to Bishop Wright's Diocese of Worcester to address some two

thousand people in a program sponsored by the
Friendly Sons of St. Patrick. At 8:50, he was standing on the stage of the Elm Street Theatre delivering
his speech when suddenly he stopped speaking to
turn and look back at Bishop Wright. Then he began to sink to the floor. The Bishop and others on
the platform leaped forward and caught him as he
collapsed.

Carried to the wings of the stage, he lay unconscious for about five minutes. Then, to the immense relief of all, he revived and refused to be
taken to the hospital in an ambulance. His own car
would be perfectly fine, he said. At St. Vincent's
Hospital, he consented to lie down, still wearing his
robes adorned with the traditional green carnation
of St. Patrick's Day. But two hours had not gone by
before he was leaving the hospital to go home to
Boston.

Although it was obviously exhaustion and weakness following his recent operations that had caused
the collapse, Archbishop Cushing said he felt well
enough to carry on his scheduled public appearances.
The spirit would dominate the body, and despite
fearful predictions to the contrary, slowly, gradually, it did. The hollows began to disappear from
under his eyes, and color came back to his face.
Newspapermen who had been watching him carefully, afraid of being scooped on a picture of another fainting spell, began to relax. (Once he had
noticed their reluctance to leave after taking the

usual shots at a gathering, and he had called out: "I'm not going to faint, so you fellows don't need to stay!")

November of that year, 1954, marked the tenth anniversary of Richard James Cushing's installation as Archbishop of Boston. Never one to take time out to count the accomplishments of the past, he would have paid little heed to the anniversary, but his grateful flock would not allow him to forget it. Years before, just nineteen days after his installation, in fact, he had said to parishioners of his own parish, St. Brigid's, South Boston:

"To you there is nothing important about the fact that I am your Archbishop. Archbishops live and die and the Church goes on just the same. I am God's instrument to love, serve, support and help. May God and His Blessed Mother be with us all the way."

Now, ten years later, the *Pilot's* commemorative supplement, Nov. 6, 1954, carried a letter to his flock which is perhaps one of the clearest statements of his own attitude toward his life and accomplishments and toward his people:

"MY DEARLY BELOVED CHILDREN IN CHRIST:

"On November 8, 1944, the crozier of jurisdiction over the Archdiocese of Boston was placed in my hand. Ten years have since passed—years filled with work and responsibility, disappointment and satisfaction, sorrow and joy. . . .

"To God we offer thanks that he has given us this anniversary. To God's representative on earth, His Holiness, Pope Pius XII, who appointed us your Archbishop, we give our love, loyalty and prayers. To you, dear people, I give my life and service. The history of the past ten years is yours, not mine. To you, after God, be all its glory.

"We have done many things, as the pages of this Special Supplement show. Some of it is in new and shining construction, and in properties acquired and dedicated to the service of God and mankind. All this has cost a great deal of money, every cent of which came from your open purses and your yet more open hearts. It has represented a willingness to sacrifice your own desires, even your own necessities, in favor of the poor and needy. It has spoken of great faith and of extraordinary good will. It has paid me the compliment of your trust in my judgment and in my desire to live for others. I thank you.

"Those of you who recall my words on the occasion of my installation as Archbishop know that I had no idea then of embarking on a great building program. No one was more astonished than I by the magnitude of the construction problems which were lurking around the corner, waiting for me to pull out the chair behind my desk. But since not one cent of the tremendous financial outlay involved could I have supplied myself, why then, should I think of the program as *mine*? It is *yours*, my dear people of the Archdiocese, especially the modestly paid working men and women among you; it is *yours*, also, my friends not of my own faith. It has been an honor to formulate the details of its expenditures, the manner of its implementation.

"My own version of my apostolate was expressed in my motto: 'Ut Cognoscant Te,' That they may know Thee, O Lord! It is the continuance of the mission that Christ gave to His Apostles: love one another as I have loved you. Unless we know God, we cannot love Him. This is a truism we all acknowledge. Through prayer, study, and an intensified Christian living of the commandment of love, we all grow in our desire for holiness, and in our earnestness to realize that desire.

"I could not be complacent about the attention I have given to material needs had I not the assurance that through the cooperation, good will and hard work of pastors and their priestly assistants, of nuns and brothers, and of the men and women of the laity, young and old, Our Lord is better known, better loved, better served today than He was ten years ago. On the pages of this Special Supplement, you will find the story of a more fervent parish life, of more people among the faithful dedicating themselves to the poor and the needy, giving of their time, their services, their money, their love, their example of holiness—giving, if not their very *all*, at least very nearly this, to God.

"Herein are the sources of my joy, and I take this opportunity of thanking you all, lay, religious and clergy. As for myself, let me continue with work and prayer and sacrifice the labor of restoring all things in Christ. With my heart full of love and devotion to everyone, with a special measure for the poor, the shut-ins, the handicapped, I thank you for your prayers, your good will, your generous support.

"Let us go forward together, ever mindful that our sojourn here is but a pilgrimage, and our destiny the throne of God. Let us pray that in the time that remains to me, and to you, that we will do our utmost to make God better known, more loved and served.

"Pray for me, as I pray for you. Ut Cognoscant Te.

"And thank you for ten years of happy leadership. God reward you all."

Devotedly yours in the Lord

✠ RICHARD J. CUSHING

Archbishop of Boston

13

A FAITHFUL HOUSE

"Sometimes people say to me: 'Don't you ever get tired of raising money and asking for help?' My answer is: No! As a matter of fact, everyone gets tired rushing about in the business of life, but everyone takes new energy from the thought of the reasons why he is rushing about, particularly when those reasons are God's reasons."

The speaker swayed back on his heels and lightly tapping his fingertips together for emphasis, continued:

"I am a great believer in the idea that trouble is the best thing that ever happened to us. If all the troubles in the world were eliminated and all the problems solved, we'd be more tired than work ever made us; we would be bored to death.

"As you know, every bishop has a coat of arms. My coat of arms should include a wolf. The wolf to whom I am indebted and who has kept me going all my life is the old, familiar 'wolf at the door' . . . and so he deserves a place on my coat of arms."

This provocative introduction led to some unforgettable remarks by Archbishop Cushing at a banquet for one thousand men and women who had gathered to present him with $125,000 toward the construction of Nazareth, the home for homeless children of every race, creed, and condition. On that evening of April 26, 1953, the Archbishop's jocund observations provided a key to his success as a provident Father of the needy:

"The wolf at the door is not a restful animal like the house cat nor an attractive beast, like a favorite horse. . . . But he has been a spur to achievement. He has been a warning against sloth, complacency and 'taking it easy.' He has kept us from going soft. . . . People save instead of wasting; they improve themselves instead of going to seed; they become successful, spurred on by our old friend, the wolf at the door.

"Now the believer in God is a man who worries about the wolf at the other fellow's door. That's

how he differs from the self-centered materialist
or pagan. . . . If there were no wolf at our door, we'd
all grow fat, lazy and dull. If there were no wolf
at the other fellow's door, we'd all grow selfish. . . .

"How can I despise the beast who gave me so
many friends, so much pleasant work to do for God,
so much opportunity to serve Him? Sometimes it
is exhausting, this battle to keep the wolf from the
door, but if we were having toasts at our dinner tonight, I'd lift my glass to the wolf at the door,
and say:

" 'I hope you never get so close that you can
sink your teeth in my arm and keep me from working; but I hope you never go so far away that I can
no longer hear you howl and thus be reminded of
how much work there is to do, for my neighbor, for
the underprivileged, and for God!' "

This unusual tribute to the proverbial beast
made such an impression on one non-Catholic Bostonian who read it in the paper that he had it printed
for distribution among his friends. In his introduc-
tory remarks, he said: "Archbishop Cushing is, of
course, a Catholic, but he has won the affection and
admiration not only of his own people, but of Protestant and Jew, for his spirit of service, his broad
understanding, his friendly way. That night, at the
Bradford Hotel, he uttered an address that to my
mind is a gold mine of inspiration for all of us. I
want to share the hope, the inspiration, the help
contained in it with many others."

Perhaps those who had heard or read this speech were less astonished than countless others when the incredible record of the Archbishop's achievements was published in connection with the Tenth Anniversary of his installation as Archbishop. They had been given an insight into the driving force behind his deeds. For in his mind, the wolf stood not merely for material evils, but for sin, ignorance, prejudice, spiritual indifference—and even melancholy. Only such an understanding of the enemy could explain the multiplicity of endeavors revealed in that ten-year record.

To begin with, fifty new parishes had been established, because the Archbishop recognized the increasing movement away from crowded Boston to the suburbs, and he was anxious to provide the newly developed communities with the churches they needed. And as the population increased steadily, new schools were required, plus more teachers. Twenty-one new parochial elementary schools, twenty-three new private elementary schools, ten new central high schools—so the list ran, and it took an estimated thirty million dollars to provide classroom space for the thirty thousand more children being given a Catholic education. Twelve new religious communities were brought in to help provide teachers for the ultra-modern edifices.

Central or diocesan secondary schools constituted a plan initiated by the Archbishop with both foresight and courage. Few parishes could afford to build and staff high schools, yet many areas needed them badly. Hence, the Archbishop began constructing centrally located schools to serve whole districts. Some the diocese supported entirely; others were financed by the group of parishes benefiting from the school. All were impressive schools.

Annual teachers' institutes, programs of in-service training, reshaped curricula, Archdiocesan-wide art and science fairs to stimulate initiative, special music programs, participation in international activities sponsored by UNESCO—all these indicated the vigorous new life in New England's largest educational system.

In the field of higher education, three new colleges had been established, and new buildings added to the three already on the scene. Every June found the Archbishop on each campus to deliver the commencement address and urge students to rise to the challenge of a Christ-centered life. A greatly expanded Newman Club program had been developed for Catholics in secular colleges, under the direction of the Paulist Fathers. The Dominican Fathers of Providence College were conducting the unique "Archbishop Cushing School of Theology for the Laity," which had met with an enthusiastic response. The Newton School of Liturgical Music, another unusual educational opportunity, implemented the zealous efforts of the Church Music Commission and the nationally acclaimed Boston Sacramental Apostolate, devoted to promoting greater understanding and participation in the liturgical life of the Church.

Always ready to support new methods of treating old problems, Archbishop Cushing listened intently one day in 1950 while Sisters of St. Francis of Assisi explained the operation of their Reading Clinic during his visit to their Milwaukee Motherhouse. About seven months later a similar clinic, called the Archbishop Cushing Educational Clinic, was already functioning in Boston, to aid both children and adults suffering from reading disabilities.

Under his leadership, the Catholic Guild for the Blind had become the largest in the country, and in addition to providing religious instruction to blind youngsters, religious literature in Braille, and a home for elderly blind women, it had opened the unique St. Paul's Rehabilitation Center. This Center offered a training program to help newly blinded adults return to normal activities in their own communities. Planned primarily to assist any blinded person of the six-state New England area who could benefit by its program, St. Paul's became the object of intense study by social workers all over the country. Archbishop Cushing was frequently on the scene, perhaps trying out the technique of walking blindfolded with a seeing-eye dog, under the guidance of a blind expert, or perhaps sampling a pie baked by one of the elderly blind ladies living at the Guild's St. Raphael Hall.

Religious education for deaf children and a wealth of apostolic activities on behalf of all the deaf or hard of hearing in the Archdiocese were provided by the Boston School for the Deaf, run by the Sisters of St. Joseph, and the Catholic Guild for the Deaf, established as a diocesan unit in January, 1949. Moved by the fact that so many deaf people cut themselves off from the hearing world, from their friends and even from their Church, the Archbishop sent specially trained Sisters on a spiritual census of the known deaf, and as a result, hundreds returned to the practice of their religion and to a happy social life again.

Of all the groups of the handicapped, it is safe to say that those who most completely won the Archbishop's heart were his "forever children," the retarded youngsters to whom he also gave the name of "exceptional children." For them he built St. Coletta's School. Staffed by Sisters of St. Francis of Assisi, it offered a home-like residence and school for boys and girls who were considered social outcasts years ago. Here their potential, low though it might be, was developed to the fullest with patient skill.

To St. Coletta's, the Archbishop often went for his birthday celebrations, and he let it be known that he would like his final resting place to be there near the children for whose care he felt especially responsible to God.

"They're brighter than we think," he often remarked. "Once I asked a group of them, 'Why are
you here?' and one little fellow popped up with,
'Because we're not all there!' "

Through the years, it would give the Archbishop singular pleasure to see his exceptional
children stage "professional" entertainments at the
Archdiocese's "Donnelly Memorial Theater." He
himself would be their Master of Ceremonies to
plead their cause before his generous people. Once,
he roared with delighted amazement when one lad,
delegated to present him with a check, held on tight
to it instead of handing it over! That was not part
of the act, but it brought the house down.

On the property of St. Coletta's, the Archbishop
built an exact replica of St. Mary of the Portiuncula,
the little Chapel in Assisi restored by his beloved
St. Francis. Situated atop a nineteen-foot elevation,
its huge front mural depicting St. Francis' profes-
sion—in multicolored enamel, baked on ceramic
tile—it is an arresting sight. All the materials for the
Portiuncula Chapel were imported from Italy at
the expense of an anonymous devotee of St. Francis.

The Kennedy Memorial Hospital, made possible by generous gifts from the Kennedy Foundation
in memory of their war hero son, was another dream
realized by the Archbishop. Staffed by Franciscan
Missionaries of Mary, this was not a custodial institution for handicapped youngsters but rather a
combination hospital-school in which children crip-

pled by the devastating effects of polio, paraplezia and the brain damage of cerebral palsy might be helped to develop according to their capacities. These children, too, would amaze Bostonians who viewed them on the stage and on TV, with the Archbishop, their inimitable MC, putting on a musical operetta. Wheelchairs and crutches only added to the poignant beauty of the song and drama festival of "Rumpelstiltskin."

It was a prized theory of the Archbishop that many of his unfortunate children were capable of distinguishing the Holy Eucharist from ordinary bread. Hence, under his direction, numbers of them were prepared and he went personally to give them their first Holy Communion to the great joy of fathers and mothers who had never thought this radiant ceremony of white veils and Christ's extraordinary gift of Himself would be for their little ones.

The night Archbishop Cushing delivered his "Wolf at the Door" address, the thought uppermost in his mind was Nazareth, his new haven for homeless children. No austere institution by any means, Nazareth, as he envisioned it, was to be a real home, designed to provide ten individual cottage-type units to shelter children of all ages, complexion and belief, homeless either because of divorce, death or any of the varied causes of family breakdown. To build this home, its accompanying chapel and Holy Childhood school, the Archbishop directed every source of revenue available—paper drives, donations from guilds, field days, and so forth. Situated on a beautiful suburban hilltop, Nazareth finally stood as a living proof of Archbishop Cushing's vital love for the youngest of his flock.

Under the heading, "A Marine Comes Home," he once included the following story in a "Newsnotes" column of *The Pilot*:

"Four years ago a mother, caring for her children with financial help from 'Aid to Dependent Children,' was taken very ill and had to go to the hospital. Tommy was then around fifteen years of age and the two girls were a few years younger. The mother wanted them placed together under the care of Sisters. It was arranged that the three children would come to Nazareth. After some months she died and a grandmother and grandfather took the children. Meanwhile, Tommy left school and went to work.

"One evening, around 7 P.M., Tommy came back with his two sisters. The grandparents were seriously ill. Tommy joined the Marines about two years ago and was doing very nicely. Each furlough he headed straight home—to Nazareth. Friday evening, February 21, he had a ninety-six hour leave and was speeding along with some other boys to make 'home' when the car skidded over an embankment and into the river. Tommy was drowned.

"His body was recovered. He was brought 'home.' All the children, Sisters and employees at

Nazareth welcomed him with tears of love. His
funeral Mass having been offered, he was laid to
rest. Please say one 'Hail Mary' for Tommy, the
Marine. Nazareth was his 'home'."

Each institution he established in these years
began its career of service debt-free, for the Archbishop made it a rule to finance every building as
it was under construction. In addition, his various
Guilds were organized to labor on behalf of those
charities once they were under way. Moreover, he
himself, with unflagging concern, kept their needs
before the public eye through speeches and press
publicity. From time to time, for example, *The Pilot*
would contain an eye-catching notice: NAZARETH
NEEDS YOUR HELP NOW! New initiatives never decreased his care for those already realized.

Benefit shows were one of the "more spectacular" methods the Archbishop used to implement
the "Archbishop Cushing Charity Fund." Again and
again Bostonians filled Boston Garden to see famous
stars or hear singers like Dennis Day, knowing that
proceeds of the event would reach those who most
needed it. Horse Shows, benefit dances, fashion
shows, one day's profit from racetracks, fairs put on
by various organizations all over the Archdiocese—
all these brought funds in a steady stream to the
man who seemed to have a genius for firing people
with his own enthusiasm. It became common to
hear people in every station of life speak of what
they were "doing for the Archbishop." And no one

ever thought of asking what his or her gift would be used for. Bostonians had been given overwhelming proof of Archbishop Cushing's staggering works for his fellow man's welfare—he would know best where to place the money.

Since 1944, two new hospitals, in addition to Kennedy Memorial, had been established in the Archdiocese, and $2,800,000 had been spent on great St. Elizabeth's, the largest of all the Catholic hospitals. New wings and facilities had been added to three other hospitals, while the old Carney—to which a reluctant Richard James Cushing had long ago dragged his little sister one wintry day—had been moved to a new plant. Spearheading an all-out drive which he had called "Save the Carney," the Archbishop had succeeded in building an ultra-modern hospital at a cost of over $8,500,000. Hence the growth in the Catholic hospitals almost matched the ceaseless building activity in the school and college area. Needless to say, all this construction provided numberless job opportunities throughout the state, thus making an invaluable contribution to the economic well-being of the area. And the great variety of names on architects' drawings and contractors' signs at construction lots evidence the fact that the Archbishop gave everyone a chance, even smaller firms just starting out.

Archbishop Cushing was often a visitor to the wards of the many hospitals, especially on holidays. He stopped by every bed to bring his own brand of cheer to each patient, delighting the down-hearted with the inevitable: "Why, my dear, you look better than I do!" Knowing the importance of good nursing, he had organized the Archdiocesan Council of Catholic Nurses, addressed their meetings and conventions, and helped them begin publication of *The Catholic Nurse.*

Home nursing was another feature added to the Archdiocese's program of charity. Dedicated communities especially devoted to this apostolate opened centers in various sections of Boston and neighboring areas.

The Catholic Charitable Bureau, Massachusetts' largest private child caring agency, greatly increased its activities under Archbishop Cushing. This Bureau, with its departments for unwed mothers, for the placing of children in foster homes or for adoption; with its services to problem children, to refugees and displaced persons, its settlement houses and camp program for underprivileged children, worked in close conjunction with the Society of St. Vincent de Paul. The latter charitable organization had been operating in Boston for eighty-four years when Archbishop Cushing was installed, but its men declared it had never expanded so rapidly as in the ten years from 1944 to 1954.

Of one particular charity directed by the Society and called St. Francis Refuge, the Archbishop wrote:

"A small, unpretentious, one-story building, made of cement blocks, located at 470 Albany Street, Boston, was dedicated on Wednesday, December 28, 1949, and given the name of St. Francis Refuge. Its purpose was to serve free meals to poor, homeless and unfortunate men.

"A good, hot, substantial meal is served daily, including Saturdays, Sundays and holidays, to an average of 600 men a day. On Thanksgiving and Christmas, turkey dinners are served to 1,500 men. In addition, on Christmas Day, small gift packages, donated by good friends of the Refuge, are distributed to the men.

"The Holy Sacrifice of the Mass is offered at the Refuge every Sunday and holy day of obligation, and about one hundred men are present. Confessions are heard there on Saturday afternoon and Sunday morning before Mass.

"There are few rules and regulations at the Refuge, but one is enforced and that is silence so that the hungry and the homeless who enter may eat a hot meal in peace and quiet. All are welcome, no one is refused, no questions are asked, no payment is accepted.

"An anonymous note, postmarked Worcester, was received with the following message, 'A year ago while in Boston I was broke and hungry. St. Francis Refuge fed me. Please accept this little gift for St. Francis being so good to me. Thank you.' Signed, 'A Stranger.'"

Hundreds of elderly men, whose birthplaces included every state in the union and nineteen foreign countries, had found shelter at the Catholic Men's Home, formerly the Soldiers and Sailors' Club during World War II. The Archbishop had had the necessary renovations made and brought in the Hospitaller Brothers of St. John of God to staff it, while its supervision, like that of the Refuge, was entrusted to the St. Vincent de Paul Society. Men of all races and denominations had been accommodated there since it was opened in 1949.

Other buildings to serve varying needs, all products of the Archbishop's zeal, included community centers, rest homes, homes for the aged, a residence for working women, and homes for students. The Boys' Guidance Center on The Fenway now had its feminine counterpart in the Catholic Girls' Guidance Center. The Archbishop had also continued in his efforts to help the girls at the Good Shepherd Home.

Still another group for whom the Archbishop had done much were the servicemen. His efforts were re-doubled at the outbreak of the Korean War, but even before that he had shown his affection by saying Mass in military hospitals for wounded servicemen and by visiting camps to speak to the boys. When the Korean War brought the horrors of death and destruction into American life again, the Archbishop set up the Catholic Serviceman's Bureau to care for the spiritual and moral needs of military men and women. Over twenty thousand rosaries were distributed to them and each Christmas, the Archbishop sent over thirty thousand greetings to the men and women in uniform. He visited bases and camps to speak with them and inspire them with heartfelt messages. In what has been called another "first," he appointed a priest to cover the departure of the young men for military service. To provide the continuing devoted care he could not give personally, he organized a group of volunteers, under the auspices of the National Catholic Community Service, to visit disabled veterans weekly and serve them in every way possible.

Among the teenagers, the Archbishop inaugurated a Pre-Induction Training program, operating in Catholic High Schools and CYO groups, to prepare youth spiritually and morally for their future. That purpose, in fact, was behind all the support he gave the CYO in all its activities. He himself was National Episcopal Moderator of the CYO for five years.

For high schoolers thinking of the priesthood, the Archbishop designed a new program of assistance in the form of St. Botolph's Guild. Through it, priests of the Archdiocese guided prospective vocations. At regular monthly meetings, the boys heard enlightening talks by priests engaged in every type of apostolate and service. The Guild was thus successful in providing many future priests with the guidance they needed.

Archbishop Cushing also created an office of the Director of Vocations and personally seized every opportunity—creating opportunities where they were non-existent—to encourage vocations, just as he had done as Auxiliary Bishop. For instance, he was still using the administration of Confirmation as a chance to plant or water the idea of total dedication to Christ in youthful minds—along with the missionary spirit. On this custom, he once wrote:

"One never knows how God will use a word, instruction or kind service for His Kingdom on earth. It has always been my custom to say at least a brief word on vocations every time I administer the Sacrament of Confirmation to a class of boys and girls. Time and again, I have learned that such words fall on fertile ground. For example, at Christmas I received a card from a Boston priest now on the island of Formosa. He wrote: 'Many thanks for being so mission-minded. Personally I owe you a debt of gratitude: your talk at Confirmation in 1941 played an important part in my own vocation. Please continue to pray for us and the missions.' "

The Archdiocese of Boston became proverbial, under Archbishop Cushing, for its abundance of priestly vocations. A new minor seminary was built at a cost of a million and a half, and St. John's, the major seminary, expanded its facilities considerably, to become the largest in the country. In the ten years of Archbishop Cushing's leadership, its enrollment had been doubled, to number four hundred and sixty.

There was also a Jesuit-conducted St. Philip Neri School for Delayed Vocations, which had proved a great success in helping older men toward the goal of the priesthood.

Many vocations from the Archdiocese, of course, went to religious orders of priests, brothers and sisters. The young people had an opportunity to see a great variety of apostolates in action since the Archbishop had brought in seventeen new orders of men (priests and brothers) and twenty-seven new communities of religious women. With these orders came new efforts for the CCD catechetical apostolate, an Eastern Rite seminary, retreat movements, cloistered life, medical, domestic and social work, and a variety of missionary and teaching apostolates.

Three great mission exhibits were held in Boston to depict the work of home and foreign mission societies, to maintain the mission spirit and promote vocations. The Archbishop had continued, without any decrease in interest, his great support to the missions and the Society for the Propagation of the Faith. Not only did he help many missionary orders build novitiates and seminaries in his own Archdiocese, but he continued financing innumerable mission chapels all over the world. With the same frequency, indeed even more so, the appeals for help arrived at 2101 Commonwealth Avenue, as they had once crossed his desk at the Propagation office.

None went unanswered, unless the request were absolutely impossible. In those cases, the Archbishop, while dictating a reply, spoke brusquely, almost impatiently to his secretary, to hide his anguish at being powerless to respond to the appeal.

In Boston itself, through the "Missionary Cooperative Plan," the missionaries were given the opportunity to preach in churches of the Archdiocese on behalf of their work, and thus to receive contributions and support. The Archbishop directed the re-establishment of branches of the Propagation and encouraged appointment of parish priest directors. A "Jaricot Club," named for Pauline Jaricot, the young French woman who began the Society for the Propagation of the Faith, was founded to promote mission interest among high schoolers.

"If you want God to bless your work," the Archbishop often said, "give to the missions." Thus, when making plans for his many endeavors at home, he always assured their success by sending support to the missionaries.

For all his initiatives the Archbishop of Boston had made extensive use of the press right from the start. Each week one of his two squads of secretaries typed up a copy of his coming schedule and sent it to the Archdiocesan paper, *The Pilot*. More copies would then be run off and addressed to editors of the local press, to be used as a basis for assigning reporters and photographers. *The Pilot* estimated that an average allotment of space—text and pictures—might total some ten thousand words and over twenty-five pictures a week in the Boston press alone. National and international news agencies had also acquired the habit of checking daily on the activities of the Boston prelate.

The Archbishop's interest in the press, however, was not restricted to its value as a method of publicizing his charities, by any means. He had a great esteem for it as a medium of the apostolate in its own right. "The Catholic Press is a number of buildings, machines, filing cabinets and people, but these particular buildings have a kind of consecration about them," he declared in an address to the National Convention of the Catholic Press Association held in Boston. "Like a church, these buildings stand out in the community. These machines sing a kind of sacred song—we cannot imagine blasphemy or obscenity issuing from them. These filing cabinets have the look of reliquaries, they contain sacred history and blessed records. And these people—they have sanctifying grace, and they subtly turn buildings, machines and cabinets into almost-sacramental instruments of supernatural good. . . . Everyone will know what I mean when I call the Catholic Press the Fifth Gospel, the Gospel which records the activity from day to day of Christ and the Holy Spirit in the world."

No wonder then that he had given full support and free rein to *The Pilot*, making it a highly readable and lively newspaper. No wonder there was an annual Journalists' Mass in Boston and an active Archdiocesan News Bureau. Given the Archbishop's attitude, no wonder he had welcomed into the Archdiocese the Daughters of St. Paul, missionary Sisters of the modern media of communication, whose Founder had written: "Consider your pressrooms and binderies as 'second Chapels,' where Christ is present in His teachings, and your presses as 'pulpits,' from which the Word of God is multiplied and preached to millions."

Although they were not to build their Boston Novitiate, where they would actually print and bind their hundreds of books and pamphlets, until a few years later, the Sisters did open a St. Paul Catholic Book and Film Center in the heart of the city, and began their distribution apostolate of bringing the Word of God directly into homes, factories, offices and institutions, offering their inspiring publications to all men. "Religious running Centers and diffusing religious books—it was a daring thing to do in one sense," said the Archbishop, "but it was a necessary thing that had to be done. And so, once you started, you were well received, and you made a modern contribution to the works of the Church in this country. You can never fully realize all the results that will follow.

"Truly you have the spirit of St. Paul himself, because I believe if St. Paul, who was the greatest of all missionaries, were on earth today, he would utilize every modern means of communication for spreading the good tidings of great joy that our Blessed Lord came upon this earth to preach."

It was because of this deep appreciation of the mighty potential for good in the mass media that Archbishop Cushing organized the Radio and Television Apostolate in his Archdiocese. Soon, over twenty-five programs weekly were originating in local stations, chief among which were the thrice-daily broadcasts of the Rosary from the Archbishop's residence, with the Archbishop personally leading the cherished devotion most of the time. In 1948, a daily Catholic Newscast was begun, a "first" in the radio field, and the Archbishop's addresses were frequently being carried by the national networks.

The first regional telecast took place on Christmas Eve in 1949, with the Archbishop celebrating Mass in the Cathedral. A series of regular telecasts began on one of the local channels. It was the second of these telecasts which produced another "first" in television—the first televising of Mass in a TV studio. For this unique "live" Mass, a special altar and sanctuary had to be built in the studio. The worry as to the propriety of the action was quickly dispelled by the end result—a highly inspiring presentation which stimulated thousands of "shut-ins" to write their thanks.

One "first" which received widespread publicity was the televised Nuptial Mass. An Archdiocese couple were actually married by the Archbishop in the TV studio, in a very beautiful presentation. Refusing all offers from advertisers to turn it into some kind of "Bride and Groom" show, Father Walter Flaherty, director of the Archdiocesan Radio and Television Apostolate, said: "The purpose of the telecast was not to appeal to the curious or to furnish entertainment, but only to explain the Sacrament of Matrimony to as many viewers as possible."

Other "firsts" in TV were the presentation of the Ordination and Confirmation ceremonies. The latter gave thousands a unique chance to see the Archbishop "close-up" as he quizzed the children on their catechetical knowledge in his friendly way, before administering the Sacrament.

The enrichment which radio and television had brought to the spiritual life of thousands was but one phase of the fervor awakened all over the Archdiocese through the inspiration of its Archbishop. Many facts gave evidence of it—the Nocturnal Adoration Society, through which almost three thousand men took turns adoring the Blessed Sacrament during the night hours; the use being made of the new retreat houses serving men, women, and youth; and especially the attendance at the new workers' chapels.

The phenomenal growth of these chapels placed in strategic spots throughout the city made daily devotions available to thousands of working men and women who otherwise would not have been able to get to church except on Sundays. Noon lunch hours found men and women from the factories or offices near each chapel pouring in for Mass, confession, novenas, or just a visit with Christ. Archbishop Cushing had made no mistake when he opened these "first-of-their-kind" chapels on the theory that if his people had the chance to draw close to the Lord, they would make good use of it. "At such times all the problems that confront us are solved and all the graces and inspiration we need to carry on, are bestowed in abundance upon us," he himself wrote.

For the working man and woman, he had provided another source of spiritual, educational and social enrichment in the form of the Catholic Labor Guild of Boston. Shortly after his elevation, a group of Catholic machinists had come to him with a problem, and this incident inspired him to appoint them a priest-director. Before long the group had expanded to take in any Catholic trade unionist who wanted the chance to learn more about the Church's social teaching and how it applied to his own occupation. After work, hundreds of union members attended their own night classes in ethics, labor history and law, economics, public speaking and parliamentary procedure, taught by expert Jesuit professors from Boston College.

In their homes the men and women met to discuss with a priest the application of the Gospel to their situation, and in monasteries they met for special workers' days of recollection. In Holy Cross Cathedral they met also, to receive Holy Communion in a body.

Then there came the day in 1953 when the official labor movement of Massachusetts and the Catholic Labor Guild filled Boston Garden for "United Labor's Reception to Archbishop Cushing." This was their tribute to a leading spokesman for their rights, and the theme of his talk to the eight thousand who had gathered there was "We Belong Together."

Indeed, if one stood off to consider the Archbishop and the greatly diversified groups within his flock, was there any one group which could not proclaim a strong bond of union with him? He truly belonged to all. In the ten years since he had become Archbishop, that had been proven beyond doubt. Those ten years had brought many joys and satisfying achievements—as well as much hard work.

In introducing the Tenth Anniversary commemorative issue of *The Pilot,* its editor. Rt. Rev. Francis Lally wrote: "Even the casual observer will find within these pages a memorial of monumental proportions and, while we ourselves may recall some events in isolated occasions, this first attempt to bring them together in a single record has an effect that is almost staggering. The simple statistics speak for themselves and they tell a story of immense labor and depthless charity. . . .

"Behind the ten glorious years that have just passed stands the extraordinary person of Archbishop Cushing. . . ."

To those who wished to call the roll of works of charity, it seemed appropriate to begin with Gospel quotes: "I was sick . . . I was in prison . . . and you visited me"; "Whatever you do for one of these my least ones, you do for me," and the like. No great effort was required to see in the Archbishop the living exemplar of Christ's teachings. Yet if anyone tried to voice such thoughts in his presence, he would be apt to dispel all such sublime comparisons with a disparaging joke directed to himself. He might well gaze long and reflectively at his would-be praiser and then ask with mock seriousness: "Do you really think we'll save ourselves in the end?"

He was still following the advice his revered rector had given him: "Take the priesthood seriously, but never yourself."

Moreover, he was too interested in praising his "good people" to listen to any lauds for Richard James Cushing. Witness his own remarks in one of his Newsnotes columns:

"Who, if not 'good people,' are the unmarried women—young and not so young—in offices and factories, in schools and hospitals, who give generously and steadily to missions and all charities, answering demands and volunteering when no demands are voiced?

"Who, if not 'good people,' the men and women who find time to rush to any one of a dozen downtown chapels for morning or noonday or evening Mass?

"Who, if not 'good people,' the men and women —retired, some of them, but not all—who visit Our Lord in the Most Blessed Sacrament every day?

"Who, if not 'good people,' the men of our Nocturnal Adoration Society?

"Who, if not 'good people,' the members of the St. Vincent de Paul, of the Legion of Mary, and of a score or more of other societies who take care 'of the least of My little ones'?

"Who, if not 'good people,' those who make constant sacrifices for our charities? Read the roster of my Guilds.

" 'My good people'?—They are 'the very best people'! The Salt of the Earth."

Perhaps the most appropriate summary of those ten years being commemorated in November of 1954 lay in the lines one large Boston store chose for its congratulatory message in the special *Pilot* supplement. The lines placed under a full-length photo of Archbishop Cushing read:

"And I will raise me up a faithful priest, who shall do according to my heart and my soul; and I will build him a faithful house. . . ." 1 Kings 2:35.

14

IN PRINCELY RED

"His Eminence, William Cardinal O'Connell."
A pause. "His Eminence, Richard Cardinal Cushing . . . yes, that's the way to write it!"

When his signature was needed for the printing of his thirty thousand Christmas cards, the newly named Cardinal of Boston had to think back to the days of his Predecessor to determine the proper way to write his latest title. His people might have been looking longingly towards the honor of a red hat for their Archbishop, but it was obvious that he himself had never given it a thought. He had not even stopped to study the way a Cardinal's coat of arms is drawn.

"Say, Bob," he began, when the Chancellor, Rt. Rev. Robert Sennott, answered his phone call, "this coat of arms changes now, doesn't it? I think we need another row of tassels, don't we?" In the meantime, his secretaries were searching correspondence files to find the emblem from some other Cardinal. When Monsignor Sennott replied that the coat of arms would, indeed, have to be re-done, the Cardinal said: "I had to know, because it goes on my Christmas cards and they've got to be printed now for mailing overseas to the servicemen."

The news of his elevation to the Cardinalate had been communicated to him on Sunday evening, November 16, 1958 by the Apostolic Delegate, Most Rev. Amleto Cicognani, himself designated a Cardinal.

"I thought to myself, whatever happens, God permits it for one reason or another," he told newsmen the following day. "I was bewildered, though. So I thought I would call some of our very capable priests who are well trained in public relations and editing. But I found they were all asleep. So I went to bed. There was nothing else I could do.

"While I was saying Mass this morning for the Sisters of the Archbishop's household, I heard the phone ringing. I sensed then that the news had become known."

Indeed it had. Coming over the wires at 6 A.M., it had sent through the city a current of excitement unequalled in years. The new Cardinal walked off the altar after saying his Mass and faced the bevy of reporters and photographers who had rushed out to his residence. After lights and television cameras were set up in the conference room, the Cardinal responded to tributes by passing all the merit of the honor to the people he felt privileged to serve.

In homes, schools, convents and rectories across the great Archdiocese, people congratulated themselves in delight at the news. Two nuns sitting in their car at Boston College saw a U.S. mail truck draw alongside them, and the carrier gesturing excitedly. Surprised, they rolled down their window only to hear his jubilant shout: "Have you heard the news? They've made the Archbishop a Cardinal!" Everywhere it was the same. Classes came to a halt at the Major Seminary, when the students rushed up the hill to the Cardinal's residence and surrounded him with gleeful cheers. "Take the rest of the day off!" he told them, as he stood quietly beaming while they clapped heartily. His whole attitude throughout the day, as photographs show, echoed the sentiments he expressed in his first formal statement:

"In behalf of all the priests, religious and faithful of the Archdiocese of Boston and throughout New England, I am grateful to Pope John XXIII for the honor His Holiness has conferred on me. In this expression of gratitude, I include the people of all religious faiths and their spiritual leaders. They have always been most friendly to me and I have endeavored at all times to cooperate with them in whatever pertained to the welfare of the community.

"The honor of being a Cardinal belongs not alone to me, but especially to all those for whom and with whom I have worked, in whatever position was entrusted to me. In very truth, they have prayed me into the various phases of my priesthood. . . .

"Trying at all times to live as a simple priest, I have endeavored to fulfill whatever duties my place in the priesthood required. That program will be continued.

"Please pray that I may succeed so that I shall be a better instrument of God, to bring souls nearer to Him, the source of all sanctity, happiness and peace."

Congratulations pouring into the residence at 2101 Commonwealth Avenue came from state and church officials, from priests and sisters, from families and individuals. Governor Foster Furcolo wrote: ". . . I know that people of all faiths will hail this news"; Rt. Rev. Anson Phelps Stokes Jr., Episcopal Bishop of Massachusetts: "I have come to know personally Archbishop Cushing's warmth and friendliness, and all of us in this area know his dedication, ability and tireless energy in service of his Church. So, as a friend, fellow citizen and fellow clergyman, I join the general rejoicing at the honor which has now come to him"; John E. Powers, president-elect, Massachusetts Senate: ". . . You represent all that is highest and holiest in the sacred Priesthood and all that is noblest in American patriotism. . ."; Most Rev. Daniel J. Feeney, Bishop of Portland: ". . . You are universally esteemed by the bishops of this country as well as by the missionary bishops and clergy throughout the world for your many years of generous personal service to the foreign missions of the Church"; Very Rev. James E. Coleran, S.J., Jesuit Provincial of New England: ". . . Yesterday, when declared a founder in this Jesuit Province, His Eminence told us that the honor thus conferred on him made him feel that he was one of us. Today we feel that a member of the family has been made a Prince of the Church"; Mayor John B. Hynes of Boston: ". . . Certainly no prelate of the Church has been more deserving and more worthy of the great honor which has come to Cardinal Cushing and to the great Archdiocese of Boston"; Rev. Dr. Albert Penner, President, Massachusetts Congregational Conference: ". . . It is an honor and distinction to have one of the great spiritual leaders in our state in this high office. I pray that he may long continue to render high service as a leader in world Christendom."

These and many more expressions of joy—from Jewish War Veterans, from his former theology professor in the seminary, Rt. Rev. Charles A. Finn, from his "good people" all over—kept him busy reading that first day, when he was not answering the telephone. The papers the next day paid attention to hardly anything else but news and praise of Cardinal Cushing. However, none of all this changed his own convictions about the reason for his elevation. That evening, Tuesday, the 18th, in speaking to the Ladies Catholic Benevolent Association, he surprised his audience by declaring:

"I don't want anyone to conclude that I have been named a Cardinal because of the work I have done. It was through the efforts of the priests, the extraordinary priests, religious and laity of the Archdiocese. No matter who had been Archbishop, he could hardly have been passed by when the Sovereign Pontiff made his selections. So the honor does not belong to me, but to you.

"Psychologically, intellectually, and by nature, I am not equipped for this honor." At this point, his audience rejected that assertion vehemently, but the Cardinal insisted: "I know full well I am not. And I know that as a result of this honor, my way will not be made easier.

"But for one reason, and one alone, I am thankful to Pope John XXIII for naming me, although he could have named many others far better equipped for the appointment by their make-up and natural endowment. "I'm grateful because the Archdiocese of Boston and the Church throughout New England merits the best from the Holy See; it merits a member of the College of Cardinals."

The talk to the Catholic Ladies Benevolent Association that evening had been scheduled long before, and the Cardinal had not cancelled it, as he had refused to make changes in any other part of his week's schedule. He told the women and Monsignor Finn that when a reporter had asked if he could not cancel this appointment, he had replied, "No, I'm going to get a check there!"

On entering the banquet hall, the Dorothy Quincy Suite of Boston's John Hancock Building, the new Cardinal had been met with a tremendous ovation, which was repeated twice before he began to speak. Even the caterer's waitresses came out of the kitchen to join in the applause. Monsignor Finn began by saying with great emotion: "To have one of my own boys made a Cardinal! It is so well deserved, for never have we had such a laborer in the vineyards of the Lord."

In his reply, Cardinal Cushing referred to the Monsignor by saying, "Surely, in my wildest dreams never did I think the time would come when the student, in a way of speaking, would be elevated above the master. To men like Monsignor Finn and the others who taught me in the seminary, I owe a great debt. They inspired me to go all out for God and the priesthood."

In what was obviously a reference to exultant press statements such as: "This is a great day for the South Boston boy who became Archbishop of Boston, a great day for Richard James Cushing,

Boston's latest Prince of the Church," the Cardinal said: "The most important day in the lives of all of us is the day we are baptized, the day we are made children of God—for without it, we would not be able to receive the Sacraments." He went on to declare: "Whatever comes in my life doesn't make a great deal of difference, because my happiest years were spent as a simple priest. Ever since I was elevated from that grade, there has been a multiplication of work of all kinds and worries of all varieties that were never there in my days of the priesthood as such."

In the light of this honest revelation of his view regarding honors, it was not difficult to understand the complete truthfulness of his constantly repeated affirmation: "I am very happy mainly because the appointment made so many other people happy."

Just a few days before, he had been given a vote of confidence by his fellow American bishops at their meeting in Washington when he was elected to the National Catholic Welfare Conference's administrative board. He had also been named Episcopal Chairman of Lay Organizations, N.C.W.C. This news, however, had been relegated to a brief notice in the papers by the far greater honor. Now the Boston spiritual leader belonged to the Catholic Church's highest senate, the College of Cardinals, the Pope's chief advisors. As a prince of the Church, his would be the privilege of taking part in the election of the Vicar of Christ.

"Your Eminence" was now his official title, but he took all the formality out of it the first time people began using it, when he announced that one lady had come up and addressed him as—"Your Elegance!" However, it was not too hard for folks to remember, because it was only fourteen years since they had last used the title for the "old Cardinal," as they now began to refer to Cardinal O'Connell.

Cardinal O'Connell had often been in the new Cardinal's mind in the last year, as indeed all his predecessors in the See of Boston, for 1958 marked the Archdiocese's 150th Anniversary.

In connection with the Sesquicentennial celebration, many historical articles had been published, the Archbishop himself leading the way with biographical sketches of his five predecessors in his *Pilot* Newsnotes. He had become familiar with their personalities and had made the predominant characteristic of each the subject of frequent reflection. "We do well to thank God," he had written, "for the qualities He has given our diocese through the men who shaped its corporate personality and who still give us so much of themselves ... the genial patience of Cheverus, the urbane erudition of Fenwick, the aggressive valor of Fitzpatrick, the mellow stability of Williams, the Roman cosmopolitanism of O'Connell. . . ." In the year which had begun with the launching of the first U.S. earth satellite, Boston and its Archbishop had been

reverently looking backward through their eventful
past to gain inspiration for the furtherance of God's
cause in the present day.

Always a lover of history and research into the
beginnings of things (had he not looked up the
word, "cardinal," in the dictionary to probe its root
meaning of "hinge" and meditate on its application
to his relationship with the Holy Father?)—the
Cardinal had encouraged journalists to delve into
the early years and make the works of their ancestors known to modern Catholics.

In special commemorative supplements put out
by Boston papers, all the rich variety of institutions
and activities of the Archdiocese had been recorded
and described, together with the fascinating stories
of the Archbishop's unprecedented deeds. In those
pages, he could be seen presiding at a debutantes'
cotillion—of all things—which, however, had the
serious purpose of raising money for Nazareth, his
children's haven. He could be seen tapping out an
Irish jig with two old ladies at the Thanksgiving
Day party for lonely old folks at Blinstrub's Village.
This gala holiday affair, held in Boston's largest
nightclub, through the generosity of its owner, had
received national attention, and pictures of the
Archbishop slicing the turkey or singing with his
priests in barbershop quartet fashion to entertain
the old folks had been printed all over the country.
Each year the numbers of elderly, blind, lame, and
deaf folks who wanted to come increased. To the

Archbishop's desk came a flood of letters: "Only a few lines asking you to please send me a ticket for the Old Folks Dinner at Blinstrub's. I am all alone. I received a ticket last year and really I never had such a good time—or a better dinner."

"May I please have three tickets to your Thanksgiving Dinner? We are three people alone that will not have any Thanksgiving Dinner unless you remember us. I don't know what we unfortunate folks would do without you."

"I felt like the President, getting such a nice invitation as that!" The frequent comment of his guests at these parties was: "May God bless him! We must say a prayer for him!"

That was the best gift they could have given him. Spiritual bouquets and offerings of Masses were the only personal gifts the Archbishop had ever wanted. That his people were given to prayer— in every situation—was a source of great satisfaction to him. He was always especially pleased to receive letters like the following, from a city inspector whose duty brought him into many homes:

"Never have I seen such a display of Faith, in beautiful homes as well as in humble ones. . . . There to greet me in hallways, living rooms, even kitchens, were statues of the saints, Our Lord, and His Blessed Mother. I made no comment, Your Excellency, and as I left, many said to me: 'God bless you. It's been nice talking to you.'

"I was also very much impressed with the children. On the way to school, they pay a visit to the church and in the afternoon, the little folks make another visit on the way home. These children were alone—not a grown-up with them—going in to pray of their own volition. Really, Your Excellency, I was very much impressed, and thought how proud you must be of your flock."

This letter the Archbishop published in his *Pilot* Newsnotes. He shared everything with his people, even the jokes being circulated, which he knew would be read with delight. His March 15th column (1958) carried such an item under the title, "That's Unemployment:"

"Did you hear this one? It seems to be going the rounds.

" 'Two nuns were very much interested in some of the functions of Government and very interested to know how various phases operated. A member of their parish who works in the Unemployment Compensation Department invited them to call during the February vacation to see it. While they were there looking around and learning about the way things worked, a man at a desk who was applying for Unemployment Compensation noticed them. He looked at them carefully and turning back to the clerk who was helping him exclaimed:

" 'You can say what you like about the opportunities for employment, but when Archbishop

Cushing is laying off nuns, that's proof of unemployment.' "

In February of that Anniversary year, the Archbishop shared an idea of tremendous import with his flock. "In Latin American countries, we have over one-third of all the Catholics in the world," he wrote . . . ," and they have only about one-ninth of the priests . . . I hesitate not to say that some 40,000 priests are needed at the present time in order to meet the needs of the Church throughout the Latin American countries. . . . For many years to come, I think that we of the United States should try to supply these priests as soon as possible. . . . In the light of this conviction, I am considering the sponsorship of a new society to be known as The Society of St. James the Apostle.

"As of the present, I don't know how far I am going to get with the project. It is merely in the planning stage. . . . I will keep you advised of progress. By Eastertime we should have a definite decision one way or the other. Meanwhile, give this great idea, please, some prayerful mementos."

Later, he could report: "At the present about ten priests are interested in becoming affiliated with this Society. It is expected that the first contingent will go to South America in 1959. Please keep the project in your prayers and recommend it for charitable alms from your friends." By May of 1959, not ten but fifteen priests were already laboring in both Peru and Bolivia. In response to the plea of Pope

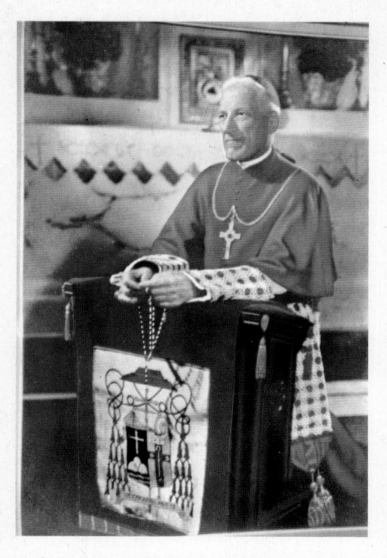

The Rosary—his cherished devotion to the Mother of God

Official Portrait after elevation to the Cardinalate

Pius XII to help him save the Faith in Latin America, Archbishop Cushing had founded a Society of diocesan priests destined to be a living proof of his concern for the universal Church. As he himself had said, it was a "wonderful memento of the 150th Anniversary of the Diocese."

But 1958 was the year that saw the death of the great Pope who had inspired the Society. On October 9th, Pius XII passed away, and nineteen days later, was succeeded on the papal throne by Angelo Cardinal Roncalli—Pope John XXIII. On November 4th, Archbishop Cushing held a pontifical high Mass of thanksgiving and petition in honor of the coronation of the new Pope. As yet he did not know the man with whom he was one day to feel so close and to whom he was to give the now famous title of "Good Pope John." In his sermon at Holy Cross Cathedral that day, he said:

"When we pray for the intentions of the Pope let us keep *this* intention also in mind, that through his outstanding personal leadership, Pope John XXIII may continue to make Christ our Lord better known and loved. Let us pray, too, that ever increasing numbers of those outside the Church may look up to the new Vicar of Christ as a man of God, dedicated to the service of his fellow men and zealous for the promoting of peace in a world which strives today so desperately—it may be at the eleventh hour—to recover from the effects of partisan strife."

How prophetic those words were no one could possibly have guessed that day.

The whole tone of the Archbishop's sermon evidenced his habitual thought of the suffering, persecuted Church. How else could it be when November 4th marked the second anniversary of Khrushchev's bloody smashing of the Hungarian attempt to win freedom? He had taken immediate action to help the freedom fighters by calling on those who were his right hand in Catholic social action—the Archdiocesan Councils of Catholic Men and Women—who, together with the Catholic Charitable Bureau, found haven for more than three hundred refugees and provided for their every need. And the anniversary of the tragic event each year was to find him seeking to keep alive the remembrance of the pitiful plight of the Hungarian people, as well as all the other nations behind the Iron Curtain. In view of all this, it was not surprising that in his sermon the Archbishop should speak of "a world made dark by heavy clouds." That darkness was his concern.

"Archbishop Cushing is only tethered in Boston," wrote Most Rev. Fulton J. Sheen in a tribute to him; "his pasturage is as wide as the priesthood." This article by Bishop Sheen, entitled "The Priest's Bishop," appeared in the *Boston Sunday Advertiser's* special 150th Anniversary Supplement. It contained the declaration that Archbishop Cushing's name was the one heard most frequently when gatherings of priests discussed the ideals of the priesthood. One reason, in Bishop Sheen's opinion, was the suffering he constantly endured: "From a physical and medical point of view, Archbishop Cushing has no right to be alive; he lives because God willed him to have an indomitable spirit in a suffering body. . . . His influence, his radiating charity, his power to communicate wisdom and to invoke love from sheep and lambs, have come not from a 'healthy mind in a sound body,' but a spiritual mind in a broken body. . . . In his broken body [the priests] see the continuing Christ as the Bishop of our souls."

The second reason Bishop Sheen gave for the affection felt by priests for Archbishop Cushing was his practice of poverty—not only regarding material goods but also time: "It is easy to give up money; it is hard to give up the hours and minutes in which one is exhausted. . . . Each priest [has seen] in him that new vow of poverty of the twentieth century: the impoverishment of time, energy, and repose for the glory of the Church. . . . Another reason why the priests consider Archbishop Cushing as their ideal is his total indifference to praise. . . . [They] know well that the Archbishop like a giant ship moves uneasily in the shallow waters of human praise. . . . Thus he who never sought to be nationally known is nationally loved . . . greater still, he who never sought to be internationally known is the most beloved of all in the far-flung missions of the Church in Africa, Asia, Oceania, and Latin America."

And now he had become a Cardinal—a month after those laudatory words were published. A great writer and Bishop had aptly portrayed the "inner man" that was Richard Cardinal Cushing.

Before leaving for Rome to receive his red hat, he wrote, in answer to inquiries, that anyone and everyone was welcome to come, as far as he was concerned, but each would have to make his own arrangements. He added:

"Others have inquired about a collection, a drive or some other kind of campaign for a gift to the Diocesan Charity Fund, Diocesan Expansion Fund, etc. I would not be interested in any project of this kind. The same people who are always giving to me would be asked to give again and again. Our Charity Fund functions every day in the year. Contributions to it can be made anytime. With regard to receptions on a large public scale, here again, I am not interested. I shall be moving about as usual in all parts of the diocese when I return from Rome and in that way I shall greet and meet more people than I could meet in any stadium or auditorium. . . .

"Let us take it all in stride. God doesn't need us. But we can do nothing without Him. The Kingdom of God is not of this world."

The Cardinal was to leave Boston on December 10th. He prepared to go by a characteristic gesture: he cleaned out the drawers of his old wooden desk and gave away the few little gifts they still contained—a pair of red rosary beads, a miniature Cardinal's mitre, a box of candy, and other small items. "Whenever he goes away," one of his secretaries once said, "he cleans house as if he were never going to return."

He was extremely weary and feeling quite sick, too. Rubbing his aching legs, he remarked to friends, "If I don't stop, I won't even get to Rome." Then surveying the room with evident satisfaction—it could not have looked poorer or barer, with its worn rug, old-fashioned chandelier, and empty tables— he put out the light and started down the long corridor. In his hand he still held a tiny key chain with a fish dangling from it, something apparently given him at one time or another and left in the desk drawers—those drawers that had to be pulled and tugged before they would open.

"No one would believe that this is the office of the Cardinal of Boston," someone said, after noting that one light switch was taped, to prevent unnecessary use, and that his chair looked as if he had had it for twelve years—as indeed he had. The Cardinal just chuckled at that and made no comment.

His mind was on the trip ahead. With his usual distaste for travelling, he was not looking forward to it. After saying that both Cardinal Cicognani and the other American just elevated, Cardinal O'Hara of Philadelphia, would be coming to Boston to leave with him, he dangled the key chain fish playfully in front of him, and said: "Not that I care about myself, but it's crazy to have us all in one plane! If the thing ever went down, they'd lose three Cardinals, not to mention other notables!" Then after a moment's silence: *"I'm taking my fish!"* Caught by surprise, his listeners broke into delighted laughter, in which he joined no less heartily. That grin made one forget how thin and white his face was, and the way he carried himself, erect and straight, effectively hid the pain that racked every limb. What he obviously needed was a good rest before the trip, but with the schedule he followed, it was out of the question.

Yet, as he afterwards confessed, it was he who handled all the arrangements for the other members of his party and saw to it that everything ran smoothly. At the Boston airport, crowds of well-wishers were on hand with placards to give them a clamorous send off. The same warmth surrounded their arrival in Rome. The corps of cameramen and reporters kept Boston and America informed of the Cardinal's activities from that moment on. In keeping with his opinion that this was the people's honor, he willingly sat for several press conferences during his stay in Rome, so that all could share the events with him. Newsmen assigned to the story testified that his elevation to the cardinalate and trip to Rome, complete with the formal ceremonies involved, formed the biggest story of interest to readers in the Archdiocese and throughout New England since the Second World War.

With the Cardinal on the trip to Rome were Bishop Wright of Worcester, Auxiliary Bishop Jeremiah Minihan of Boston, Monsignor Robert Sennott, the Chancellor, and Monsignor Lally, editor of *The Pilot*. His family too, had come to the Eternal City for the great occasion, with the exception of Elizabeth, the Cardinal's older sister. In the midst of their rejoicing, the tragic news reached Rome that Elizabeth had passed away suddenly. So, as a grieving Prince of the Church offered Mass for the repose of his beloved sister's soul, his family flew back to Boston, their trip and their joy cut short by the sudden loss.

The first official ceremony took place at the North American College, where the Cardinal was staying. The papal messenger arrived with the "biglietto" or note from the Holy Father officially informing him of his elevation to the college of Cardinals. Then the hundreds of well-wishers gathered for the occasion expressed their congratulations. Later in the day, the Cardinal received Cardinals, Bishops, religious, priests, and friends among the laity. Bostonians, indeed Americans in general, who noted the reception given him everywhere he went, realized that he was being treated with a kind of "super-respect, given to a man internationally known for his complete dedication to charity and good will," as one Roman correspondent put it. Speaking of the reception following the biglietto ceremony, a *Pilot* writer noted: "For all the historical importance and dramatic pageantry of the scene, there was yet a typically American friendliness about it all."

On December 17th, in a semi-public consistory, the new Cardinals were brought into the presence of Pope John to be given their mozetta (short cape-like garments) and their new birettas, the square-shaped red hats for everyday wear. Photographs of Cardinal Cushing kissing the Pope's hand in sign of filial respect reveal a warmly smiling Pontiff regarding the Boston Cardinal with affection. Later Cardinal Cushing was to confess that he felt at home with "Good Pope John," even though in every picture of his with the Holy Father he appears with bowed head and very modest aspect. "I hope I'm not being irreverent," he was to say on his arrival home, "but he is somewhat of my type. He likes people. He likes to be of service to people."

The great consistory in St. Peter's Basilica took place the next day, December 18th. The Mother Church of Christendom was filled with thousands who had been waiting for several hours for the ceremony that was to begin at nine. Enthusiastic cries of "Viva il Papa" greeted the entrance of Pope John on his portable chair. After he was seated on his throne facing the great altar of the Confession, the Cardinals approached to kiss his foot and hand reverently and to receive his embrace. Then they

took their places, from whence, one by one, the new
Cardinals ascended to the papal throne to receive
the "galero," the wide-brimmed, tasselled red hat
that is never worn, but is placed on the Cardinal's
catafalque at death and then suspended from the
roof of his cathedral until it disintegrates. Heavy
applause hailed Cardinal Cushing, when after having the hat placed over his head and having em-
braced the Holy Father again, he walked back down
the aisle to take his place formally among the Cardinals. His erect figure, still somehow conveying his
deep humility, was striking even in that colorful
scene of myriad lights, shining marble, stunning
paintings, the ermine capes and red trains of the
Cardinals, the flashing helmets and silver swords of
guards. It was in all truth an unforgettable ceremony in which a Prince of the Church was made.

A special papal audience for the Cardinal and
the American party—four planeloads of them—was
the highlight of the following day, together with the
ceremony in which Cardinal Cushing formally took
possession of St. Susanna's, his titular church. This
church was the scene of eight simultaneous Masses
for the Cardinal's deceased sister, Elizabeth.

Several hundred people braved a bitter New
England winter temperature to be at the airport
when Cardinal Cushing returned home on December 21st. After greeting his family and friends, he
went to Our Lady of the Airways Chapel to say
Mass for the members of his party, commenting,

"These people are fatigued and so am I. But I'm going to say the ten o'clock Mass for them at the chapel here so that they can fulfill their religious obligation today [Sunday]."

"I'm happy to be back!" he added, as he stood there before newsmen, wearing his scarlet cape and red-banded, black "capello." And he obviously meant it.

In the days that followed the Cardinal reiterated his belief that the honor was not his but his people's—"Good Pope John's Christmas gift to the Archdiocese." Speaking in his Cathedral, he said: "If the Cardinalate will help me be of more service to the Church, to the missions, to you who are my first care and responsibility, then I'm happy."

Even his wardrobe, in his mind, was not his to keep to himself. Knowing that his faithful wanted to see them, he wore the various robes of his new office. "Come see me in my glad rags!" he laughingly told a friend. "Do you recognize me in this?" he asked a group of Sisters. And his opening remarks to a TV audience, whom he was addressing for the first time as a Cardinal, began with: "There is a saying in Scripture: 'Fear not, it is I!'"

Asked to give his impressions of his trip, he willingly took the time to do so, in order to please his questioners. He described Italy and the people he had met. To friends, he admitted that he had received many appeals for help: "They thought I

had the United States Treasury with me!" Perhaps
the most humorous summary of his trip was contained in a letter to a friend:

"I came back from Rome with a red hat, a bad
cold, and an empty purse. *The honeymoon is over!*"

The Roman trip was indeed over, but a very
different description of what it had meant was giv-
en by Monsignor Lally in a special *Pilot* article:

"For Bostonians it was an especially proud occasion because the majestic figure and warm personality of the Archbishop of Boston gave special
meaning to the ancient ceremonies. In the hushed
tribunes of the public consistory, at the edge of the
crowds as the solemn procession passed, many of
us could hear the voices of our neighbors from other lands, as they pointed to the tall, lean American,
'That is Cardinal Cushing.' We never knew there
were so many ways that such a simple name could
be pronounced.

"All of those qualities which we have learned
to take for granted here at home—the affability of
spirit, the warm gesture of friendship, the love of
little children, the humble, self-effacing phrase, the
undisguised generosity toward others, the grandeur
of carriage and eloquence of voice—all of these
were part of the glory of these days in Rome. For
us they were part of the man and surely part of the
reason for his being here; for the others they were a
revelation of greatness, an experience never known

before, an inspiration for the soul and a proud ornament for America. . . .

"How typical were his words as he landed back in Boston in the bright, chill Sunday morning of New England. 'We are grateful . . . we are grateful . . . we are grateful . . . and now, back to work!' "

THE MAN

BENEATH THE RED

They were as excited over the trip as any other children would have been, even though their facial expressions or leg braces revealed that these little ones were different. A big crowd had packed the overseas section of Logan International Airport that April day in 1959 to see them off, and in the confusion some of the little ones turned for reassurance to one of the many Sisters with them. Others felt safe when shepherded about by the leader of this unique pilgrimage to Lourdes, Richard Cardinal Cushing.

289

For a while all was silent there in the waiting room as he began the recitation of the rosary. Then the voices of the parents and friends of his "exceptional children" rose and fell in the prayer to Our Lady, to whose Shrine their little ones were being taken. Afterwards, to the stirring music of the police band, the children were helped aboard their plane, and another of Cardinal Cushing's "firsts" had entered history.

Not long before the day of departure, he had said to an audience of three thousand Sisters: "As the time approaches, everyone is getting worried except me!" It was decidedly an unprecedented venture, but doing something new was nothing new to the Cardinal. He emphasized that they were not going in the hope of obtaining miraculous cures, but rather to pray and to manifest faith in God.

The newsmen covering the pilgrimage reported that Europeans were greatly surprised by the Cardinal's informality. The sight of him walking with his "forever children" and stopping to talk with everyone brought tears to many eyes. One woman remarked: "He could only be an American."

The Cardinal and his little pilgrims landed back in the U.S. on April 27th, fifteen hours and twenty minutes late. The plane had developed engine trouble and made a forced landing in Newfoundland. Undaunted, the Cardinal had kept his charges happy during the wait and had proclaimed them great little travellers. Now, as he alighted at

Logan, his arm around one of them, a burst of applause greeted him.

The newsmen were on hand, with their microphones set up in the waiting room and their cameras ready. Once he had seen his children safely off the plane and under the care of the Sisters in charge, he stepped up to the mikes and spoke at length. His words, full of his characteristic optimism, faith and love of God, came rapidly, accompanied by energetic gestures, even though under the camera lights he looked very pale and wan.

When he finished, people called out: "We're glad to have you safe on the ground!" A photographer who had climbed up on a counter shouted: "Your Eminence, please, this way!" Obliging as ever, the Cardinal turned, took off his wide-brimmed black hat, waved and smiled.

Cardinal Cushing had received the *Jewish Advocate's* Man of the Year Award, the New England Variety Club's Great Heart Award, the Knights of Columbus' Lantern Award, honorary citizenship in Ireland, a command in the Order of the Cedars of Lebanon, a citation from Italy, membership in the French Legion of Honor—and so the list went on. More than a dozen universities had conferred degrees upon him and more were to do so. All these honors had been bestowed in recognition of his merits, and due notice had been given them in the press. But the praise that came in the wake of his exceptional pilgrimage was quite another thing. Yet once the event was over, though pleased that it had gone so well, the Cardinal promptly settled back into his work, with no more thought to the additional fame attained.

One word of praise that came to him with regard to quite a different occasion, however, he himself gave to *The Pilot* for publication. It came from a former prisoner of war. Willy Vellen of Aachen, Germany, wrote to congratulate him on his elevation to the Cardinalate and to thank him for having gone to Fort Devens in July of 1945 to administer the Sacrament of Confirmation to the German prisoners there. "I didn't forget Your Eminence, all thirteen years long," wrote Vellen, "because You have given us a great courage and a powerful hope as a Catholic priest and bishop during the hard life in our imprisonment in the time after the second world war."

This letter and a photo of the memorable prison camp scene appeared in the first 1959 issue of *The Pilot*. A note from the Cardinal on prison visits in the same issue was a fitting companion:

"I have accepted every invitation to meet, help and encourage prisoners everywhere within our jurisdiction. I was fearful that when I became Cardinal this would not be in accordance with tradition. Happy I was to read that Good Pope John XXIII visited Regina Coeli Jail (Queen of Heaven Jail, Rome) on Christmas Day. That visit thrilled me because long ago I arranged to visit the prisoners at

the state prisons at Walpole and Norfolk. I shall go
to both of them on New Year's Day."

"I will not change—I couldn't if I wanted to!"
he had exclaimed to the John Hancock Employees
branch of his charity organization. Indeed, he
moved at an even more killing pace after becoming
a Prince of the Church. It was enough to ask a favor
by prefacing it with a hesitant: "I don't know, now
that you're a Cardinal, if you can. . . ." That would
do it. He would be sure to say yes, and to add, "You
can ask me anything you want!" As a result, his list
of engagements was longer than ever.

Everywhere he went, of course, he had to wear
his red watered silk, in those first months, because
his audiences would have been highly disappointed
otherwise. "I feel like Santa Claus!" he remarked
ruefully on one occasion. Another time, glancing at
his square-buckled shoes, he said: "Don't I look
like one of the Pilgrim Fathers?"

Though always impeccable in his attire and
appearance, the Cardinal has never worried at all
about "injuring his dignity" by being too informal.
One day, two visitors noticed that while talking with them, he kept twitching his cassock, a new
one which formed part of his cardinalatial wardrobe. Suddenly, he queried: "Do you know of anything that can be done to get the electricity out of
this thing?" He continued to pluck at it patiently,
until finally he gave up.

It has always been his delight to share embarrassing experiences with his friends. There was the time he was travelling in a foreign country and had given away all his clothes to the point where the day before he was to return home, he was down to the pair of wrinkled trousers he had on. So, before retiring that night, he asked a priest in his party to have the pants pressed by the Sister-housekeepers where they were staying.

To his dismay, the Cardinal discovered in the morning that she had ironed them as if they were pajamas—no crease! Back to bed he went, (with photographers and officials waiting for him at the airport!) while the priest explained to the nun that she must press the trousers with a damp cloth and get a neat crease down the center. At last the pressed pants were duly ready and the Cardinal could get out of bed and catch his plane.

On the flight, he suddenly became aware of cold air on his legs. "Some draft here," he said to himself and glanced down. To his horror, he caught a glimpse of his knee showing through a wide split in his trousers! The nun had pressed a bit too hard and too long! There was nothing to do but to take off his suit coat and put on the long cassock, so that Cardinal Cushing could alight from the plane at its destination without causing a mild sensation.

Referring to some formal portrait of himself in *cappa magna,* he is apt to say, "Here, have a comical valentine. Nobody will know who it is. They'll probably think it's Napoleon!" The fact is that thousands upon thousands of pictures of him are distributed and requests arrive constantly for permission to reprint this or that photo in every form, from wall-size portraits to bronze busts or small gold medallions.

All this interests the Cardinal not in the least. His self-mockery is typified by the following tale:

"This morning I preached at St. ——— Church. When the Mass was over, I delivered the sermon and then started down the aisle. An usher stopped me and said that while I was preaching, a lady from out of town had come up to him and asked, 'Who's that man up there?'

" 'Why, that's Cardinal Cushing!'

" 'That's him?' With that, she had turned around, gone back in, stood stock still in the aisle and looked long at me. Then she had exclaimed, 'For the Lord's sake!'

"I don't know what she meant with that," laughs the Cardinal, "but I suppose she was shocked to see what I really look like!"

It was a hot summer day when he told this joke on himself, together with other self-disparaging remarks. Finally his listeners protested: "That's the way the Saints talk about themselves, but. . . ."

The Cardinal had a quick retort to that. "The heat's got you!" he laughed.

He was at his story-telling best one afternoon when he told some friends about going to a banquet in a country where customs are quite different from his own. He lowered his voice to a stage whisper as he related in mock horror how much they talked and how long they stayed at table. "At last, after everyone had finished dessert," he said, not looking at his listeners but raising his eyes to the ceiling as though to symbolize the constancy of the martyrs, "at last we all stood up and I thought the ordeal was over. 'We'll say grace and leave now,' I said to meself." (He often mimics the brogue for added effect.) Here he paused, and then with a resounding thud of his fist on the desk: "Nothing doing! They sat down and started right in talking again!" When his listeners had all had a good laugh, and he had watched them with pleasure, he added, "They've got a custom there, to stand up and then go back to it again. I thought I'd die!"

These moments of relaxed conversation in his office are very few and far between, however. How could it be otherwise when there are secretaries working until nine or ten at night, replacing the "day corps" and when the desk is piled with a stack of mail, either incoming and therefore to be read and answered, or outgoing, and still necessitating reading? Friends who call never know whether he will be able to give them a minute or not. Often he is writing rapidly, his thin hand, weighed down by the big ring, moving swiftly over the back side of a typed sheet as he inserts a new thought in a forthcoming address. In those moments he is apt to glance up, nod, and go right back to his writing until he completes his thought. Having dug the pencil vigorously into the paper for the last period, he will push his swivel chair back from his desk, pull off his glasses, and ask, "What's new? Sorry to keep you waiting but I've got to get the final copy of this speech typed tonight and the typist will be here any minute."

It has been said that Cardinal Cushing enjoys listening to classical music. This is true, but he always combines his listening with his work. He puts a stack of records on and then lets them play on low volume while he attacks his correspondence. Even while watching a football or baseball game on TV, he keeps at his desk work. At times it seems as if he had forgotten all about the ball game, until at the crucial moment, his head comes up and he gives his full attention to the play.

After so many years of dictating hundreds of letters daily, the Cardinal still sends off personal messages free of stilted phraseology. Certain words or expressions have, however, become habitual with him, as for example, "mighty mite," "poorest of the poor," "the least of the flock," ". . . with which I am identified," and "prayerful memento." Invariably, after signing his name, he pens an extra word or two. It may be "Hi!" or "God love you!" or "See you soon."

Quick to grasp a situation himself and to act promptly, the Cardinal expects the same of his associates. Having asked someone to take an envelope for him from one of the shelves, he will call a second later, "Did you find it?" His schedule is so tight that every moment is precious, and those who see him wading through piles of letters that require his complete attention marvel at the patience he shows when the telephone constantly interrupts him and visitors with appointments arrive before he has accomplished what he had planned. About his telephone manner, which often consists in getting things said in a hurry, he remarks: "I'm terrible on the phone, aren't I?"

Sometimes, having arrived home late, and seeing a visitor sitting in the reception room, he walks into the dining room, eats a few grapes or a little cup of cold custard, on which he sprinkles salt, and calls that supper. Then he goes in to greet his visitor without giving another thought to himself.

The Cardinal's daily mail comes from all over the globe, from high Church and state officials and from the ordinary members of his flock. Sometimes, in the midst of much that requires deep thought, there is a delightful little note like this one from a youngster in one of the Archdiocese's parochial schools:

"I am writing to you because you are the top man. Sister N.N. was transferred from our school to St. ————'s. She was only here three years. If she is happy, you can leave her there, but if she isn't, please send her back. The whole seventh grade will be very happy."

To this the Cardinal replied:

"I was very pleased to hear from you. Yes, Sr. N.N. is very happy. She remembers you and prays for all of you. Now, study hard, etc." He then sent the boy's letter plus a copy of his reply to the Sister, with this note: "I thought you'd like to see these."

Another day's mail brought a letter from an elderly lady who had once owned a milliner's shop frequented by the Cardinal's mother. In his reply, he wrote: "I well recall the store in South Boston and I well remember my beloved mother speaking of 'Cassidy's' in referring to the famous milliner. In memory of old times I am sending you the enclosed spiritual bouquet witnessing to a Mass I will celebrate for you. God bless you and be with you always."

Letters that might simply be routine replies become very often delightfully self-revealing messages which are treasured by their recipients. A Jewish businessman responded to an "Old Jewelry for Charity" drive sponsored by the Cardinal and sent a ninety-seven-year-old watch which had belonged to his father and another given him on his Bar-Mitzvah. In his accompanying note, he wrote that he had always admired the Cardinal's charitable work, and added: "Although my folks were Orthodox Jews, they were liberal in their religious

thinking. I have followed the same practice throughout my life. I know you will make good use of the
jewelry, and good luck on your humane venture."

"I thank you for your letter and the two watch-
es you sent to me in answer to my appeal for old
jewelry," the Cardinal replied. "You certainly sent
me two historical time pieces. Appreciating the fact
that they are precious heirlooms, I assure you that
they will be used in accordance with the brief appeal I printed in my *Pilot* column.

"There is no need of telling you of my cordial
affiliation with all Jews, Orthodox and otherwise. I
have a sister who was married to a Jewish lad and
they lived most happily for thirty-five years, until
his death. He was a great example to me and in all
honesty, a girl could never have a more devoted
husband.

"You will be interested to know that the other
night a Jewish taxi cab driver, who brought me
home from a hotel where I gave an address, told me
I was the best Rabbi in Boston. I suppose the poor
fellow didn't know what else to call me, but it was
a tribute, I assure you, that I appreciated."

When an elderly resident of County Cork, Ireland, wrote to ask him if a long-lost uncle of hers
who had gone to Glanworth, County Waterford,
might not be his own grandfather, the Cardinal
replied:

"Thank you for your note and the interesting
data of the Cushing Clan.

His Eminence and Most Rev. Thomas J. Riley, D.D.,
Auxiliary Bishop of Boston, with Pope Paul VI,
at the opening of the second session of Vatican Council II

His Eminence and Boston Prelates with Pope John XXIII
during the first session of the Second Vatican Council

"I don't know whether I am identified with those prominent people or not, but it really doesn't make much difference as of the moment, because I assume all the forbears are enjoying the Beatific Vision—where I hope they are praying for me.

"My Easter greetings to you and yours go by way of the enclosed spiritual bouquet card witnessing to a Mass that I will celebrate for you, and the autographed photo. God love you and be with you always."

Many of the letters that cover the Cardinal's desk concern his building projects; others are from some of the more than eight thousand priests and sisters of the Archdiocese; still others bring offerings for his many undertakings. Then there are the letters from missionaries the world over, besides many comments coming from the thousands who have heard or read one of his timely addresses.

After his first best-seller, *Meditations for Religious*, was published in the early part of 1959, the Cardinal's mail always contained dozens of appreciative comments from Sisters all over the country. Refreshingly simple, encouraging and timeless in their application of consoling truths to daily life, the meditations have been in great demand. National attention focused on the book when it placed high on *America* magazine's best-seller list.

Meditations for Religious was to be followed in the next few years by other volumes—*Christ in Bethlehem, Christ in the Eucharist; Pope Pius XII;*

Mary; St. Catherine of Siena; Spiritual Guideposts; The Sacraments; United in Giving; The Mission of the Teacher; St. Martin de Porres; Call Me John (on Pope John XXIII), plus innumerable pamphlets on such subjects as vocations, the role of the Christian intellectual, Communism, psychiatry, nursing, parents and teenagers, the Bible and the Christian, the Rosary, and religion in education.

As one of his books after the other began to come off the presses at the Novitiate of the Daughters of St. Paul, the Sisters devoted to the apostolate of the modern communications media, admiring hundreds asked: "Where in that fantastic schedule of his does he find the time to write?"

The answer is simple: the pamphlets are, in most cases, reprints of addresses delivered on various occasions. The books, however, are compilations of speeches or retreats or even religious instructions given by the Cardinal since his first days in the priesthood. These addresses, so carefully prepared—often at the cost of working until one or two in the morning—had all been filed by subject matter in an old cabinet over the years. The Cardinal had thought of finding the time someday to compile them, but since that time could never be found, he had permitted the Daughters of St. Paul to do the initial work of grouping them for him. Once galley proofs of a book are before him, he reads quickly, often making extensive changes so as to ready the material for the press. All that pertains to the particular event which occasioned the address is omitted; repetitive sections or matter no longer apropos are also deleted, and the total content blended until it represents the Cardinal's thinking on a given subject.

Riding to and from some ceremony, the Cardinal often reads and corrects galleys of his books. Amazingly, he can work oblivious to all distractions. One Sunday afternoon, he told the Sisters, he had worked six straight hours that day on a forthcoming book. Another time when they called, he was writing a moving treatment of "our first and last Communion" to be included in a book and while they waited, he covered two pages with his slanted, vigorous writing. Then handing it to them with a "See how this sounds," he hurried off to say the rosary with the thousands who follow the evening radio broadcast. Though written almost without a pause, the profound reflections seemed a spontaneous outpouring, perfectly expressed, of thoughts often mulled over and relished.

When a new book comes out and the Sisters bring him the first copy, he invariably denies himself the pleasure of looking at it at once. He will leave it on one corner of his desk and continue with his mail or the preparation of some new address. Only after a time will he call the secretaries to have a look at it. He will then say, "The Sisters did a nice job with it, didn't they?" A few days later, he may add, "Everyone likes the new book" (never "my new book"), but that is just about the last time he will mention it.

The Cardinal's mountainous work is carried on despite frequent suffering. In July of 1959, to his chronic asthma, and muscular pains was added a severe case of shingles. Referring to the flaming red sores which had sent him to the hospital for a week, he once said: "I don't like to complain, but the pain is terrible. It's internal, like a raw nerve."

The shingles finally left him, but the asthma, constant exhaustion, and ulcers provide him with limitless opportunities for hidden penance. His asthma is so acute that an oxygen tank is always at his bedside to give some relief in the long hours when his weary body often can enjoy no sleep. He reads, then, or prepares speeches in advance, working at an old brown desk which in antiquity and utter plainness matches perfectly the nearly empty bureau that holds his few clothes. In his bodily suffering, work is his only salvation; when full of enthusiasm for some apostolic undertaking, he can forget every pain. Once in a moment of candor, he was heard to say: "All I've done is work, work, work. For thirty-eight years [since ordination], I've lived for nothing but Christ. That's my way of living. And all there is ahead of me is more work." Another time he declared, "I haven't got a dime. I'm sick. I can't eat. I can't sleep—and yet I'm happy!"

"Your Eminence tries to do too much," someone close to him protested one Good Friday, when
the pain was more intense than usual.

"Nothing's too much for God on Good Friday,"
he answered quickly. "You have to suffer. Nothing
good comes without suffering."

He has said that he lives to give and this is literally true. Just before leaving for the North American College Anniversary reunion in October, 1959,
he wanted to give something to a missionary, so he
tugged open one of the wrapping paper lined
drawers of the old-fashioned bureau in his bedroom,
only to find nothing but a new black hat and a new
leather briefcase. Giving these both away, he then
tried another drawer. Here there were three little
piles of linens. Taking one, which consisted of three
shirts, he handed it to the stunned visitor, overriding
his protests by saying, "Take whatever I give you,
because I'll only give it away anyway."

At times, particularly with his secretaries, he
commits the unforgivable social sin of offering them
as a gift ("I can't use *this!*") something they themselves gave him.

"Do you want this box of funny candies?" he
asked one secretary one afternoon. "They're supposed to be a delicacy." He held out the fancy box
to her and then sensed that something was amiss.
Glancing up (he always hands things away without
looking at the recipient), he saw a queer smile on
the secretary's face. "Thank you very much," she

said. "Yes, I'd like them. I think they're delicious.
It was I who bought them for you!"

This same secretary has had that happen before. On rare occasions, but not as much as in past
years, the Cardinal takes a few hours off to go fishing. Knowing that he was planning a fishing trip
the following day, the secretary and a friend decided to try to find him a couple of nice sport shirts
—light and cool, but not too loud. They tramped
from store to store in sweltering heat, until at last
they found just what they had in mind. Triumphant,
they made their purchase and gave the shirts to the
Cardinal on time for his fishing trip.

Some time later, the Cardinal's brother, John,
went to the secretary with two sport shirts. "Do
you think the Cardinal could use these?" he asked.
"Someone gave them to me, but I don't remember who."

Taking one look at them, she said, "I can tell
you, because I bought them for the Cardinal—and
if he didn't keep them the first time, I guess he
won't keep them now, either!"

With the sure instinct of one who knows he
enjoys the sincere affection of those with whom he
works, the Cardinal delights in teasing and is not
above a practical joke now and then. Not even the
Rt. Rev. Monsignors who live on the top floor above
their Chancery offices, just down the knoll from
him, are exempt from his good-humored pranks.

One Good Friday night, a very inebriated gentleman rang the Cardinal's doorbell at an unearthly hour and shouted: "Christ is risen!" Over and over again he repeated his message. At last the Cardinal called out, "Listen, fellow, you're two days too early!"

But the intoxicated caller persisted, so the Cardinal said, "You go on down to the next building and tell those people down there all about it."

The following morning, the Monsignors indignantly informed the Cardinal that some crazy man had kept them up all night with his shouting. "You don't say!" said the Cardinal, the picture of innocence. "You don't say!" he repeated, with just the hint of a smile.

It might be true that everyone in his orbit has to keep moving at top speed, but it is undeniably true also that life in his company is anything but boring.

Should someone attempt to voice sentiments of appreciation to him, the Cardinal puts an end to that soon.

Likewise, it is generally hard to discover just how he is feeling. To a query about his health, he is apt to reply: "I'm dying fast, but I'll bury you all!" Or if a friend remarks, "Your Eminence looks quite good today," he replies, "I guess you can get used to any face if you look at it enough!"

Yet there was no doubt about his run-down condition when he collapsed at the 1959 National

Catholic Youth Council Convention in Kansas City, Missouri, November 14th. After his return from Rome the preceding month, he had kept going from one engagement to another, and the day he flew to Kansas City, he first made two appearances in Boston. Moreover, it was only a few months since he had come out of the hospital following the bout with asthma and shingles. Prior to entering the auditorium, where thousands had gathered for the convention banquet, the Cardinal suffered a brief fainting spell but quickly recovered and went into the hall. Then during the banquet, the great number of prelates, priests and youth were shocked to see him suddenly slump down on the speaker's table.

The attack lasted five minutes and a doctor said he could not get a pulse from him. "He was whiter than white," one priest stated, "and we did not know whether he was dead or alive." A stretcher and resuscitator were brought into the auditorium, and a priest stood ready to administer the Last Sacraments. But, as once before in Worcester, the Cardinal snapped out of the seizure, waved the doctor away, and stood up to deliver a stirring address.

Later, at the residence of Bishop Cody of Kansas City, he told reporters that he had been in the hospital, but he said, "I'm in pretty good shape now, though I've lost a lot of weight." He also noted that it had been quite cold in the small, private plane that flew him to Kansas City from Chicago and that by contrast, the auditorium had been very hot. Bishop Cody told the reporters he thought the first fainting spell, at least, had been due to fatigue and to the fact that the Cardinal had not eaten in several hours.

The following day, the Cardinal preached to ten thousand boys and girls at the Convention's closing Pontifical Mass, warning them that the values of Christian life are falling under the influence of a pagan culture of materialism. "It is only when your faith is a source of energy, a principle of action, a blueprint for life, that people who see you will also see Christ," he concluded.

From Kansas City, he went on to Washington for the bishops' meeting, with no more thought to his health than if nothing had happened. And once back home—as if he did not have enough to do—he told a young Jewish girl who came to see him about becoming a Catholic that he would instruct her himself! The very evening she called he made the appointments for the series of instructions.

With such a schedule, it is understandable that a few days before Christmas in 1959, he who usually has addresses ready far in advance was still working on his Christmas message. "I'm way behind," he admitted, as he tried to write between trips to the reception room to accept one gift after another. He receives every conceivable present—even Christmas trees made out of cookies.

Christmas morning he celebrated Mass at the newly opened Sisters' Residence for student nuns of various orders, and then went on to the Cathedral to preach at the Pontifical Mass. At four o'clock, he said another Mass on TV and preached again.

In addition, over the holidays he worked hard on his book "Questions and Answers on Communism," a text to acquaint people with the atheistic nature of Communism and its tactics. In one day, he read proofs of this book three times.

Thus passed Richard Cardinal Cushing's first year as a Prince of the Church—not that it was much different from his other years in the service of God. He was still striving to fulfill the program "Thy Will Be Done," as expressed in what had once been published under the title, "Archbishop Cushing's Special Morning Prayer":

"Sweet Jesus, lay Your wounded hand upon my head and bless me. Stretch forth that same dear hand and bless each one at home. Give me Your staff. Help me to go around in Your fold just for today doing Your work in Your way. Push me back when I would go wrong and make me go forward when I am afraid to do right. Be with me in my dealings with each soul with whom I come in contact and grant that each may know, love and serve You better for having passed me by.

"I want to know, love and serve You above all things. And when life's little day is ended and its task complete, give me a place at Your feet to rest for all eternity.

"My dearest Lord, what do You send me today? Humiliations, contradictions, physical sufferings, bad news which I do not expect; an aching heart, a failure? Shall I see myself misjudged, wrongly suspected, despised? All that You wish. O my God; I accept it all in advance, and if I weep through weakness, oh, regard it not; if I murmur, check me; if I am forgetful, punish me; if I am discouraged, raise me up. But through it all, teach me to say, 'Thy will be done.' Amen."

16

FOR THE GOOD

OF THE CHURCH

AND SOULS

They called the place the "City of God," but the name was hardly suited. It was one of the worst slum areas to be found in any city of man.

The Cardinal looked at the people and the shacks they lived in, without electricity, without sanitation; his eyes took in the sights, while his smile warmed suspicious glances, and his fertile mind began planning . . .

Richard Cardinal Cushing was in Peru as Pope John's Legate to the National Eucharistic Congress

312

of 1960. In this official capacity, he had been feted
and honored with red carpet, presidential welcome, and cavalry escort. All these he had accepted in good grace, but as ever, his chief interest
was in the people—the people among whom his
priests of the St. James Society were laboring. He
had come to Peru not only as papal legate, but also
as the Founder of the Society of priests whose parishes comprised the poorest of the Peruvian poor.

"Keep us in your prayers!" the Cardinal had
called to friends before leaving for South America.
Not knowing Spanish, he felt somewhat at a loss.
Unaccustomed to indirect communication with an
audience, he worried about the speeches, working
on them over and over again so that they might be
translated readily. Nor did he want to mar in any
way the honor bestowed on him by Pope John in
naming him his personal representative. Despite his
uneasiness at the thought of his new role, the Cardinal was anxious to go to Peru in order to see for
himself how his St. James' priests were doing. Thus
it was with mixed feelings that he set out.

Once there, however, he adapted himself
well, despite the language barrier. Here, too, he
demonstrated his ability completely to master a situation and sense what gesture would be most appreciated. His love for people guided him to do
things that won hearts. A murmur went through the
crowd when on his arrival, met by the color guard,
he gathered the folds of the Peruvian flag in his

hands and reverently kissed it. Passing by flocks of wide-eyed children, he stopped to pat them on the head, and at times the littlest ones were lifted up in his arms.

What need of a common language when thousands of Peruvians saw the picture of the tall figure resplendent in red delighting in the company of their children? What need of a speech to the squads of soldiers at the Congress after he had crowned the statue of their Patroness, Our Lady of Ransom, and kissed her hand in the best Spanish fashion? His interest, his devotion, his decision personally to give Holy Communion, despite the heat, to every one of the hundreds desiring it, made the papal legate popular and the Church prestigious.

At a dinner he gave for the American priests and religious in Peru, the Cardinal solicited news about their health and their apostolate. He spoke with each of his St. James' missionaries and inquired about the difficulties they were meeting, as well as their needs. "They're happy," he later reported, "because they're busy!"

The Cardinal returned to the States highly satisfied with his trip. He was especially pleased that he had been able to give his priests encouragement and to see for himself the religious situation. "We are in business," he would often say in speaking of Peru, "to go out of business." He would then explain that the American priests are only a temporary solution to the shortage of clerics in Latin

America. Ultimately their goal is to furnish the Church with enough native priests to make missionaries unnecessary. "When that time comes, we shall step out." Although it costs him over $500,000 a year to support his missionaries and their churches, schools and clinics, he will gladly release control of organization and buildings whenever the native priests are ready to assume charge. And to provide more of these priests, he has financed the construction of new seminaries.

"The picture is dark, but I believe the future will be bright": with these words the Cardinal often concludes his remarks on the South American situation. It is a phrase typical of his undying optimism. "This is just the springtime of the Church," he thunders. "She is not old; she is eternally young, and out of persecution or apparent failure, she will rise again. Let us confidently sow the seed, and others will reap the harvest."

The St. James Society constitutes his "field hands." Since its beginnings, the Society has grown steadily until it now numbers over ninety priests in Peru, Bolivia, and Ecuador. Reportedly, the Cardinal begged Pope John to let him resign as Archbishop of Boston and go personally to labor in Latin America, but the Pope's reply was that he could do more for the cause by staying at home. Thus he has become an indefatigable recruiter of manpower and collector of funds, as well as a kind of unique publicity agent for the plight of the Latins.

The Cardinal's own nephew, Rev. William Francis, son of his sister Anna, joined the Society; but it is characteristic of him and his uncle that no mention was made of their relationship when the Boston *Record-American* ran an article on Father Francis' work in a Lima slum area, as part of its dramatic series entitled "Cardinal Cushing's Lonely War in Peru." This series, another instance of the Cardinal's utilization of the press, presents a memorable story of the poverty, disease, ignorance and Communist influence against which the dedicated priests struggle to save the people from material and spiritual death.

"Coming to Peru was the most worthwhile decision I ever made," wrote seventy-one-year-old Archdeacon Thomas Duggan, who gave up a distinguished position in Cork, Ireland, to become a St. James Missioner. The Cardinal was so moved by this great priest's zeal that he publicized his sacrifice in a leaflet entitled "Typically Irish." And when Archdeacon Duggan died suddenly, the Cardinal rose from a sickbed to go to Lima for his funeral. To take his place came other Irish priests who have declared: "The work here is the most worthwhile we ever did."

The priests of St. James and their Founder have a humorous little ditty—some might call it a publicity number—which, home for a visit, they sing to their fellow priests on rare festive occasions:

"I work in the mountains of Peru
The land that God forgot,
Where the mud is sixteen inches deep
And the sun is scorching hot.

I've peeled a million onions
And twice as many spuds.
And when I have some spare time
I always clean my duds.

You can have your Jesuit classrooms
And Trappist monasteries too.
Here's a different type of priest
I'll introduce to you.

When he dies and goes to Heaven,
To St. Peter he will tell,
Peru reporting in, sir,
I've served my time in Hell."

With this light-hearted outlook and the father-ly support of a prelate who never fails to keep his word and to follow up what he begins, the diocesan priests of the Cardinal's Society have brought a renewal of faith and hope wherever they labor. "The presence of the Society of St. James in Peru is one of the greatest blessings God could bestow on the Church here," said Archbishop Romolo Carboni, Papal Nuncio to Peru. "For his mind and heart, for his ideas, suggestions, and programs, for his extremely generous contributions and especially for founding the Society of St. James, I consider Cardinal Cushing a great Father of the Church in our times, helping the Mystical Body of Christ throughout the world and especially here. . . . Surely, there has seldom been a Prince of the Church with a more catholic viewpoint—and I use 'catholic' with a small 'c.'"

"Keep giving of yourself to the Lord, despite the advice other people hand you," the Cardinal once wrote to some zealous lay co-workers. "None of us could do more than that. The greatest thrill of a lifetime is to go to bed exhausted after having given yourself to help others."

Someone might conclude that remark with the observation that Cardinal Cushing speaks from personal experience.

"For the good of the Church and souls, he makes himself God's beggarman," wrote an Irish Jesuit, Reverend Robert Nash. "No one who contacts him can doubt that this is a man of dedicated life. He has a vivid understanding of the value of an immortal soul, and, like 'a saint in a hurry,' he turns every moment to advantage for his divine task." These lines were penned shortly after the first exceptional children's pilgrimage to Lourdes, which had included a stop-over in Ireland. "There have been many spontaneous expressions of admiration and affection for Cardinal Cushing since his recent visit," said Father Nash. "The sight of that man, great in physical stature and great in mind and heart, carrying a little negro girl of seven down the gangway in his arms, has moved and captivated all who witnessed it. Clothed in the robes of a Prince of the Church, he bore his precious burden, explaining that the bones of the child were brittle and that great care was necessary, and showing by his whole attitude, and especially by the tense expression in his face, the love and anxiety he felt for her."

In May, 1960, the Cardinal went to Lourdes again with his exceptional children. He had had so many requests from parents all over the country the preceding year that he had had to turn many down, since the quota was necessarily limited. However, just a few weeks before this second Lourdes trip, he fell very ill, and after X-rays revealed internal abcesses, he had to undergo surgery. Everyone protested that he must not think of travelling to Lourdes after that, but he would not hear of cancelling the trip. Friends who came to call on him during his sickness found him as usual unwilling to talk about himself. He appreciated their concern, but wanted no one "losing time," as he put it, over him.

Upon his return, the Cardinal remarked to intimates that he and his doctor, Richard Wright, Bishop John Wright's brother, had their hands full, for the children seemed harder to handle. In Lourdes, he himself had carried the monstrance containing the Blessed Sacrament throughout the whole procession of the blessing of the sick, although normally a priest would have performed this function. "I wanted to carry it myself," the Cardinal said. "And then I preached one of 'my' sermons—even though I knew not many understood English."

As a footnote to this sermon, he added that while he was talking, one of the retarded children, a born mimic, watched him intently and then suddenly began imitating his every gesture—even making the sign of the cross with his left hand!

On the return flight, there had been a short stop in Shannon, Ireland, and while everyone else went on a shopping tour, the Cardinal and the doctor stayed on board the plane with the children. At that point, the Cardinal's sickness caught up with him, and to find some relief, he made a kind of bunk on top of two seats, and lay down on that for a while.

He had been home but a short time when he began travelling again, to keep engagements on the West Coast for various commencement exercises. His schedule was very tight and required flying at all hours, losing sleep, and being on the move constantly. He gave himself thoroughly to each address as though it were the only one, and stayed not a minute extra. As always, as soon as he could, he set out for home, where he knew work had accumulated.

For one stop, he had prepared a devotional address on the Holy Eucharist, but finding that the talk was to be televised, he set aside his carefully prepared address and delivered instead one that might be appreciated by a more general audience.

"It was so hot, no one knew what I was saying, anyway," he joked afterwards.

Earlier in the year, Cardinal Cushing's first Pastoral Letter had been issued and distributed in every parish of the Archdiocese on the first Sunday of Lent. It was a challenging portrayal of the active role of the individual Christian, both in human society and in the Church. No theme could be more characteristic of the Cardinal's thinking; it might well be said that he had never given an address in which this challenge was not conveyed directly or indirectly.

Bishops and priests, state officials and scholars wrote to congratulate him on this Pastoral: "It is a comprehensive study of our present confused human condition and a clear guide to a peaceful solution of the many problems that beset us on all sides;" "one of those rare documents that one will study many times;" "should be read by everyone—Catholics and non-Catholics—throughout our land."

Over two hundred thousand copies were distributed. It was read and studied in many college and seminary classrooms, and printed in the national press. In succeeding years, the Cardinal followed it with Pastorals on such topics as the ecumenical council; moral values and American society; the Church and public opinion.

If Cardinal Cushing was already a familiar figure on the American scene, he grew even more prominent when John F. Kennedy became President of the United States, or more accurately, when the young and vigorous President was assassinated. At that time, and in the dark days that followed, the Cardinal was viewed by the nation both as an old family friend, as the papers invariably called him, grieving over the loss of still another young Kennedy, as well as an American moved by the tragic death of his President. But in January of 1961, when John F. Kennedy assumed office and the Cardinal was invited to deliver a prayer at the Inaugural, no thought of such a disaster was in anyone's mind.

Characteristically, the Cardinal had his Inaugural Prayer ready soon after the invitation arrived, but this time he showed the typed sheets to no one. He wanted his words kept out of the press until the ceremony.

While he was wondering about what arrangements to make for his stay in the capital, Archbishop O'Boyle of Washington called to tell him that he wanted to play host to him and take care of everything. This thoughtfulness greatly pleased him.

Thursday, January 19th, at three in the afternoon, the Cardinal left Boston by plane for Washington. With him went Monsignor George Kerr, who often accompanied him on his Confirmation rounds. The plane never reached Washington, however. A storm forced it back to New York, and a bus took the travellers to Penn Station. There the trains were running irregularly due to a strike, so until two o'clock in the morning, the Cardinal-Archbishop of Boston sat on his suitcase, as he later said, and just waited.

When at last they boarded the train, they faced the prospect of sitting in a coach all night. But two men from Boston whom they had met went to argue with some official and wangled a roomette for the four of them. It was so cramped that they could do little more than sit looking at each other, and to make matters worse, some time later, another official showed up to say apologetically that they were in a roomette reserved for someone else! When it came to paying for it, the Cardinal did not have enough money with him. "It's a good thing Monsignor Kerr was going to stay with relatives when he got to Washington," he commented later, "for it was Monsignor who paid."

Archbishop O'Boyle waited up all that night for the Cardinal. When at last the travellers arrived at the episcopal residence, the Archbishop himself made them some coffee.

The next morning, at the Mass he celebrated at the National Shrine of the Immaculate Conception, the Cardinal recited a moving prayer to beg God's blessing for John F. Kennedy:

"Father of Nations, Sovereign Lord of all creation, Thy people in the United States have been strengthened from the beginning by Presidents who, without exception, entered upon their exalted office with humble but confident prayer to Thee.

"In the days of America's newborn vision and vitality, George Washington acknowledged at his inauguration that '... it would be peculiarly improper to omit in this first official act my fervent supplications to that Almighty Being Who rules over the universe, Who presides in the councils of nations, and Whose providential aids can supply every human defect.'

"John Adams, proclaiming Thee to be 'that Being who is supreme over all, the patron of Order, the Fountain of Justice, and the Protector in all ages of the world of virtuous liberty,' begged Thee to impart Thy 'blessing upon this nation and its Government and give it all possible success and duration consistent with the ends of (Thy) providence.'

"Thomas Jefferson publicly prayed that Thine 'Infinite Power, which rules the destinies of the universe, might lead our councils to what is best, and give them favorable issue for (our) peace and prosperity.'

"John Quincy Adams reminded himself and us that 'except the Lord keep the city, the watchman waketh but in vain.'

"James Buchanan, conscious of Thy 'kind Providence which inspired our fathers with wisdom to frame the most perfect form of government and union ever devised by man,' implored Thee to prosper our form of government 'until it shall have been peacefully instrumental by its example in the extension of civil and religious liberty throughout the world.'

In a grave hour of our national testing, Abraham Lincoln, most prayerful of our Presidents, devoutly declared that 'intelligence, patriotism, Christianity, and a firm reliance on Him who has never yet forsaken this favored land are still competent to adjust in the best way all our present difficulty.'

"Inspired by these memories, we, this same nation, turn to Thee, our same and unchanging God, in times of new trials and yet new graces. With Calvin Coolidge we declare again that 'America seeks no earthly empire built on blood and force. No ambition, no temptation lures her to thought of foreign dominions. . . . She cherishes no purpose save to merit the favor of Almighty God.'

"With Franklin Roosevelt, we give thanks that Thou hast 'given our people stout hearts and strong arms with which to strike mighty blows for freedom and truth,' and with Dwight Eisenhower we strive to accept 'the work that awaits us all, to be done with bravery, with charity, and with prayer to Almighty God.'

"Wherefore, we beg Thy blessing for John F. Kennedy that he may give to this land favored by Thy Providence and to all the world the example of religious piety which, with their patriotic devotion, has made our Presidents so admired by men and, we pray, acceptable to Thee.

"Then will Thy supernatural grace elevate and ennoble the natural gifts of our President and all his co-workers; then will the prayer be answered that is the motto of the capital city of his native state: 'Sicut Patribus, Sit Deus Nobis,' As God was with our fathers, so may He be with us! Amen."

Later in the day, at the Inauguration, the Cardinal emphasized in his prayer the principles of responsibility and cooperation:

"In this year of Our Lord, nineteen hundred and sixty-one, we ask Thee, O Almighty God, to enlighten us:—

"That we may know, as men, our personal responsibilities;

"That we may know, as Americans, our political, social and humanitarian responsibilities;

"That we may know, as citizens of the world, our global responsibilities to ourselves and our fellow men;

"That we may know, as children of God, our responsibilities to the Father of mankind;

"Enlighten us, O Lord, that we may know how to combine all of these responsibilities into a continuing Principle of Responsibility;

"Enlighten us that we may know how to put this principle of responsibility into daily practice, both in ideal and action—in these troubled but hopeful times.

"In this year of Our Lord, nineteen hundred and sixty-one, we beseech Thee, O Almighty God, to strengthen our resolve:—

"To enlarge our vision of the common good;

"To implement with personal sacrifice the objectives of our national purpose;

"To revere in every man that divine spark which makes him our brother—that human spark which can make him our friend—and that personal spark which makes him himself;

"To learn to ask ourselves sincerely in every community effort, not what we can get out of it, but what we can put into it.

"To defend my right to be myself; to defend my neighbor's right to be himself, and to defend America's duty to respect the rights of all men.

"Strengthen our resolve, O Lord, to transform this recognition of others into a Principle of Co-operation.

"Inspire us to practice this Principle of Co-operation both in ideal and action—in these most dangerous but soul-stretching times.

"On this twentieth day of January—one thousand nine hundred and sixty-one years after the birth of Christ—on the occasion of the inauguration of John Fitzgerald Kennedy as president of the United States of America,

"Do thou, O Almighty God, give him, his Cabinet, the Congress and Courts of the United States—and all of us—the grace:—

"To perform with full personal responsibility our duties as free men;

"To perform in full cooperation our duties as American citizens;

"To perform with complete vigilance our duty to prevent the spread of totalitarian terror everywhere.

"To perform with religious fervor our duty to teach, implement, and create true freedom as a way of life at home and abroad—for true freedom underlies human dignity and is a holy state of life.

"Give us the grace also, O Lord, to realize that we are made to be holy according to Thy image and likeness; *for to be holy is to be Godlike.*

"Give us the vision to realize that in Thy plan we have a self-sacrificing part to play in completing an unfinished universe; *for to sacrifice is to conquer;*

"Give us the strength to further Thy creation by our responsible and dedicated work—*for to labor is to pray;*

"Give us the charity to further Thy creation by our brotherly cooperation—*for to care is to love.*

"Finally, O Divine Ruler of men and nations, through confidence in Thee let men take hope in what is being done in this capital city of our nation, in this hour, in this month of January, in the year

1961; let hearts everywhere be lifted, and let anxieties be dispelled as new hands, in the vigor of youth, grasp the wheel of the ship of state. Put Thy Hands on his hands, put Thy spirit in his heart, put Thy justice and peace, the work of justice, in all his programs and let this land—and all lands— move forward under Thy guidance and through his leadership to new frontiers in peace, progress and prosperity. Amen."

The incident of the smoking lectern during the inauguration ceremony is history, for it clouded every TV screen. The Cardinal had noticed it before he himself stepped up to offer his prayer, and had called it to the attention of a guard. "I thought it looked like a short circuit," he says. While he was speaking, the situation grew worse. Still he went ahead apparently unperturbed.

"I thought to myself: 'This is as good a time as any to give my life for the people!'" he joked afterwards. "I also thought: 'If it blows up, I'll land on the Washington Monument.'"

The Cardinal saw little or nothing of the Kennedys beyond the inaugural itself, and did not attend their luncheon. When a minister told him that he would like to go to the affair, but did not have a ticket, the Cardinal simply said, "Here, take mine." And he gave it to him then and there.

Back from Washington, he was soon making arrangements to go to Kingston, Jamaica, another area which considered him its chief benefactor. On his return from there, he stopped at Guantanamo, the U.S. base in Cuba. The local situation was so tense, that there were those who were not eager to see him make a stop there, but the Cardinal would not let any such consideration of danger deter him.

Shortly after he returned home, he heard from the Jesuits in Jamaica of the great impact his visit had made on officials and people there: "No one has ever done as much for the Church in Jamaica as you did in your brief visit."

In that early spring of 1961, the Cardinal was thinking of another field in which he might serve the Church: he was occupied with the problem of how to make it easier for older men to study for the priesthood. In Rome there has been, for some time, a seminary especially for belated vocations, the English Beda College. It is geared to maturity and experience. The Cardinal had often felt that older men who for one reason or another had not begun studying earlier, would flock to the priesthood if they were not asked to go through a seminary training suited to much younger candidates.

Out of this conviction was to come the Pope John XXIII National Seminary for Delayed Vocations, unique in the United States. It took time to plan, courage to execute, and, inevitably, more work to raise the required funds; but the number and quality of the men who applied for admission more than justified the Cardinal's faith in this undertaking.

May 26th, 1961, marked his fortieth anniversary of ordination. A few days previous, he wrote to a friend:

"I just returned from engagements in Chicago and Notre Dame University. They were numerous . . . hence I am 'all in.'

"Don't forget to say a special prayer for me on May 26th, the date I commemorate my fortieth anniversary as a priest. I don't celebrate any anniversaries of this kind, but I would appreciate a memento in your prayers for this occasion, in thanksgiving to Almighty God for using me as an unworthy tool to perpetuate His Divine Mission on this earth. Someone once defined a slave as a living tool of his master. I hope that for forty years I have been a slave for Christ."

A kind of celebration he did have, however, "Cushing style." He filled his house on May 26th with as many little wheelchair and stretcher cases— his exceptional children—as it would hold. The anniversary was his, but the party was theirs.

On that same day two years later, in response to a request by a newspaper to express his thoughts, the Cardinal made some statements about the ideal priesthood to which he has always and everywhere aspired:

"Like every priest, I am obliged, first, to become a human reproduction of the First Priest, Christ the Lord; second, I must serve as His instrument to perpetuate His Divine Mission. Without Him I can do nothing.

"First and foremost, I have, like all others, the primary duty to sanctify and to save my soul. What shall it profit me if I gain the whole world, become all things to all men and fail to become Godlike in my own life and lose my immortal soul? This is a difficult task for a diocesan priest. At best his life is a lonely one and the higher he ascends in the ranks of the priesthood, the greater the responsibilities and with them greater loneliness.

"Sanctification is a tremendously personal effort. It is a constant battle against self; an arduous, persevering, never-ending private warfare against the world, the flesh and the devil. In some difficult phases of this struggle one loses a skirmish now and then. Human nature is weak and God chose men not angels to become priests. We all have our faults and failings, but the grace of God is sufficient for the conquest of self, for detachment from creatures and for ultimate victory in the spiritual battle of life.

"The human element in this conquest was expressed by a great saint who said: 'Agere Contra'— 'Act against self.' That is the challenge faced by every priest. It is a lifelong struggle. If we are successful, we die to the world and gain a new life reflecting that of Jesus Christ, the Divine Exemplar of the priesthood.

"The lesson of this first point of my meditation as I look back over more than four decades to May,

1921, is the overwhelming truth that the only successful priest is the priest who has conquered self and become like a plastic substance in the Hands of God to be fashioned and formed according to the Divine Model, Christ the Priest. 'You have not chosen Me,' He said, 'I have chosen you.' 'Learn of Me. I am meek and humble of heart.' 'I am sent to preach the gospel to the poor and to heal the contrite of heart.' 'Be ye holy as your Heavenly Father is holy.'

"The second meditation prompted by this anniversary is: I have not been called to the priesthood to be a 'spiritual millionaire' or to become a saint and to neglect others. The priesthood is not mine to be cherished and locked in a selfish heart. I have been called 'to go about doing good.' I have not been ordained for myself but to serve others.

"Spiritual writers throughout the ages have called the priest 'Alter Christus,' 'Another Christ.' I must imitate Him and continue in my lifetime His Divine Mission. It is a mission of love, generosity, sacrifice and total dedication to the will of God. It is the mission of the Good Shepherd, always ready to lay down his life for his flock. It is a vocation, to teach the gospel by word and example, to heal the contrite, to seek the sheep who are lost, to offer the sacrifice of the altar, to visit the sick, to clothe the naked, to comfort those in prison, to help the poor, the abandoned, the exceptional children, the helpless in mind and in body, to love and serve and to die, if necessary, for those who know not the God

Who made them; to counteract by word and example secularism, atheism, communism and to help build an economic, social and political order, where the inalienable rights of man are respected.

"Condemnation of evil is not sufficient. I must sponsor and support everything just and beneficial advocated by the precepts of the Gospel. That requires on the part of the priest of the twentieth century prayer, study and courage so that he shall support effectively social justice for all, a new order, everything that will enable men to be happy here and hereafter.

"It also presumes that we must not endeavor to solve the problems of the twentieth century with the methods and means of former ages. We must follow the social and spiritual directives of the Popes, love our fellow men as children of God, present to them divine truths in modern terms and sow the good seed of prayer and work to the end that in God's own time 'we may all be one as Christ and the Father are one.'...

"To the Catholics, Protestants, Jews and churchless people who have helped me in the fulfillment of this sublime vocation, I extend my love, prayers and gratitude on the occasion of the forty-second anniversary of my ordination to the holy priesthood. If at any time I have hurt anyone, I apologize to them. If I have helped anyone I appeal for your prayers ... that I may become a totally dedicated 'slave of Christ.'"

17

"MY ONLY INTEREST

IS IN

HELPING PEOPLE"

The Cardinal stood holding the square box with its lid upraised. He was gazing down on a jewelled pectoral cross, its heavy gold chain neatly coiled around it, but he did not really see it. Before his eyes was the white vision of a figure beloved, a man and a father who was no more.

Pope John XXIII was dead, and Richard Cardinal Cushing held in his hand the late Holy Father's pectoral cross.

"Your Eminence," read the accompanying letter from Archbishop Angelo Dell'Acqua, "I have the honor to forward to Your Eminence the enclosed pectoral cross which was destined by the Holy Father John XXIII for Your Eminence.

"This cross was used by His Holiness during the years of His service for the Holy See in the Orient, in Paris and in Venice. It was also used by Him while He was Pope."

The letter was dated June 18, 1963. Pope John's prolonged agony had ended fifteen days before, while the world he had brought closer together mourned his passing. That highly valued token of a great Pontiff's affection was sent to Cardinal Cushing the day before he entered the conclave to exercise for the first time his right to vote for a successor to St. Peter as Vicar of Christ.

Less than two days after the Cardinals entered the Conclave, they gave the Church a new Sovereign Pontiff. The man elected, Giovanni Battista Cardinal Montini, who three years previously had been Cardinal Cushing's guest in Boston, made it clear at once that he would continue the path marked out by his unforgettable predecessor.

To say that Good Pope John made a tremendous impression on the Cardinal is an understatement. He saw in this Pope the perfect model for his own aspirations.

"Pope John XXIII completed the long climb up the ladder of perfection," he declared. "He reached the summit of charity and is united with God. His epitaph can best be written by those of us who imitate those qualities of soul which he preached and practiced. . . .

"Though a man of advanced years when he was elected to the papacy, he was young at heart in every way, seeing the world in freshness and simplicity, in open-hearted candor and wondrous optimism. He was an example for our age, and though he has passed from among us, that example will linger on and glow more brilliantly with the passing of time."

Speaking on a more personal note of what Pope John had meant to him, the Cardinal confessed: "I never felt at home as the Archbishop of Boston. My background has been entirely different from all these Princes of the Church. I'm no theologian, and I never did any formal teaching. The average Archbishop or Cardinal represents various phases of scholarship far different from anything in my experience.

"But when the good Pope John made me a cardinal, I saw a picture of his brothers on a farm with baskets on their backs, and I will never forget it.

"I said to myself then, 'If Almighty God wills that a man like this who came from poor people and had extraordinary humility and a great sense of humor should be the Pope at one of the most critical periods in history, then I have this proof that I too am the Archbishop of Boston by the will of Almighty God.'

"If it hadn't been for him, I wouldn't have lasted here. I'd have gone to Latin America as a missionary and begged for those who couldn't beg for themselves. But that Pope gave me the lift I needed. I feel all right now. He inspired me to be myself and not pretend to be something I'm not."

Making the required allowances for the humility which colors every reference to himself, there can be no doubt that the Cardinal found great encouragement for his way of life and his undertakings from the man he described as "one of the most beloved, unique, and in a constructive way, revolutionary Pontiffs in history."

As another mark of his confidence and esteem, Pope John had made the Cardinal his legate to the Eucharistic Congress in Santa Cruz, Bolivia in the summer of 1961, and in a spirit of confident obedience, Cardinal Cushing had gone, despite warnings from the State Department that conditions were critical there. Planes were being hijacked and riots were feared to mark the beginning of a major revolution.

"Unless Rome tells me not to go, I'm leaving," said the Cardinal. "I'm on a mission from the Vatican."

Prior to his trip, he went to a parish in the Worcester diocese to solicit support for the missions. He preached at every Mass that Sunday morning and came home exhausted, but contented. The papers reported that his appeal more than doubled the high of any previous appeal in the parish.

For the Congress, the Cardinal carefully prepared three speeches. (As it turned out, he spoke as much as six times a day, sometimes right on the streets.) The language barrier again worried him, but he was heartened by a letter from Archbishop Carboni, Papal Nuncio in Lima, where he planned to stop to meet with the St. James Missionaries. "Recently I read in the papers," wrote the Archbishop, "that Your Eminence promised to make shorter speeches. [The Cardinal had declared that he was a man of a "few million words" and that the reason he often talked at length was because he had strong convictions to pass on; nevertheless, he had said he was going to start bringing along a buzzer to remind himself when it was time to stop.]

"I beg Your Eminence not to put that resolution into effect until your return to the United States," continued the Archbishop. "Your presence inspires our people here, regardless of what language you speak, and the longer you talk, the longer we shall have the pleasure of your company!"

The trip and the Congress went well. Thousands of Bolivians gathered at the outdoor altar before the huge replica of "Christ of the Andes" to hear the Cardinal speak of the spiritual unity of Catholics of all nations. Families consecrated themselves to the Sacred Heart. Bolivia's National Army was dedicated to Our Lady of Mt. Carmel. Throngs cheered the papal legate after he responded with great warmth to the civic and national honors bestowed upon him.

No revolution developed as had been feared. The only unpleasant aspect of the trip, in fact, was the infection the Cardinal contracted, which produced painful raw sores on his arms and legs that did not heal for over a month.

Apart from occasionally wondering how long they would last, however, the Cardinal paid little attention to them. He had long ago become accustomed to living and working to the accompaniment of pain. It was part of the total giving of self of which he once spoke in a strongly worded talk on the Sacred Heart:

"We have presented the whole thing too sentimentally," he said at that time. "We need a new approach. I tell you honestly, I don't find any appeal in some pictures and statues of the Sacred Heart. Looking at them, you cannot blame people who think that our Christ is effeminate. They have it wrong, but they can't be blamed for it.

"The Sacred Heart is not effeminate in any way. The quicker we lift this devotion out of sentimentalism, the more it will appeal to men and to women looking for a challenge. It demands sacrifice of the human will, a giving of the whole heart. It is virile, enduring, beautiful. Christ loved the rich young man, but He did not spare him. God, as man, wants us totally. We will do nothing if we do not give ourselves completely, in a perfect flowering of human life. This is superhuman heroism."

In his own life, total giving has been the secret of his ability to take sorrows and disappointments quietly and privately in stride. The whole story of what the Cardinal has suffered because of the defection of Father Leonard Feeney, for example, is known to very few. In happier times, Father Feeney used to bring his yearly group of converts to meet the Archbishop at his residence. When the priest began publicizing his heretical contention that only Catholics can be saved, Archbishop Cushing used great kindness with him while doing all he could to try to make him drop this position. Even after Feeney had been excommunicated and had returned every appeal of his Archbishop with refusals, insults, and even a public demonstration with his young followers when the Archbishop opened a Catholic Chapel at the Jewish University of Brandeis, still the Archbishop never spoke harshly of him. In fact, more than once, he laid himself open to further suffering by fruitless attempts to win him and his followers back.

"Is this what you've been going through all these years?" wrote a Bishop who had just had a painful encounter with 'Feeney followers.' "I tell you, you're a martyr!"

Yet because he is convinced that he is first and foremost a priest, and a priest is a man in search of souls, the Cardinal's only thought in the whole matter is the welfare of those involved.

The welfare of souls throughout the world was uppermost in his thoughts when Cardinal Cushing travelled to Rome in 1962 to join with more than two thousand prelates for the opening session of the Second Vatican Council.

The pastoral aims of the Second Vatican Council are of great interest to him, for his whole concern has always been with the problems of Christian living in the twentieth century—the problems of the poor, the missions, the relation of liturgy to the life of the people, and the ecumenical movement.

In an informal speech to a religious community shortly before he left for Rome, the Cardinal declared,

"It is the people at home who pray for the Council, in whom I have confidence. It is your prayers which will bring the Holy Spirit to preside over the Council."

In his Pastoral Letter of that year, "The Call of the Council," he had written:

"Every Christian must accept responsibility for his part in this gathering and no person called to membership in the Body of Christ can conscientiously set it aside. It remains now to urge all hearts to patient prayer and penance so that purified of our iniquities, we may be worthy of God's direction and blessing on our efforts for His glory.

". . . Let each of us be ready to apply the decisions of the Council to himself. There will doubtless be some changes, which will effect us in our life of worship, of instruction, of social action. Let none of us have a false sense of independence by which he may think himself excused from the universal application of the decrees of the Council."

The Cardinal's fundamental outlook is strongly evident in this Pastoral: "The common responsibility of all the Church to share in the mission of Christ to all men must be realized now in a more concrete manner. We are members of the *Catholic* church, universal and ecumenical; our horizons cannot be limited merely to the geographic area of our residence."

As a member of the Congregations of the Council, Propagation of the Faith, and Seminaries and Universities, the Cardinal exchanged points of view with many of the Council Fathers and deeply impressed them by his personal and genuine concern for the progress of the Church in every country.

During his stays in Italy, the Cardinal visited several general houses of communities laboring in his Archdiocese and, also, charitable institutions in the environs of Rome, such as the unique hospital solely for nuns, owned and staffed by the Daughters of St. Paul. In 1963, he visited *Sotto il Monte,* hometown of the late Pope John, and in keeping with a request made personally to him by the Pontiff, provided for the restoration of the facade of Pope John's old parish church. Two other little Italian towns were visited by him, to the great delight of the townspeople. Everywhere he went, "il Cardinale Cushing" met with spontaneous applause and a return of the affection his warm smile and generous gifts evidenced.

Prompted by his partiality for St. Francis of Assisi, he squeezed into his schedule a visit to Greccio, the place where the Saint built the first Christmas crib. Here in a cell once occupied by Francis himself, he sat for a while in deep reflection.

Shortly after the first session of the Council, December, 1962, a new title was added to the many that had been given to the Cardinal. This time it was none other than "the mysterious donor." Just before Christmas Fidel Castro demanded two million, nine hundred thousand dollars as ransom for 1,113 prisoners from the Bay of Pigs invasion, in addition to fifty-three million in medicine and food previously demanded. Attorney General Robert Kennedy later declared: "I made one phone call and received a pledge of a million dollars."

Who was the mysterious donor? Every newspaper wanted the answer. The Cardinal had no intention of letting anyone know. It was enough that the suffering prisoners had been released and been reunited with their families for Christmas. In replying to the Attorney General, he had said, "I'll get it for you, but just don't reveal me as the giver."

Yet the newspapers kept calling, acting on a hunch that the Cardinal was the unknown donor. At last, on January 11, 1963, the press carried his statement that he had worked day and night to raise the ransom and that he alone was "responsible for the collection of this extraordinary sum." He added: "The credit, however, belongs to my co-workers and benefactors in the United States and Latin America, who have supported my apostolic work." The reason he gave for at last disclosing his part in raising the ransom money was "rumors crediting the gift as coming from sources with which I have no identification."

Indeed, one reporter had phoned the Cardinal to say, "We have a story that you are the donor and that you are head of Catholic Charities for the whole country."

"They'll be saying next that I'm the head of Fort Knox!" the Cardinal remarked when he hung up. Another paper called to say they had heard he was head of the Kennedy Foundation, and— "Mister, I wish I were!" laughed the Cardinal.

The guessing ended with his statement and its subsequent confirmation by Justice Department officials.

This particular expenditure attracted publicity, but much larger ones have been made for charity over the years. For example, at the time of the "mysterious donor" episode, the four million dollar Madonna School for Girls was under construction to house the Good Shepherd Sisters and the troubled girls entrusted to their care.

In 1957, a reporter had hazarded what he called a "conservative estimate," that just the main accomplishments of the Archbishop over the years, might be worth one hundred fifty million. By 1964, guesses no longer could keep up with achievements.

To cite one further example, just prior to his Twenty-fifth Anniversary of Episcopal Consecration, June 29, 1964, the Cardinal appealed once more to the generosity of his beloved flock for another great project: a retirement home for the senior clergy, a home which he called, "a welcome addition to the institutional complex of our beloved Archdiocese of Boston."

On the subject of finances, the Cardinal once said, adapting the famous lines of St. Pius X to himself: "I was born poor, I shall die poor—but with all my debts paid." Sometimes, in these many building projects, he has been frustrated in his hopes, at least, for the first attempt, but despite the inevitable disappointments, he has always affirmed, "I have confidence in God."

June of 1963 had brought the Cardinal an immense sorrow in the passing of Good Pope John. In late summer, he suffered with President Kennedy over the death of the infant, Patrick Bouvier.

It was in the Cardinal's own chapel that the Mass of the Angels was said for Patrick Bouvier

Kennedy, with the prelate celebrating it in white. Later the Cardinal said that he had seen President Kennedy in tears for the first time that day: "He wouldn't take his hands off that little coffin."

The grieving mother, Mrs. Jacqueline Kennedy, who had received condolences by the thousands, wrote a deeply touching letter to the Cardinal, whose beautiful prayer at the Mass for her infant son moved her greatly.

"Help, O Lord, the sorrowing parents of this child," read the prayer in part, "to realize that begetting him was not in vain. Remind them, when they think of him, that they have been very near to a little saint who is now serving before the heavenly throne and praying for them. Give them the true parental love which desires only happiness for their children, no matter what price they might be asked to pay. Make their faith strong enough to see that they could never have brought the happiness to this child that he now enjoys . . ."

When in November, the Cardinal next saw the young President, John F. Kennedy was dead by assassination. Profoundly affected by the sudden tragedy, by the events that followed upon it, and by the heroic grief of the President's wife and family, the Cardinal brought them both priestly and personal consolations in every manner he could. When the valiant Jacqueline, as he was ever afterwards to refer to her, arrived at St. Matthew's Cathedral with Caroline and little John, Jr. for the

Requiem Mass, the Cardinal departed from the usual procedure and walked down the steps to meet and comfort her. In the days that followed the burial of the President, he kept in close touch with the sorrowing family.

Several months later, on May 29th, at a luncheon commemorating the issue of the Kennedy Memorial Stamps, he was to say:

". . . We commemorate the contribution of a great American to the history of his country and the entire world; we pay tribute to the energies and vision which he brought to the highest executive office in this land; we salute the courage with which he faced all trials in line of duty even to the demands of death itself.

"In the stamps issued today we seek to record for all time some part of the inspiration which his leadership gave to America, some memory of that grace and style which is now no longer with us.

"We pray today that these stamps, as they cross the globe in international exchange, will carry with them some of the spirit of that stalwart President whose image they bear. His pursuit of peace, his strivings for harmony among the nations, his strength in time of testing, his youthful hopes for a better world—all of these find wings in these stamps to touch anew the hearts of men in every place where people communicate with each other."

For the Kennedy Memorial Library, the Cardinal helped to collect contributions from the thousands who expressed a desire to show their admiration for the fallen President. To each of the countless contributors he sent the promised gift of a picture of JFK and a copy of the eulogy he had preached.

In an ecumenical talk written in the first months of 1964, after noting that "our task should be to inquire how we can in unfeigned love speak to one another," the Cardinal continued:

"What could be more eloquent of the way in which 'God writes straight with crooked lines' than the way in which men of every faith were brought closer together at the time of the late President's death?"

What he said of the President's death—that it had brought men closer together—might well be said of the Cardinal's ecumenical spirit. Over the years, his constant good will gestures have created a friendly atmosphere. Long before actual ecumenical contacts were earnestly programmed, the ground had been prepared in Boston. In fact, by 1962, the Cardinal could write in his Pastoral Letter:

"In our own archdiocese we have been greatly gratified by the growing ecumenical spirit among our priests and among so many of our dissident Christian brothers. Indeed many Protestant clergymen and not a few Orthodox leaders have been engaged in serious theological conversation with priests of the archdiocese. These encounters we have approved and endorsed in the warm hope that they will foster mutual understanding and true Christlike charity in our community and will lay a groundwork for ultimate union. These meetings have revealed that, although there are definite areas of theological divergence, many of our hostilities and causes for separation are in reality a vast network of misunderstanding which only patient love can cut away. They also highlight the truth which the Popes are ever wont to utter: the work of unity is the work of *every* Christian, a work of prayer, of holy example, of apostolic love. Union is prepared and effected not only in ecumenical councils: it is born and grows in the pluralistic neighborhood."

It was the Cardinal who was instrumental in bringing Augustine Cardinal Bea, head of the Vatican Secretariat for Promoting Christian Unity, to Harvard University in 1963 for the famed Roman Catholic-Protestant Colloquium. In the course of a long letter to Cardinal Bea, he wrote:

"I appreciate full well that Your Eminence has many demands and that Your Eminence has been tremendously pressed for time and energy during the first sessions of Vatican Council II, but, believe me, even though I am no scholar, I wish to say, as one who has dedicated an entire lifetime of my priesthood of forty-two years to the Church Universal and to befriending people outside the Catholic faith, that the presence of Your Eminence at the first seminar identified with the ecumenical spirit, sponsored by Harvard University Divinity

School, will be the greatest contribution that could be made to unity in this generation."

This ecumenical dialogue surpassed all hopes for its success. In an introduction to the published proceedings, George H. Williams of the Harvard Divinity School wrote: "Many of us, as we first heeded the heartening words carefully shaped on the lips of a revered scholar and beloved Prince of his Church [Cardinal Bea], listening to his words each night in the favoring presence of the Cardinal Archbishop of Boston, perceived that we of this ancient academic community . . . had personally and with a sense of solemn joy, entered now upon a new age of the Church."

If this colloquium was a stimulating experience for all its participants, it was a source of deep joy to Cardinal Cushing.

As one who has always stood for what unites men, he has also supported the cause of inter-racial justice by both example and word. In a masterful treatise entitled "Inter-racial Justice," published in 1963, he has written:

"Let us join the Negro in his eager striving for racial equality and social justice. The place to begin for each of us is in his own heart. The Christian must be sure that here, in the sacred citadel of the soul, there is nothing but love for all of God's children, that no lingering prejudice or ancient bias warps his attitude toward those who were redeemed in the blood of the Savior . . .

"But much more than our own conversion is asked of us in these critical days. Each one has a positive role to play in hastening the day when the fruits of justice are everywhere available to the denied and the oppressed . . . True Christians must support all efforts at legislation which writes into law the claims of justice for our citizens; they must not even shrink from the difficult course of demonstration, denunciation, witness and testimony, when these are required of them. In education and employment and in housing—the traditional doors of opportunity for all Americans—we must put into every day action the deepest commitments of our faith."

In view of these and many similar statements, it came as a surprise to some that the Cardinal opposed the "school boycott" method of demonstrating for Negro rights. He made it clear, however, that he opposed it because he felt it was not a suitable method of achieving the desired goal. His exclusive concern was for the inevitable harmful effect on the children. To emphasize once more his longing to see the "vast, accumulated machinery of discrimination" broken down soon, he devoted his 1964 Pentecost message to inter-racial justice. A sentence in that message constitutes one of the most unforgettable appeals he has ever made in any cause:

"I say, love all men and especially love Negroes, because they have suffered so much from lack of love."

The Cardinal once described his Good Pope John as a "Master Bridge-builder," and the title might well be applied to himself also. He has spent his life and his strength in trying to raise bridges across the chasms that separate races, religions, and nationalities; that separate the spiritually rich from the spiritually deprived; the old and lonely from the young and gay; the privileged and gifted from the underprivileged and handicapped. Consequently, many within the Church and without, locally and internationally, consider him indispensable.

Not he himself, however. When he finally acceded to the urgings of those who wanted him to re-furnish his house and provide himself with an office and reception rooms worthy of the Cardinal-Archbishop of Boston, he said, "I'll do it for my successor." Yet he never thinks of himself as growing old, even though he may joke about it. And no one around him considers him less than a dynamic man in God's good motion.

Not even the physical effects of sickness and overwork are visible to audiences wholly conquered by his personality. Witness the remarks of Dr. Scott Francis Brenner of the United Presbyterian Church, Philadelphia, after hearing the Cardinal speak at the closing dinner of the 1963 Harvard Ecumenical Colloquium:

"Cushing is a massive, muscular man with deep etched lines in his face. Hearing him I thought first of all of Al Smith, and looking at him, of Abraham Lincoln. Then as the impact of his words gripped me, I thought of Albert Schweitzer. Smith, Lincoln and Schweitzer—put them together and you have Cardinal Cushing . . . Without him there would have been no colloquium—because of him the colloquium will continue. What a man, with a heart as big as the heart of God!"

And about a year later, when the Rev. Wendell B. Tamburro, Episcopal Pastor at Highland Falls, N.Y., made the startling suggestion that Cardinal Cushing be considered for the office of presiding bishop of the Protestant Episcopal Church in the United States, he declared:

"Here is a man like the early Apostles—rugged and down-to-earth; frank and impetuous, but a saint in the New Testament sense of the word." While suggesting that the Cardinal remain head of the Archdiocese of Boston, the Reverend Tamburro said he could preside at conventions of Episcopalian bishops and give them "his fine leadership with his own peculiar, special, unique ecumenical orientation."

In declining, the Cardinal said, "It's impossible." And he added, "They have better men than me to head up their church." But the suggestion stood as a witness to the success of his efforts to create the climate "in which men can speak to one another in unfeigned love."

Unsurprisingly, one of the Cardinal's favorite Scripture quotations is: "We look for new heavens and a new earth, according to His promises, wherein dwells justice" (2 Peter 3:13). The "new" has been an integral part of his life since the day he was ordained, for he is irrevocably committed to the principle that it is never too late to begin—to begin to replace unbelief with faith, despair with hope, and suspicion or indifference with love.

* * *

There are few who could not add their own chapter to the story of Richard Cardinal Cushing, thus illuminating still another aspect of his personality, for the ways and the occasions by which his dedication to God has been manifest through his dealings with man are innumerable. Yet the portrait would still be unfinished, and the added praise would give him no pleasure.

"You are a consolation to the Church" were Pope John's last words to him. No other commendation has ever meant so much. Had he not once said with utter sincerity: "I hold the universal Church in my heart"? And in strongly rejecting plans for public tributes to himself, he has always declared: "I'm not interested in all that. My only interest is in helping people."

If this 'world's Cardinal' could speak to all continents at once, the image spontaneously rises of him concluding with the typical assurance: "Should you ever need me, don't hesitate to call!"

* * *

And were he sitting at his desk listening to this resume of projects past, beyond any doubt, he would long ago have interrupted impatiently:

"Enough of this. Let's go back to work!"